John Ackworth

**The Scowcroft Critics**

John Ackworth

**The Scowcroft Critics**

ISBN/EAN: 9783337180768

Printed in Europe, USA, Canada, Australia, Japan

Cover: Foto ©ninafisch / pixelio.de

More available books at **www.hansebooks.com**

# THE
# SCOWCROFT CRITICS

By
JOHN ACKWORTH,

*Author of " Clog-Shop Chronicles," " Beckside Lights," &c.*

London:
JAMES CLARKE & CO., 13 & 14, FLEET STREET.

1898.

# CONTENTS.

| | PAGE |
|---|---|
| The Scowcroft Critics... ... | 1 |
| The Starting of Scowcroft Mill | 19 |
| Adam and the Stars ... | 57 |
| William's Idol .. | 81 |
| Jacky's Trouble | 119 |
| Billy's Blunder... | 157 |
| A Silent Sermon | 201 |
| The Superintendent | 253 |
| A Suspicious Case .. | 291 |
| Reuben Cleans His Slate | 331 |

# THE SCOWCROFT CRITICS.

# THE SCOWCROFT CRITICS.

Scowcroft held a position in the Wallbury Circuit altogether out of proportion to its size and the number and social status of its members. Its name was a very long way down on the plan, and its financial contributions gave it no claim for special consideration. At the same time it had a distinction all its own, and was renowned throughout the district for a severely critical spirit and an exacting standard of pulpit ability. Everybody who was anybody in Scowcroft was an expert in the difficult art of sermon tasting. Even the children as they grew up learned to prop their chins on the backs of the forms before them and follow the words of the preacher with faces of such precocious astuteness that an embarrassed, hesitant, or nervous preacher was greatly disturbed. There was more than one preacher on the "plan" who dared not occupy the Scowcroft pulpit at all, and there were others who must not if they would. And when once the Scowcroft sanhedrim had pronounced against an aspirant to pulpit honours he would have been a bold superintendent indeed who had appointed such an one.

Everybody of importance sat in the gallery, which went round the four sides of the building, and was disproportionately large for the size of the chapel, and the rank of a worshipper was indicated by the distance of his seat from the front pew. The men of light and leading sat of course at the front overlooking the well, each one occupying the door seat of his particular pew, and thus having his family safely penned up inside.

There were three front pews on each side and two over the clock, and in these apartments sat eight keen, caustic, uncompromising critics, like so many impanelled jurymen, showing by their whole demeanour that the ordinary tricks and blandishments of "counsel" were entirely wasted on such experts as them.

Several of these men were preachers themselves, and preachers of more than average popularity too. There was alert, eager, quick-eyed Miles Grimshaw, who was the only local preacher who was appointed at Wallbury Chapel *every* quarter. There was Jacky o' th' Gap, the bright, humorsome, highly emotional, and anecdotal preacher, who could boast that he had once shared an anniversary with the great Dr. Newton, and who had an odd trick of breaking into singing, and even occasionally sitting down, whilst he preached. And then there were the two Barlows, "Owd Mark" and "Young Mark," as they were called, both of whom were above the average in pulpit gifts and fiercely critical to boot.

But above all these was that terrible slaughterer of the innocents, that remorseless inquisitor-general, Jimmy the Scutcher, of whom the young ministers were all afraid, and before whom even superintendents had been known to turn pale.

The rank and file of the Scowcroft critics were given to free-and-easy modes of audible approval or disapproval, and a preacher was never left long in doubt as to whether he was hitting the nail on the head or not. His words were received for the first moment or two in severe silence, then if the hearers broke into nods, sometimes at him and sometimes at each other, it might be concluded that text and exordium had been approved, and the sermon might be preached with confidence.

Jacky o' th' Gap had special licence, and often followed the preacher with a sort of ejaculatory running comment, now interrogative, now confirmatory, now sarcastic, and now flatly contradictory. If the preacher was making a favourable impression Jacky would be followed by several others in a lower key, one or two of the women even venturing so far on occasions.

But all this was only the rattling, harmless thunder which the preachers learnt to value at its true worth; but in the second front pew on the preacher's right sat a man with a long oddly-shaped head and an uneven brow over which hung a fierce-looking tuft of hair. He had full lips and a wide, almost malicious mouth, and though he possessed two eyes, you were only conscious of one, the oversized left one—but that a very fiery dragon's eye of intimidating fierceness, which never moved from the pulpit and its occupant for so much as a glance at the clock. The light from this eye was the real lightning which struck terror into the hearts of all comers; and there was no person high or low in the Wallbury Circuit but had a wholesome fear of the renowned Jimmy. In his private capacity he was of no particular account in Scowcroft, but when it came to homiletic criticism the village was becomingly proud of its great chief, and was quite conscious of the glory his presence gave to their chapel and Society. Rumour had it that Jimmy had been ambitious to get on the plan himself in his early days, and those who had suffered under his castigations asserted that the hour that saw the closing of the pulpit-door against him was the hour in which the critic was born within him.

Jimmy sat at the door-corner of his pew, with a small cube-shaped duodecimo hymn-book— for he was specially proud of his independence of spectacles or large print—and an extra large Bible covered with an outer binding of green baize before him. Nothing ever escaped him. He sat with sphinx-like immovableness throughout the whole service, and it was only two or three of his closest friends who were able to discover during service whether the great inquisitor was satisfied or not. And even they were deceived sometimes.

Most of the homiletic epicures of Scowcroft were content with a general criticism of the sermon, but not so their great head. Whether the preacher "lined aat" every verse of the hymn, or adopted the modern and depraved habit of having it sung through; whether the hymns were each of them germane to the subject of the discourse — were points noted with unerring care. All originalities in the pronunciation of Scripture names, the range and emotional temperature of the prayer, were matters also that had to be duly noted. It was a fixed principle in Scowcroft that all sermons must be delivered extempore, "hot off the backstone," as it was always phrased, but only the Scutcher could distinguish those fine shades of tone and manner which decided whether the orator had been really preaching or only "saying his piece."

"Notes" were always regarded as contraband, and awakened a severe spirit in most of the hearers, but if the preacher forgot to consult his notes or in the fervour of his oratory ignored them, he was considered to have redeemed himself for the time; but only the lynx-eyed watcher behind the green-baize Bible could have told you exactly how often a hampered preacher consulted the obnoxious "papper." On that awful night, for ever memorable, when a local preacher, newly come from the South of England, deliberately read his sermon "wod fur wod" amidst a frigid silence, any respectable Scowcrofter could tell you that Jimmy, breaking through the habitual silence of years, as far as sanctuary ejaculation was concerned, gave vent when the preacher stopped to a long-drawn "*T-h-e-e-r*," so expressive at once of profound relief and grimmest irony that the preacher not only did not wait to be spoken to in the vestry, but informed the super., whom he overtook as he went home, that nothing on earth would ever induce him to preach at Scowcroft again. "And," the respectable villager aforesaid would add, in tones of impressive conviction, "that chap turnt aat a wastril."

That green-baize Bible, too, was a most formidable book. It had broad margins, and on them were inscribed in lead pencil opposite this or that verse of Scripture the name of the man or men who had preached from it, and the date of that occurrence; so that a preacher, hard driven for time or matter, and tempted to fall back on an old discourse, knew better than to do so at Scowcroft.

Two or three of the veterans of the circuit, who were assured of Jimmy's private regard, ventured on this course occasionally, and would have felt that something was wanting if Jimmy, on the way home or over the after-service pipe at Mileses', had not rubbed his hands and cocked his head on one side and remarked with an expressionless face, save for that terribly eloquent eye of his, "Warmt-up broth's poor meit."

"Naa then, Jimmy," one of the bolder spirits would reply, "it's fowerteen yer sin Aw preached that sarmon here," but the only reply vouchsafed would be, "Let's whop (hope) it ull be twice fowerteen afore tha brings it ageean."

And then there was another thing about this inexorable record. The text of every sermon that had been preached in the chapel for the last thirty years was marked off in it. And when some poor preacher had had an unusually bad time with a text, Jimmy would remark to him in the vestry when it was over, with one of his most aggravating drawls, "Dr. Bunting wunst preached a *sarmon* here off that text"—with a very special and significant emphasis on the "sarmon." And forthwith Jimmy would glide off into a minute description of the twenty-year-old discourse, giving copious extracts and even the illustrations; so that, whilst every Scowcrofter present glowed with pride in the skill and marvellous memory of their great critic, the poor victim was tortured by a sense of the insignificance of his own utterances as compared with the quotations given.

What made matters worse was that the Scutcher was credited with a profound acquaintance with theological literature, and it was considered as the clearest possible evidence of the extraordinary nature of his gifts that he actually seemed to enjoy reading pure theology. Most of the Scowcrofters were content to possess "The Saint's Rest," "The Life of Hester Ann Rogers," and the "Pilgrim's Progress," but Jimmy owned, and was reputed to have read, Leslie's "Method with the Deists," Paley's "Evidences," and Mr. Wesley's "Notes." And when on a certain Sunday night Jimmy, before all the assembled magnates, calmly ordered the "super." to bring him Butler's "Analogy" opinion was divided between intense wondering pride at Jimmy's intellectual greatness and strong suspicion that the Scutcher was giving way to intellectual pride and descending to that, to a Lancashire man, most intolerable of weaknesses, a desire to "show off."

"Lest see, whoar is it ta-neet?" asked Noah, the grocer, as they sauntered back from a before-service stroll over the bridge one heavy summer's evening.

"Abe Whittle, fro' Puddincroft Fowt," somebody replied.

"H'm!" grunted old Matt Briggs. "We'er in fur splutter and splash ta-neet, then."

"Aye; th' poor lad doesna spur hissel', does he?" observed Quiet William, intentionally misinterpreting the last remark.

"Neaw, nor he doesna spur uz noather," retorted Matt.

"He met let th' Bible and hymn-bewk abee, at ony rate," chimed in Jacky o' th' Gap.

"Aye," assented Jimmy, with that slow deliberateness which was the surest sign that something was coming; "when owd Mixey wur i' this circuit he used say as it wur nobbut th' empty pots as rung."

By this time they had reached the chapel door, and after the smokers had knocked the ashes out of their pipes, they all entered the building, and in a few moments the service commenced.

They got just what they expected. The preacher, a tallish, thin-faced man, with watery eyes, was noted for a highly rhetorical style, and a verbosity which was often wearisome and always distasteful to the Scowcrofters, particularly to the Scutcher.

On this night, in fact, the preacher seemed to be rather worse than usual, and all his faults seemed to have become more pronounced than ever. His sermon was wordy, incoherent, and long; so that whilst the rank and file went away at the close feeling somewhat weary, the responsible chiefs wore discontented and even sulky looks.

Jimmy the Scutcher walked off by himself to the tailor's house, and the awkwardly upward angle at which he was carrying his head boded no good to the poor preacher. He said less than usual whilst the orator's supper was being "laid," but Quiet William, who was alternately watching him and studying with anxious looks the guest of the evening, grew more and more uneasy as Jimmy's silence continued.

When the oat-cake and milk and cheese were brought out, William sat down immediately opposite the preacher and was soon pressing upon him the good things provided. But the preacher did not need much encouraging to eat; in fact, under other circumstances his readiness to attack what was set before him might have attracted attention, and even as it was Jimmy's face grew harder and his eye gathered unholy light as he noticed that the preacher either did not realise how badly he had discharged his duties, or was not much disturbed by the fact.

"That's a moighty foine sarmon we'en hed ta-neet," Jimmy began at last.

Now, when the Scutcher fell upon an unsatisfactory preacher with one of his open attacks, terrible though it was, it was well known that this was not by any means his worst mood, and that he did not regard the case as calling for very drastic treatment. If he snapped and snarled it was concluded that he had only noted surface irregularities, but if he began deliberately, as now, with a compliment, it was a certain sign that there was trouble in store for the offender.

Jimmy's encouraging remarks therefore greatly disturbed Quiet William, and snatching up a knife he cut for the guest an unusually liberal supply of cheese, and began to urge oat-cake upon him. But Abram didn't seem to be disturbed; indeed, he appeared to be so engrossed in the business in hand that he gave a very indifferent sort of attention to what was being said to him.

Jimmy watched him eating and drinking with growing displeasure, and was piqued to think that his fame as a critic was having so little effect on the man at the table. "Bud Aw say," he resumed again, in the tone of a man who had appreciated as far as he could, and wanted a little difficulty or two removing in order to complete his satisfaction, "wot dust meean by th' circumnambient heavens?"

The preacher looked round with an uneasy, hesitating look, and presently answered, "Aw meean th' sky—wot else?" But as Dinah Grimshaw, the hostess, just then came forward with a bit of cold beafsteak pie, and began to press it upon him, Abram turned once more from his critic, and gave himself to more interesting business.

"Oh! the sky," drawled Jimmy, whilst his pugnacious left eye began to blink ominously and his tone indicated that he had just received sudden and complete relief from mental perplexity. He paused a moment, and then, dropping into a treacherously confidential tone, he continued, "Aw'll tell thee wot, lad, if Aw wur thee Aw'd *say* sky if Aw meant it—we're nobbut poor simple fowk at Scowcroft, tha knows," and the mock humility of his tone made more than one of the listeners squirm in their chairs, out of pure sympathy with the preacher.

Quiet William began to press more milk upon the visitor, partly to distract his attention, and partly to conceal his own growing agitation.

The preacher made no reply, and there was an uneasy sort of silence whilst Mrs. Dinah went into the pantry to replenish the milk jug.

"Then," Jimmy went on in his most dangerously seductive manner, " wot dust mean by th' hayzure canopy?"

" Aw mean the sky fur sure," and there were signs of rising resentment in the preacher's tones.

"Oh!" ejaculated Jimmy, as if he were again conscious of sudden and vast enlightenment, "then th' ' starry concave of the empyrean ' 'ull mcean th' sky tew, Aw reacon?" he asked, in a tone of modest but eager curiosity.

But the preacher had become sulky and heedless, whilst the attention of the rest of the company became divided between Jimmy's scientific heckling and the remarkable appetite of Abram. He was certainly making a most extraordinary supper. Jimmy's prominent eye now put on its most fixed and inexorable expression, whilst its owner cleared his throat, and entirely changing his tone, said, in slow and weighty manner, "Abrum, when yung parsons an' college chaps an' newspapper felleys uses 'great swellin' wods o' vanity' they makken thersels redic'lous, bud when a Lancashire weyver lad starts o' talkin' o' thatunce, it's daan-reet pace-egging, an' nowt else."

Abram, who seemed by this time to be relaxing his interest in the supper-table, and was therefore more at liberty to listen to his tormentor, flushed a little under this broadside, and was just turning round to reply when Jimmy resumed: "An' theer's another thing, Aw've allis noaticed as th' less foak han' ta say th' bigger maathful they makken on it an' th' less woth yerring (hearing) it is. Naa tha's nobbut bin preichin' six yer, an' that's thod (third) toime tha's gan' us that sarmon ta my knowledge."

Now Miles Grimshaw had been away fulfilling a preaching appointment, but happening to come in just as Jimmy was finishing his last deliverance, and guessing at once the cause of it, he plunged with his accustomed impetuosity into the subject under discussion, crying with a touch of indignation in his voice as he glared at Abram, "Tha's known as tha hed ta come here monny a wik; wot hast bin wasting thi' toime at as tha' worn't ready?"

A sudden cloud appeared upon the preacher's face; his eyes became dim as, with hasty tears, his loosely hanging lip quivered, and he was evidently struggling to keep back some emotion.

Everybody saw it and misunderstood its meaning, and Jimmy, who secretly believed that the man he had been chastising had something in him if only he would cultivate his gifts, was just preparing to give him another blast of reproof when Mrs. Dinah laid her big, soft hand on Abram's shoulder and asked kindly, "Haas yore Annie, lad?"

The look on the preacher's face darkened, a sudden flush passed over it. An entirely unexpected sob escaped him, and in fear and shame at this unwonted self-betrayal he dropped his head upon his arm and hid his face, whilst the sympathetic Dinah observed with distress that great tears were dropping upon the sanded floor.

"Is owt wrung wi' her?" asked Dinah, putting all the sympathy she could into the question.

There was a pause for a moment, and then Abram groaned out, "Hoos deein', Dinah."

"Deein', lad?—niver!" cried Dinah in shocked astonishment. "What's ta dew wi' her?"

There was a deathly stillness in the house. All the men were holding their breaths to listen. Presently Abram lifted his head for a moment and cried, "Consumshon," and then, after hesitating, he went on with a resentful jerk, "an' starvation."

"Starvation!" cried everybody at once.

"Aye, starvation," answered the now desperate preacher. "Hoos bin i' bed five munths, an' Aw've bin aat o' wark fur seven wik, an' wot wi' th' doctor, an' wot wi' th' childer, an' wot wi' seein' her deein' afoor me een, an' wot wi' clemmin Aw'm welly meythered amung it."

There were looks of deep and solemn sympathy on all the faces, and down Quiet William's cheeks streams of silent tears were flowing. Presently he leaned forward, and looking hard at Abram, he said, with an interrogative inflexion of his voice, "Tha's etten a rare supper ta-neet, lad."

But Abram didn't answer the question that was in the big man's mind, and so, after watching his face for a moment or two, William inquired softly, "Aw reacon tha's hed noa gradely dinner ta-day."

"Dinner!" cried Abram, with fresh agitation. "Aw'm tellin' thi God's trewth, William; Aw havna hed a bite o' nowt i' my yed fur welly three days."

The preacher's wife, Annie, was a native of Scowcroft, and in a few seconds everybody was talking at once about this unhappy and yet lucky discovery, and all sorts of help was offered to the suffering man.

Jacky o' th' Gap went off hurriedly to fetch

2

his trap and drive poor Abram home, and when he returned with it he had two bags of potatoes lying in the bottom of the vehicle. By this time a good stock of provisions and other things had been collected, and when the trap drove away all present sent after the poor weaver many a fervent "God bless thi, lad."

All this time Jimmy the Scutcher was sitting perfectly still at the fireside. He had a habit of biting his nails when excited and unhappy, and now seemed to have one of his worst worrying fits upon him.

The others, coming in from seeing poor Abram off, addressed him several times, but without evoking the slightest response. At last, however, he rose to go.

"Well," he said, looking shyly into the fire, and evidently trying to avoid catching any one's eye, "Aw've fund aat wot th' mooat an' th' beeam meeans ta-neet, an' Aw expect A'wst be na wur fur it." And sauntering to the door with his head down he departed. But the manager at the mill had a very persistent applicant next day, who wanted looms for a four-loom weaver, and as the Scutcher was a very old "hand" he had his way, and a week later Abram, the preacher, had been removed to Scowcroft, where his sick wife's last days were made sweet by many tender little attentions.

# THE STARTING OF SCOWCROFT MILL.

# THE STARTING OF SCOWCROFT MILL.

## I.

THE engine of Scowcroft Mill had just "slackened" for a moment as an intimation that in a short time it would stop for the week-end. The mill-gates, usually closed during work hours, were thrown wide open. Just inside the gate was a little office at the pigeon-hole window of which a number of men were receiving their own and others' wages. Here and there within the yard were little knots of workpeople "settling up"—minders paying their piecers and bobbiners, and cardroom overlookers distributing wages to their subordinates. Outside the yard were a number of wheeled stalls, retailing tripe and trotters, hot pork pies, hot peas, and the like. At the near end of the long row of houses nearly opposite the gates a tall woman was standing inside a doorway receiving "tay-wayter money" from a small but constant stream of customers, and moving about amongst the groups of hands standing here and there round the gates were two or three club-collectors and the Scowcroft knocker-up gathering in their dues. Just as the engine was giving a sort of dying groan, as if painfully reluctant to stop even out of respect to the approaching Sabbath, and you began to see the short spokes of the pulleys in the shafting as they slowly slackened speed, a heavy pulley-and-weight door was opened in the side of the mill, and a young woman, evidently a weaver, stepped out. She was not the least bit like the typical Lancashire lass. Her hair was light and her eyes large, grey, and dreamy. She had just colour enough in her face to make it piquant, and though her features were not particularly regular there were lines in them suggestive of much more than appeared on the surface. She had a seductive grace of movement which made her almost independent of the art of dressing, and which even factory clothes could not conceal.

As she approached the mill-gate a side door in the office where the men were being paid was opened, and a young man whose clothes, though they bore unmistakable evidences of contact with cotton manufacture, at once distinguished him from those about him, stepped into the yard, and in a moment was walking by the girl's side.

He was a medium-sized but strongly-built young fellow, in whose face keen business shrewdness was somehow blended with a softness that neutralised the effect and made the observer uncertain in his judgment.

The girl started and flushed when he spoke to her, and, checking her pace, glanced uneasily around as if afraid of being seen in such company; and then, turning her great eyes with a sudden flash in them, she said something to her companion which was evidently very unacceptable, and which compelled him to stop in the middle of the road, and begin to plead, heedless altogether of the fact that many pairs of eyes were now fixed curiously upon them. The young master, for such he was, seemed to be very much in earnest about something, and yet very much afraid of being overheard; and the girl listened with wavering manner one moment, and glanced round with fidgety impatience the next, and was evidently very restive under the popular gaze. Thus they stood for some moments in close conversation. Presently a man with a flat, open cart containing earthenware, sand-barrels, and bags of rags and bones, and drawn by a ragged-looking pony of uncertain yellow colour, came round the corner at the lower end of the croft, and screwing his mouth to one side of his face he cried out in round, ringing tones, "Wey-shin-up-mugs! Stew mugs! Whaaite sand an' rubbin' stone.—Whey! will ta?"

The animal addressed in the last sentence made a feint at stopping, and then settling down into a slow professional sort of saunter moved slowly along the front of the row and past the chapel. In a moment or two they had reached the mill-gate end of the row, where the pony stopped of itself, and the man, turning his back to the mill, but moving gradually round towards it as he cried, began again: "Wey-shin-up-mu——" But there he stopped, and whilst the lips of his big mouth still retained their trumpet-like shape he stared scowlingly and amazedly before him.

As he began his professional refrain his eyes caught sight of the weaver and her companion still engaged in earnest conversation. His trade-cry died on his lips; a sudden fiery glare came into his eyes; every feature of his strongly-marked and shaggy face tightened into rigidity, and he stood there glaring at them in undisguised anger. Just then the girl caught sight of him; she flushed, spoke hastily to the young man, who was still urging something upon her with intense earnestness, and turning abruptly, left him, making off towards Lark Lane, with a startled and downcast look.

The hawker was still standing looking at her, and just as she was approaching the end of the row, and in another moment would have been lost to sight down the lane, he raised his whip a little, and, jerking it beckoningly, called out to the evidently frightened girl, "Here! Aw *want* thee."

The girl turned pale, hesitated a moment, glanced hastily down the lane as if meditating flight in that direction, and then, turning, stepped slowly towards the cart and its driver.

The hawker did not move an inch to meet her, nor did he speak when she stopped a moment at some little distance from him as if afraid of coming within reach of his whip, but simply stood looking at her with a cold glitter in his eyes, his hands the while twitching nervously about the stock of his heavy whip.

When she had come close up to him, and was preparing to speak, he stopped her with a gesture, and, looking almost through her, said, sternly, "Pike off whoam, an' if tha stirs aat o' th' haase afoor Aw come, Aw'll gi' thi some o' this," and he gave a significant twirl to his whip.

Dropping her head, and blushing afresh as she realised that many eyes in the croft were upon them, the girl turned slowly round, and increasing her pace as she went quickly disappeared round the corner.

The hawker was Reuben Tonge, one of Scowcroft's most notorious characters, and the girl he had addressed so harshly was his only living child, Grace.

A stranger moving about in Scowcroft would never have suspected that there was more than one class amongst the inhabitants, but the native Scowcrofter knew of several, and could have drawn the line between them to a nicety, and in any such classification Reuben Tonge would have been included in the lowest; if, indeed, he was not placed in a still lower grade all by himself. Not that he was poor, though his appearance would have justified such an inference, nor that he was dishonest; rigid business integrity, indeed, was the one virtue in which he prided himself. He was not by any means a drunkard, though he had occasional violent drinking spells, and he was not a blasphemer, but that may have been because his marvellous command of the vocabulary of vituperation relieved him of the necessity of resorting to such clumsy implements as oaths. He was not neighbourly and made great display of his lack of "bowels," and yet there were two or three incidents in Scowcroft history which were inexplicable, except on the assumption that he had a soft place somewhere. He was never seen inside the chapel, and was ostentatiously opposed to his daughter's attendance; and yet somehow she always had gone, not only since she had grown up but from earliest infancy. He appeared to treat his daughter with a roughness verging on cruelty, and yet she not only never complained, but seemed on the whole as comfortable at home as most of her girl associates, and had quite as much liberty.

Reuben had been brought up in the Sunday-school, but since the day Alice Pollitt married Jacky o' th' Gap instead of him he had never been inside the chapel doors, and on all possible occasions jeered and scoffed at religion and religious institutions so relentlessly that when any of the leaders prayed in the prayer-meeting for all scoffers and gainsayers, everybody thought of Reuben Tonge. Of late years he had become conspicuous as the only avowed sceptic in the parish, and was also suspected of holding Chartist and other revolutionary opinions. He boasted constantly of his views on social equality, and practised them to the indecent length of "thouing" the vicar and even his good wife, who was cousin to a lord. And yet there was nothing that so quickly aroused his unrivalled powers of abuse as any attempt on the part of a Scowcrofter to aspire to a social grade higher than the one to which he or she originally belonged.

It was in harmony with this last of Reuben's many inconsistencies that he acted on this particular occasion towards his daughter as he did. He had been free enough with his sneers at the new owners of the mill when first they came to Scowcroft, and called them "hupstarts" and "clug swells" whenever he had occasion to allude to them, and had carefully collected a stock of more or less reliable stories of the early life of Mr. Westall, senior. And yet when he saw "th' yung mestur" in such close converse with his daughter, his sense of the immense social gulf between them created in him intense anger that his child should even appear to suppose that she could by any means cross that gulf; and, on the other hand, he was angry that she should be so lacking in proper pride as to be flattered by his attentions. For Reuben made no manner of doubt in his mind as to the meaning of what he had seen.

It was dark when he had finished his rounds and reached his house, which was about half a mile down Lark Lane on the way to Wallbury. Presently, having groomed the unkempt "Pablo," he turned into his house with a hard look and his nearly perfect teeth set in grim resolution.

He opened the door quietly, for his anger was not of the explosive kind, and stepped slowly across the threshold. His daughter was nowhere to be seen.

"Grace." No answer.

"Grace." Still no sound or sign.

Another man would have grown furious and plunged about in search of the disobedient one, but Reuben never turned his head, but sat down in his chair and quietly lighted the lamp with a hard set about the mouth that boded ill for the absent daughter. Reuben sat thus for a couple of hours, but no Grace appeared, and presently, though only a little past nine o'clock, he got up, went out quietly and took a look at Pablo, and then came back into the house and slowly locked the door, so that when the wanderer returned she would find it closed against her.

But she did not return. During Sunday Reuben so far departed from his usual manner as to cast a cursory glance behind the pink-and-white curtain that screened off the corner next to her bedroom chimney, and thus made it into a wardrobe. A deep sigh that angered him as he made it escaped the rugged hawker as he discovered that all the girl's clothes were there except her Sunday best; and he went out and down into the village, where, standing amongst the members of the open-air village Parliament at the "brig-end," he learnt that his daughter had eloped with the young master, and had that morning been married at a small church in the suburbs of Wallbury.

That night poor Pablo got no supper, for his master went home so preoccupied and depressed that he forgot all about his patient pony, and sat down by the expired fire sick at heart, and nursing a fierce resentment against Westall the younger. Just as the old verge watch hanging on a hook under the mantleshelf reached the hour of nine, and whilst Reuben still sat gloomily thinking by the cold fireplace, he heard the latch of the door gently raised; but as he had turned the key in the lock when he came in, the applicant, whoever it was, was disappointed. Reuben turned his head slightly round to listen. In a moment or two the latch was raised again, and a soft, anxious voice outside said, "Feyther!"

The hawker rose slowly to his feet, stepped to the door, and, half opening it, put his own burly body into the aperture. It was bright moonlight, and there in the lane stood Grace, tearful and trembling. Reuben fixed her with a steely eye, and looked her over with slow deliberation.

For some moments neither of them spoke, but at length Reuben said, "Aw knowed as they made hypocrytes an' scandal-mongerers at the chapil, an' naa Aw see they makken harlots tew"; and with the same stony look he stepped back, closed and locked the door in the girl's face, and walked calmly to his seat.

Poor Grace burst into a wild cry, and rushed forward as if to stop the closing door. But she was too late, and in a moment she was alone in the lane, with the knowledge that that door was closed against her for ever.

For a few moments the unhappy girl stood in the lane, sobbing and trying to collect her thoughts. Then she began to move back along the way towards Wallbury, from whence she had come. Then she stopped, hesitated, turned back, and passing her father's house, with another burst of sobbing, she walked slowly along the lane towards Scowcroft. In a few minutes she had reached a little cottage, standing on the edge of the footpath, and noticing that the door she would have to pass was wide open, and that a tall, stout man was standing smoking in the doorway, she crossed the road, and was stealing past under the shadow of the opposite garden fence when a thick, husky voice called out, "Wot! Grace, wench! is that thee?"

Grace stooped lower and began to run, but in three or four strides the big man was across the lane and had taken her by the arm.

"Let me goa, William," cried Grace, piteously; "Aw want ta *dee*—ta *dee*."

For answer, the man addressed put his long arm around her, picked her up as if she had been a baby, and carried her gently into his house.

A little quick-eyed old woman, in a spotless granny's cap and a natty bedgown, rose hastily from her seat as William came in with his burden, and when she saw what her husband carried, her frank face became suddenly over-clouded, a soft chirping "Hey my!" escaped her, and she hastened forward to make the girl a resting-place on the check-cushioned long settle.

Now the ponderous William—known popularly as "Quiet William"—had dropped his pipe in the effort to bring Grace into his cottage, and so as soon as he had placed her upon the settle he went back into the lane to seek it. The garden hedge opposite his house kept the moonlight from the road just where he had dropped his comforter, and so he had to grope about awhile before he recovered it. When he did so, however, he stuck its short stem into his mouth and, staring down the lane in the direction Grace had come, he held up his huge fist and shook it threateningly towards Reuben's house. Then he crossed the road, and was re-entering his house, but overcome by his feelings he turned back, shook first his left fist and then his right in the same direction as before, and then, shaking them both together until he went red in the face, he stepped softly into the house and closed the door.

Whilst William was thus engaged, old Betsy, his sharp little wife, was fussing about their inconsolable visitor. As she glanced curiously at the dishevelled Sunday clothes she cried under her breath, "Hey, my!" then, looking intently at Grace's left hand and finding it ringless, she cried still more sorrowly, "Hey, my!" and then stooping over and tenderly smoothing back the wavy golden hair and wiping the tearful eyes with her white Sunday apron, she went on, "Hey, my! Hey, *dear* my."

But by this time William had returned, and Grace suddenly sitting up began to beg to be let go.

"Aw'm disgraced!" she cried; "Aw'm turnt aat o' whoam. Aw'll throw mysel' i' th' cut" (canal).

"Hey, dear, my wench," cried old Betsy, "thaa munna talk loike that; God's pitiful, tha knows, an', an'"—with a glance of inquiry at William—"ther's a whoam here fur thi till tha con get a bet-ter."

The big William, standing where Grace could not see him, threw up his arms with a gesture of delight, and nodding triumphantly at Betsy, stepped quickly behind the little draught screen near the door, and relieved his feelings by shaking his fist once more in the direction of Reuben's residence.

Much more was said, both by Grace and Betsy, with an occasional monosyllable from William, but neither he nor his little wife showed the slightest desire to pry into Grace's secret. Eventually, the unhappy girl was persuaded to go to bed, and next morning all Scowcroft knew that Grace was not married, and had returned; but having been turned from her father's door, had found refuge at Quiet William's. And on Tuesday morning Grace, with dark circles round her eyes and a white cold face, was found at her looms in the mill.

## II.

Now the Methodist Church at Scowcroft was managed on somewhat peculiar principles. The leaders' meeting was, of course, the fountain of all authority, at once its parliament and its high court of justice, and was held as occasion required after the week-night service, so that the superintendent minister from Wallbury, or one of his colleagues, could preside.

But somehow this meeting had always a very formal and perfunctory air about it, and was usually got through with quite remarkable celerity. Ostensibly because the minister had a long way to go, but really because everything had been arranged beforehand. The fact was, it was a fixed idea amongst the ecclesiastical officials of the society that the less the ministers knew about the actual internal working of the church the better, and so there was an informal leaders' meeting—a sort of irregular "House of Commons"—of the church, where all important matters could be debated at becoming length and with unrestrained liberty. The conclusions of this council were generally reached without any such artificial arrangements as formal resolutions, and once settled thus nobody ever dreamed of appealing against them to the legal court. These irregular meetings were held at irregular times and places. They were never formally convened, but any time after the Sunday-night or week-night prayer-meetings they might take place around the vestry fire, and if any emergency meeting was required such a gathering might be held either at Miles Grimshaw, the itinerant tailor's, or at the house of Jimmy the Scutcher, next door to the chapel. The conventions thus held were generally summoned by Jimmy standing at his door and looking across the croft until he caught the eye of some one of the authorities lounging at the bridge end, when he would jerk his thumb over his shoulder, and then walk inside and wait until the court assembled.

On the Wednesday night after Grace Tonge's return nobody needed to be told that there was to be a solemn inquisition on Grace's conduct and her relation to the church, and so as the rank and file dispersed the rest resumed their seats and waited until they were alone. There were five of them, a full complement. Jacky o' th' Gap, who, by reason of his position as a very small freehold farmer, was nominal chief; Miles Grimshaw, the only remaining local representative of the race of itinerant tailors, once so common in North-country villages, and the real ruler of the Scowcroft Society; Jimmy the Scutcher, whose obliquity of vision extended to his mind and prevented from him ever seeing things exactly as others saw them, and made him therefore a thorn in the side of Miles and an inveterate obstructionist all round; Noah, the grocer, and Quiet William, who has already been introduced.

Whilst these potentates were settling themselves in their seats as comfortably as stiff-backed and cushionless forms would permit, Miles took the lid off the top of the little stove and began violently stirring the fire.

He was a very small man with a large, long beard, sharp green-grey eyes, sharp features, a wide, thin-lipped, aggravating mouth, and hair that stood out in such irregular points as to make him look what he really was, a sort of Methodist terrier. When he had been pounding away for a minute or so at an obstinate piece of bass that had somehow got into the stove, he suddenly stopped, and turning round with a jerk and looking fiercely at Quiet William sitting against the wall under the window, he demanded, "Well, wot's yond wench say fur hersel'?"

William in a conciliatory and apologetic tone answered, "Aw durn't know."

Another savage plunge with the poker into the little stove which sent the greater part of the contents flying through the little door at the front, bringing with them a puff of sulphury smoke; and then: "Wheer wor hoo a Setterday neet an' Sunday?"

"Aw durn't know."

Miles stood up, placed one foot on the bench near him, and eyeing the abashed and melancholy William from head to foot, twirling the short poker as he did so, he proceeded: "Is hoo marrid?"

"Aw durn't know."

Miles looked very much like throwing the poker at William's head, but after taking another deliberate inventory of the big man's clothes, he drew a long breath and launched out his final question: "Is hoo goin' back to her feyther?"

"Aw durn't know."

"Tha doesn't know! Hast a gradely pow or nobbut a biled turmit for a yed, dust know that?" And flinging the poker down in a pet, Miles resumed his seat in high dudgeon.

Now, Miles and William were brothers-in-law twice over, a brother and sister having married a brother and sister, and there was a big man and a sharp little woman in one house, and a big, tender-hearted woman and a sharp little man in the other. And Miles, always sensitive on the point of undue influence, and jealous, above all things, for independence, always made it a point to put on his most worrying manner when dealing in public with his brother-in-law, between whom and himself there was an attachment of the strongest kind, which seemed to grow stronger by being so constantly strained and tested.

Nobody, therefore, was much disturbed by the apparent harshness of Miles's attack on the peaceable William. But gathering from Miles's attitude what was the official view of the grave question of the hour, Jimmy the Scutcher at once prepared himself for conflict. He was sitting next to Miles on the same form. He paused a moment, dropped his folded hands and clasped them round his knees, cocked his head at the angle of contradiction, and turning his eyes up towards the lamp hanging high above head, he said, slowly, "Aw yerd a chap preich t'other Sunday off 'Judge not, that ye be not judged,'" and then, after slowly taking his breath, "An' it wur a gradely good sarmon, tew."

A grin went round the room, even Quiet William making a peculiar sound with his tightly pursed lips that was suggestive of enjoyment.

Miles was momentarily nonplussed. He, of course, was the preacher referred to, and pride in his pulpit power was his greatest earthly besetment, so that whilst the latter part of Jimmy's observation broke the force of the reproof, it also in another sense increased it. He gave a little gasp, whipped round sharply towards the Scutcher, and was evidently just about to extinguish him when Jimmy, who had not moved a muscle, went on drawlingly and with a sly smirk of relish: "Th' preicher that

## STARTING OF SCOWCROFT MILL. 39

neet said as an aance o' practice wur wurth a ton a preiching."

"By Gow he did," shouted Jacky o' th' Gap, smiting both knees at once in recollection and enjoyment. Miles waited until the faces were all straight again, and then, taking a solemn, reproachful look round, he sank back against the bench side, and said in tones of weary resignation and despair, "When th' leets o' th' church con grin o'er a wench's faw and a church's shawme it's toime to write Ichabod up."

This sobered everybody at once. The painful subject they were discussing came back to their minds and brought a cloud to every face. There was an uncomfortable pause, and then Jacky, looking across at Quiet William, asked, "Has hoo towd the *nowt*, William?"

William leaned his head back, and looking steadily at the long stove-pipe answered with a sigh, "Nowt."

Miles, whose face seemed to say that he had said his last word and that torture could not wring another from him, suddenly jerked out: "He's ne'er axed her."

This charge was so exactly characteristic of William that everybody knew it was true as soon as it was stated, and deep sighs, expressive of reluctant resignation to the inevitable, escaped from three or four.

Then the conversation became more general

a long, tortuous discussion took place, and finally Miles, as usual, had his way. Discipline must be maintained at all costs, and though many roughly kind things were said about Grace, it was finally acknowledged that there was nothing for it but to dismiss her from the choir and remove her name from the class-book.

"Whoa's class is hoo in?" asked Miles, who was trying to conceal his dislike of the business behind an inexorable insistence on law and discipline.

"William's!" answered Jacky o' th' Gap.

Three pairs of eyebrows went up quickly, and a flicker of amusement passed over Jimmy the Scutcher's face; for everybody present suddenly realised that the whole debate had been so much wasted breath. They could guess what William's attitude would be; and though he had never spoken save as reported here, it was perfectly plain to everybody that he would not consent to Grace's expulsion. And if he didn't they knew full well that it was no use reporting the case to the ministers, for they all seemed to have a regard for the big man altogether out of proportion to anything he ever either said or did.

A few minutes later the meeting broke up; and whilst the rest adjourned to Miles's for a smoke William stole quietly, almost guiltily, away towards home.

When he had got into Lark Lane he dropped into a saunter, as if he felt safer; and presently pulling up as if struck by a sudden thought, he ejaculated, "Well, Aw'll be bothert. Aw've read mony a time as 'a mon should be fur a hiding-place,' but Aw ne'er thowt as it 'ud be me. Hay, Aw'm *fain* it's me."

Meanwhile Grace, with cold, averted face, was braving things out as best she could in the mill. She was conscious all day long that curious eyes were looking at her from all parts of the room, and every time she lifted her eyes and saw two weavers talking together she dropped them again with a guilty consciousness that she was the subject of their conversation. On the afternoon of the day after the leaders' meeting a girl, a weaver from the opposite side of the room, paused as she passed Grace's loom ends, and after a glance round the room, as though attracting all the spectators she could, she stepped into the loom-alley and said to the embarrassed Grace, "Arta goin' to the practice ta-neet?"

The girl was a fellow-singer of Grace's, who had been very jealous because Grace was always asked to take the solo parts.

Grace flushed painfully, turned her head away, and said as softly as the rattling looms would permit, "Neaw, no' ta-neet, Aw think."

The girl took another glance round to assure

herself that the other weavers were still watching, and then, looking into Grace's timid eyes with a quiet, hard insolence, she said, "Neaw; Aw wouldna if Aw wur thee," and then, picking up her cop-skip, she passed jauntily on her errand, whilst poor Grace dropped her head over her loom with the added bitterness of not being able to conceal her tears.

That same night as she was going home to Quiet William's just about dark she heard a footstep behind her, and then a low but significant clearing of the throat. She slackened speed, and presently the young master came alongside her, saying as he did so, "What a little fool you are, Grace."

The pretty weaver stopped, stepped back into a little by-lane they were passing, and then, suddenly turning round, replied, "Aw'd sooner be a little foo nor a big sinner, Mester George."

"But they are all sneering at you, and whispering as you go by. Any other girl would be having grand dresses and gay times now."

Grace did not answer for a moment, but then she said, "Yo con stop their whispering if yo'n a moind, Mester George. An' if yo'n ony feelin' fur me yo will. An' that's the fost an' last thing Aw'st ever ax off yo."

But Mr. George only laughed. He knew his

## STARTING OF SCOWCROFT MILL. 43

power over her, and hoped that the disgrace she was feeling would drive her to him in spite of herself. But for once he overreached himself. Grace drew herself away from him, and standing up to her fullest height she answered, "Mester George, yo made me loike yo, an' me luv an' me nowty pride made me think as wun loike yo 'ud marry a poor weyver lass. Bud yo've oppened my een fur me. Aw've lost aw my friends, an' Aw've lost my charickter, bud Aw hav'na lost me—me—mysel'; an' there's One aboon as knows me, an' Aw winna vex Him even fur *yo*'; and with a smothered cry she swept past him, and in a moment was in safe shelter in Quiet William's cottage.

A muttered curse broke from the young man when he found himself alone. "I'll have her!" he cried, with a passionate jerk of his clenched hand. "The proud little Methody, I'll have her yet," and returning to the lane, he strode away, still muttering as he went.

When the wages were paid on the following Saturday the overlooker told Grace that her looms had been "shopped," and that she need not come any more, and Grace went home to William's nearly broken-hearted.

Very soon, however, Grace and her troubles were forgotten in Scowcroft, for the following Sunday morning the old master of the mill was found dead in bed. Then it was discovered that the Westalls were not so well off as had always been supposed, and as Mr. George had long before quarrelled with his only sister, and had now to pay her out in cash, it was soon realised that the firm was in straitened circumstances, and that, with the young man's wild habits, made it very doubtful whether he would long carry on.

There was no other factory within three miles, and, consequently, dark days seemed to be in store, and anxiety reigned in many a Scowcroft home.

## III.

THREE anxious pinching years passed away, and the fears of many had been realised. Mr. George, released from the restraining oversight of his father, and harassed by financial worries, had plunged into reckless excesses and become a helpless drunkard. The mill, after running irregularly for months, stopped altogether. The hands had, some of them, found work at Wallbury Moor and other places still further away, and had to walk to and fro every day. Many had been unable to find regular employment at all, and so whilst heavy scores were being run up at Noah's shop everybody in the village was feeling the pinch of poverty. Rumours that the mill had been sold and would be started by the new owners sprang up every now and again, and were eagerly believed, but no sign of such a welcome event ever showed itself; whilst the present owner, having got to the end of his resources, was no longer able to keep his place amongst people of his own rank, and loafed about the "Red Cat," a slinking, disreputable wreck. One day, however, the bailiffs arrived at the mill and took possession, and a fortnight later large bills were posted on the gates announcing a sale by auction. The mill was to be offered first in one lot as a going concern, or, failing sale in that form, it was to be done piecemeal. Scowcroft received the news with divided feelings. To some it was the sign of the end and the inevitable parting from the place of their birth, and to others it was the promise of a new master and better times.

Grace still lived with Quiet William. He and she had found work at Wallbury Moor Mills some three miles away, and Grace could never quite understand the curious coincidence that William should have grown tired of "th' Shop" just about the time that she found work elsewhere, but had she known how frequently Mr. George haunted the dark lanes between Scowcroft and Wallbury Moor, about the time when she would be returning from her work, the mystery might have been less obscure to her.

The sale was fixed for a Monday and the two following days, and all the week before the auctioneer's clerks and assistants were busy on the premises. Late on the Saturday afternoon Mr. George, shabby, prematurely aged, only a wreck, in fact, of his former self, turned up at the mill in a state of wild, pugnacious drunkenness, and in a few minutes was embroiled in a reckless quarrel with the men in charge.

As it was Saturday afternoon the Croft, as the large, irregular square of open land by the side of the mill and in front of the chapel was called, was more than usually thronged. A travelling stall or two was moving along the front of the "long row" overlooking the Croft. A small knot of men stood against the bridge end at the lower corner, and in the middle of the open space a number of boys were playing "piggy."

Just as Reuben Tonge and his everlasting pony came round the top corner of the row with the inevitable cry of "Weyshin-up mugs," &c., "Stew mugs," &c., &c., a sound of angry voices was heard coming from the mill lodge. Everybody turned round to look and listen. The sounds grew louder, and the listeners looked at each other in mingled perplexity and alarm, and a crowd of small boys made towards the point where the sounds came from. All at once the low half door of the mill lodge crashed open, and out came three men struggling and cursing and fighting together. The middle man was Mr. George, bleeding and blaspheming, but still struggling violently with his ejectors, and just as Reuben's cart reached that end of the row one of the men sprang angrily at the young master and struck him a furious blow in the face, which sent his head violently against the stone gate-post, from which he reeled to the ground, and fell insensible, whilst his assailants slunk back into the lodge and locked and bolted the door.

A sharp exclamation broke from men and women alike as they stood in their doorways and beheld what took place.

The boys left their "piggy" and raced up to look at the fallen man; but old associations prevented them going very near. Reuben, who had evidently seen everything, gave vent to an exclamation which might have been taken for either a sneer or a groan; and leaving his faithful steed to carry on his business, he sauntered slowly up towards the fallen man. As he did so a woman, still young and fair, came rushing breathlessly down Lark Lane, and pushing swiftly through the little crowd cast herself on the ground with a wild cry, and taking the fallen man's bleeding head upon her lap began to wipe it tenderly with a soft Saturday afternoon apron, and to kiss it the while in a perfect passion of grief and fear.

## 48 STARTING OF SCOWCROFT MILL.

The little knot of people now gathered stood looking on in pitiful interest, and the rugged Reuben, stepping slowly up, glanced over the boys' heads at the woman and her patient, then stepped back, stood gazing fixedly for a moment at the ornamental top of the lightning conductor of the mill chimney, and then, returning to his cart, began to pat and stroke his antiquated and astonished pony, keeping an eye meanwhile on the little excited crowd a few paces off.

A moment later the tall fat form of Quiet William appeared on the scene. He, too, took but a casual glance at the two on the ground, and was just stepping back when he caught Grace's eye fixed beseechingly upon him. Not a word did he speak, but striding into the ring he picked up the bleeding and still unconscious man, and hugging him to his breast as a mother might her child he strode rapidly off towards home, Grace walking tearfully at his elbow.

The drunken and bruised young master was very soon restored to consciousness and put to bed, his head was bound up by the doctor, and in an hour or so he was sleeping peacefully.

On the following Monday the great sale commenced; but when the bidding for the concern in one lot could not be got anywhere near the reserve price the auctioneer, to the surprise of all and the annoyance of the brokers, announced that his instructions to sell piecemeal had been withdrawn, and the proceedings were therefore at an end. The few Scowcrofters present felt inclined to cheer, for so long as the machinery remained in the mill there was always some hope of better times; but if that had been taken out it would have meant dark days indeed for the village.

A fortnight after this it was announced that Grace Tonge was going to marry the young master, broken and ruined though he was.

He had recovered from his injuries and began to look respectable again. Grace and Quiet William had induced him to "sign teetotal," and he was going about seeking work with a quiet earnestness that left no doubt as to his sincerity.

There were, unfortunately, plenty of empty cottages in Scowcroft just then, and Grace had saved a little money. How much she did not know, for William was her banker, and whatever thing she wanted there was always just enough left to buy it, so that before the wedding-day came she had a neat little house ready, of which she felt sufficiently proud. She still kept on going to the Moor Mills to work, and thus escaped much of the gossip that was going in the village. But whilst the women all shook their heads and spoke with looks of dark mystery about the matter, the men were united in applauding her splendid forgiveness and courage in taking such a doubtful lot as Mr.

George, so much so that Miles Grimshaw, who was never known to retract anything he had ever said, was one night surprised into conceding, "Hoo's a wench in a thaasand, if hoo is a backslider."

"Backslider!" jerked out Jacky o' th' Gap. "If that's backsliding, Aw wish aw th' wenches i' th' Schoo wur backsliders."

Then Mr. George, as he was still called, and Grace were married quietly one day at a little church in the suburbs of Wallbury, and came back to their cottage to start the world afresh.

When they had been married about a week George was sitting one night by the fire with Quiet William for a companion, whilst Grace busied herself in little household duties, when the door opened and, without the least warning, Grace's father entered the house. He looked perfectly cool, and was meditatively chewing a straw. He walked straight up to the fire and, stopping right before it, stood looking thoughtfully down upon it, whilst William, with a look of most unusual fierceness on his big fat face, rose softly from his seat as if preparing for action.

"Grace," said Reuben at last, without turning to look at her and altogether ignoring William's significant actions, "wot did ta leeav whoam fur?"

"Ta get married," gasped Grace, white to the lips with fear and excitement.

## STARTING OF SCOWCROFT MILL.

"Then haa is it as tha wur married ageean t'other day?"

"Aw wurna—Aw meean Aw—Aw—didna——" began Grace, but just then George broke in.

"I'll tell you, Reuben. I coaxed her away under the pretence of marrying her, making sure I could persuade her to be content with—well, with something less. But I couldn't, and now I thank God I couldn't. She came back as pure as—as an angel of God."

A gleam of concentrated anger shot out from under Reuben's heavy brows as he looked at his son-in-law, and his hand twitched ominously, but he restrained himself with an effort, and was still oblivious of William, who stood behind him ready apparently to fall upon him. Presently he proceeded.

"Aw yo'n letten her bur th' shawm of a fause report aw this toime?"

"Aye! God forgive me," cried George, with a flush of keen shame and a gesture of despair. "But——"

But Reuben put up his hand and stopped him, and, turning round from the fire and looking for the first time at his daughter, he asked, "An' if tha'd a' towd, it 'ud a shawmed him an' getten him inta trubbel wi 'th owd mestur?"

"Weel, bud, feyther——" began Grace, but Reuben interrupted her sternly.

"Aye or neaw, is it soa?"

"It is, Reuben, it is!" shouted George in a choking voice, and with tears of passionate grief. Another gesture of haughty impatience from Reuben, and then he proceeded, looking now at George, "Aw, yo leet her be turnt away fro' th' shop, an' still yo didn't speik?"

George dropped his head into his hands, and began to sob piteously; whilst Grace, looking past her father at the conscience-stricken man, was just about to step across to him, when Reuben seized her somewhat roughly by the arm and said: "An' efther aw that tha picked him up i' th' loan (lane) yond, an' naa tha's marrit him."

Grace dropped her head quickly, like a child caught in mischief, and as her father was evidently waiting for her answer she replied, with a sudden impulse of emotion, "Aye, an' Aw'd dew it ageean ta-morn."

Reuben suddenly dropped the girl's arm, leaned one elbow against the mantelpiece, whilst a sort of convulsion seemed to shake his sturdy frame.

There was an awkward silence for a moment, and at last he turned and looked down into the fire and said, as though talking to himself, "Fur twenty-five yer Aw've bin saying as ther wurn't sich a thing as trew religion, an' naa my own dowter's shown me as ther is. Aye, this *is* religion."

There was a low cry, and in a moment the white arms of Grace were round her father's neck, and she was kissing him passionately. Quiet William disappeared into the back scullery, and stood looking through the window and making all sorts of grotesque grimaces, with the object, apparently, of concealing from himself the fact that he was crying. George jumped to his feet and stood looking at Grace and her father in a sort of happy bewilderment, and presently he glided off into the scullery to William and began to shake him excitedly by the hand, as if he must find some means of relieving his feelings.

Reuben stayed a couple of hours after that, and then began to talk of departure. As he did so, however, he turned easily to George, who had resumed his place by the fire, and said, "Wot arta goin' ta dew fur a livin'."

"I don't know; I'm willing to do anything, but I get no chance somehow."

Reuben stood looking down at George and evidently reflecting. Then he turned and studied the fire again, and then once more scanning his son-in-law's mournful countenance he asked, as indifferently as he was able, "Haa mitch would it tak' ta get them 'bums' (bailiffs) aat?"

"Them," cried George, with a weary indifference, "three thousand pound at least, but I don't know where to get three."

Reuben began to move towards the door. When he had got half-way he stopped and turned round, saying as he did so, "Then, if yo'd a pardner as could put three thaasand in, yo could start?"

A look of momentary curiosity flashed into George's face, and glancing up he said, "Yes, if I *had*."

Reuben had reached the door and was toying with the sneck in a hesitant, absent manner. Then he turned, and with his hand still on the door-fastening he said, slowly, "Well, if yo'n a moind yo con start Westall and *Co.* i' th' mornin', wi' aar Grace theer as *Co.*, an' Aw'll foind th' brass," and before anybody could stop him he was gone.

Next morning Reuben turned up before eight o'clock, and pretended to be rather astonished that George was ready to accept his offer. But what seemed to please him most of all was the fact that neither Grace nor anybody else seemed to have any idea that he had money.

A week later the mill started, and Reuben, having previously bound over the others to strict secrecy, went on his rounds as usual, asking everybody he could get into conversation with wherever George had got his money from, and had they any idea who this mysterious *Co.* was? But the secret couldn't be kept. George could not hold it if everybody else could, and in a short time Grace's praises were being sounded throughout the neighbourhood, and everybody knew that her patient heroism had brought about the starting of the Scowcroft Mill.

As they sat over the vestry fire one Wednesday night about this time, Jimmy the Scutcher turned to Quiet William and said, with a short laugh, "Well, Aw reacon yond woman's name 'ull ha ta goa back upo' th' class-book."

"It's ne'er bin off!" was the quiet reply.

# ADAM AND THE STARS.

# ADAM AND THE STARS.

A LITTLE spare old man, with thin grey hair, which curled out at the ends, and with a well-worn walking-stick in one hand, and a large basket swung on the opposite arm, was trudging meditatively along Twiggy Lane on a certain Christmas Eve. It was an exhilarating night, the ground was hard with frost, the air crisp and light, and the moon and stars seemed to have shifted their quarters, and drawn considerably nearer to the earth to be ready to take their part in the Christmas festivities.

The old man looked pensive, and now and again cast despondent glances at his basket, which contained a few tempting looking oat-cakes. But presently, as he climbed the rugged road, the quickening influences of frost and stars began to affect him, and at length pulling up and looking hard into the shining sky he burst out—

> The opening he-e-evens around me-e shine,
> With bee-ems of sa-a-acred bliss.

The music excited him, the basket began to sway up and down upon his arm, and he commenced to beat time by striking the heavy ferruled end of his walking-stick upon the hard ground. Then he stopped suddenly, the stars were too many for him, and altogether too fascinating.

"Hay bud, yo *arr* pratty," he cried, addressing them; "yo looken loike angils as is coming a Kessmassing, an' has na getten near enough fur us ta see their wings," and then, breaking off again, he murmured to himself, "Shur up, thaa owd gabble maath! Dust think as they can yer *thee*," and turned to face the hill again towards home.

He was approaching a short row of cottages on the right, and as he did so a door opened and a gleam of light shot across the lane. As he heard the latch, the old man gave a little start and went nearer the hedge on the opposite side, as if wishing to avoid being seen, but a little child, a sturdy boy of five, came and stood in the light of the doorway, and catching sight of the passer-by, he cried: "Heigh! felley, merry Kesmus!" And then, getting a glimpse of the stranger's face, he suddenly retreated, crying as he banged the door: "By Gow! it's my grondad!"

The old man proceeded a few paces up the hill until he was quite past the cottages; and then, stopping and turning round to look at them he cried: "Aye, lad! it's the grondad! An' a bonny grondad he is! He's ne'er spokken to thee sin' tha wur born, neaw, nor thi mother nother." And there was passion and tears in his voice as he turned once more homewards.

## ADAM AND THE STARS.

But the child had given a very unhappy turn to his thoughts, and his face grew sadder and his step heavier as he plodded abstractedly along the lane.

As he reached the top of the hill, where the lane opened out a little and gave a fuller view around, he stopped again; addressing the gleaming stars above him he cried: "Aye, yo met weel stare at me. Aw've nobbut wun gronchild, an' *he* dar no' speik to me. Oh, Lord!" he continued, turning a haggard face toward the heavens, "we said we wur reet, an' ween allis stuck tew it as we wur reet. An' we've towd them as coom aat wi' uz as they wur reet; weel, if we wur Aw wish we hadn't a bin. Aw dunna cur," he cried, raising his stick as if to hold off some invisible objector, "if we wur reet, *Aw* want ta be wrung, an' ha' me dowter an' her little 'un back in my hert; aw'd rayther be wrung nor reet. Some folk can leeav feyther and mother and childer fur Thy sake, but Aw canna. Aw've bin trying for eight yer, and it's welly brokken my hert." And turning his face upwards to the stars once more he continued: "If yo *arr* angils coming to sing abaat peace, bring peace into Scowcroft Chapil, an' peace between me an' mine." Gazing half resentfully up at the stars for a moment, and then turning and looking wistfully back at the cottage he had just passed, he sighed heavily, and resumed his journey homeward. He lived at Spindlepoint, a full half-mile out of Scowcroft village. In early life he had been a handloom weaver, but on the introduction of the power loom he had been driven to seek some other method of getting a living, and after several unlucky experiments he had finally started business as a baker and hawker of oatcake.

His name was Adam Hargreaves, but he was most commonly known as "Adam o' the Point." He had always been poor, but his character had given him influence among his neighbours quite out of proportion to his worldly condition. He was a local preacher with a turn for anecdote, and enjoying considerable local popularity. For many years he had been one of the leading spirits at the Scowcroft Chapel, but some eight years before the time of which we write a most painful dispute had arisen.

A number of the young people had proposed the introduction of an organ into the chapel, and all the elders were up in arms against it at once. It was worshipping God by machinery. It was pride and "nowtiness" of heart. It was Popish. The conflict waxed hot, sides were taken, parties formed, harsh and severe things were said, and at last at a trustees' meeting Adam got hot and angry, and declared that the day the organ came into the chapel he would go out and never return. The meeting decided in spite of Adam's protest to have the instrument, and there was nothing for it but for Adam to carry out his threat. Of course he never intended to do so, but when his threat was defied it angered him afresh, and what was even more serious still, it angered his wife too. Now Mrs. Adam would have made two of her husband, not only in cubic proportions, but in strength of character. Adam's threat was an instruction from her, and she was all the more chagrined, therefore, when the trustees were not overcome by it. When it was done she insisted on Adam fulfilling it to the letter, and so on the following Sunday Adam's pew was empty, both morning and night. Another Sunday came and still no sign was made, and Adam, though he went about with an exaggerated assumption of vivacity, was eating his heart out with regret at the step he had taken, whilst Sarah, his daughter, openly protested as much as she dare. Then the new organ arrived and was opened with great ceremony, and still no sign of *rapprochement* came from the victorious innovators.

By this time Adam and those in sympathy with him began to feel that they had stayed away so long that they could not go back of themselves, and Mrs. Adam threatened her husband and daughter with penalties of unheard of severity if they even hinted at it. To make things worse, Mrs. Adam never went into the village without getting into some kind of squabble with one or other of her old friends, and one day, after spending a whole evening at the house of Miles Grimshaw, the itinerant village tailor, and one of Adam's chief opponents, she came home late, and kept Adam up until after midnight trying to compel him to agree to start a new cause. Adam was horrified, and resisted his strong-minded wife more than he had ever done before since they were married. At last, after calling him by every opprobrious name she could think of, she fell to coaxing and then to crying, and finally she reminded him that, having resigned his membership at the chapel, he had of course lost his place on the plan, and would now be unable to preach. This argument touched Adam's weakest point, for preaching was as the breath of life to him, and seeing in the proposal an opportunity for resuming his beloved work, he reluctantly consented, and a fortnight later opposition services were commenced in Joany's (Jonas's) loft, a large room which had once been used for weaving in the old handloom days.

Now the rubicon was crossed, and Adam, though he was almost perpetual curate at the "loft," felt so keenly about the matter that he never passed the old chapel without heaving a heavy sigh and suffering fierce pangs of remorse and self-reproach.

Then, as if to close for ever the gate of

repentance, a serious domestic difficulty arose. Adam was sitting one evening by the fire engaged with the Bible open before him preparing his Sunday sermon, when Sarah, his daughter, a comely, round-faced girl of two-and-twenty, came near her father's elbow, and, touching his blue shirt-sleeve nervously, said, shooting a quick glance of fear at her mother as she did so, "Feyther, dun yo' think yo' could spur me?"

Both parents lifted their heads quickly, and the mother in her usual brusque tones demanded: "Spur thee! We'er dust want ta goa? Thart allis aat. When Aw wur a wench——"

"Aw dunna meean that," interrupted Sarah, avoiding her mother's eye, and appealing humbly to her father.

"Aw meean, could yo' spur me for good? Aw want to get marrit."

Adam shot a glance at his wife and another at Sarah, and then, taking off his glasses with hands that shook unwontedly, and slowly closing his book, he replied: "Marrit, wench; whoa tew?"

"Aw thowt theer wur summat up wi' Aw them ribbins an' faldals, an' gooin' aat o' neets, that desateful hussy thaa! Aw reacon it's sum wastril or other tha's picked up wi'. When aw wor a wench——"

"Huish, 'Tilda!" cried Adam, closing his eyes wearily, and then turning to his now white and trembling daughter, he asked, gently: "Whoa is it, wench?"

"Abrum Briggs, feyther."

And then there was an explosion. Never in all the years of their married life had Adam seen his wife so utterly overcome with wrath, and never before had he guessed the power of quiet courage that slumbered in the breast of his daughter, for she stood up to her mother, and quietly and almost disdainfully defied her, and a war of words, such as Adam had never heard before, took place in that little sanded cottage. For Abram Briggs was the village butcher, and organist of the new organ, and son of the leader of the movement in favour of procuring it.

It was a terrible blow; even Adam felt that his daughter had been wanting in proper sympathy with him in his greatest earthly trial, and, though he spoke softly and tried to mollify his furious wife, he went to bed that night feeling grieved with his daughter and fearful as to what his wife might do.

'Tilda soon settled that. She got up to see Sarah off to her work next morning, and just as the girl was leaving the house she called her back, and, standing between the door and her daughter, said in words of cruel deliberateness: "Sayruh, thart gooin' aat o' th' haase thaa wur born in, an' wheer them as curs fur thee lives. Naa, if thaa comes back ta-neet it meeans as tha's gan yond organ-playing wastril up. Naa, then, which is it ta be, Whoam or Abrum?"

Sarah turned deadly white, paused a moment, drew a long breath, and then said: "Abrum, mother," and then glancing up the stairs at the foot of which she stood, she called out, "Good-bye, feyther, an' God bless yo'"; and in another moment she was out in the lane sobbing as if her heart would break as she made her way to the mill.

But she did not come back. She was married a little later on, and though eight years had passed she and her parents had never spoken to each other. Adam was for a time almost beside himself, and would have gone to his daughter for reconciliation many a time during the first year after her marriage but for his wife, and when he heard that a baby had arrived, and then that it was christened Adam, it took all Matilda's arguments and threats to keep him from going and "makkin it up."

Latterly, however, he had settled down to a dull sort of endurance, except that occasionally he had fits of longing which more than once took him to Sarah's door, but on each occasion his heart failed him, and he returned as he went.

Besides all this, Adam's customers fell off. He either could not or would not call at the houses of his former friends to sell his cakes, and, when this became clear to them, they retaliated by inviting an oat-cake man from Cartwistle to supply them, and as this worthy added the additional attractions of muffins and "pikelets" to his stock-in-trade, he not only got all Adam's customers who belonged to "th' owd body," but several others as well. And so for the last five years Adam had been going steadily down the hill, and now, as his patched and shiny clothes indicated, he was in real poverty. And his religious venture had not fared any better than his worldly one. One by one his chief supporters in secession fell away from him. Some died, some went back to the enemy, and some lapsed entirely, and were the subjects of much heart-searching and remorse to their leader. Only a few now remained, and these found it increasingly difficult to maintain the "cause" in the loft; and but for the fact that they could not bear the idea of giving the enemy cause to rejoice, would have been back long ago.

This statement of affairs is given to enable the reader to understand poor Adam's soliloquy as he wended his way home on Christmas Eve. The crisp air, the shining stars, and the suggestive and heartening season all tended to exhilarate him, but behind it all there was a depression and uneasy self-accusation which refused to be pacified. A moment more and he has arrived at Spindlepoint, and approaching the first of the half-dozen houses which made up that place of residence he opened a back kitchen door, and, with an apologetic cough, stepped inside.

"Theer's noabry wants whot (oat) cakes at Kessmas, wench," he said, anticipating deprecatingly his wife's first question, "it's aw cock-chicken and sparr-rib, an' pork-pie an' pudding."

"Aye, cock chickin and pork-pie's fur other fooak's wives," was the hard reply, "an' whot cake—and whot cake tew it—for thine."

Adam winced and glanced furtively through the back window at the stars, as if afraid they might be listening, and then, hanging his basket on a hook in the joist above his head, he heaved a heavy sigh and went quietly to his seat at the fireside.

"Aw ne'er thowt," resumed Mrs. Adam, fretfully, "when Aw left my good whoam up i' th' moor yond as Aw should iver come to a Kessmas dinner o' whot cakes."

"Ne'er mind, wench," replied Adam, in low, coaxing tones, "wee've a roof o'er aar yeds, an' a bit o' feire an enuff ta keep uz fro' clemmin. Let's be thankful!"

Thankful! But words seemed too weak to express 'Tilda's disgust at the whole business, so she whisked back into the kitchen, angrily slamming the door as she went.

A look of dull sadness sat on Adam's face as he cowered over the tiny fire, and very soon he was in profound and evidently not pleasant cogitation.

Presently his wife, who though she had grown hard and raspy of temper of late was an excellent manager, brought her husband his "baggin" (tea), and placed in the middle of the table a big plate containing the cakes which he had brought back. She did not sit down with him, but retired in grim dudgeon to the kitchen again, where Adam could hear her talking rapidly and angrily to herself. Then she seemed to relent, for she returned into the house and flopped down under Adam's delighted nose a steaming dish of toasted cheese.

"Bless the wench, tha *art* good ta me," cried he in eager tones, but 'Tilda curled her lip and disappeared again into the back regions.

An hour or two later the two sat before the fire in silence. Adam kept glancing at his wife's clouded face in hope of finding signs of relenting there. Presently he said in a tentative sort of tone, "Aw seed little Adam as Aw come whoam." There was no answer, but the lines about 'Tilda's mouth tightened.

After a long silence Adam ventured again, "Kessmas is rayther a looansome toime for— them as has na mony relations."

No reply. Another long pause, and then staring steadily into the fire and becoming suddenly quite husky and faltering in his tones, he said, "Aar Sayruh used trim th' haase up wi' pink papper, and holly and ivry. Dust think hoo'll be thinking abaat us ta-neet?"

And Matilda, with a face as hard as ever but with a traitorous quiver on her lips, rose hastily and went out to bring in the chips for next morning, but never a word did she speak.

Next morning as usual Adam was up first, and on his wife joining him her practised eye noted some change in him. He seemed to be struggling to suppress some excitement; he had put on his "blacks," now very threadbare, but still having an air of distinction about them, and was busy blacking his Sunday Wellingtons.

'Tilda saw all these things with secret wonderment, but never a trace of that feeling showed itself on her face, and she persistently ignored all Adam's palpable attempts to provoke a question.

There was certainly something the matter with her husband. His hand shook as he toasted the oat-cakes, he spilt his coffee upon the white clothless table-top, and would have flopped the milk into the sugar bowl but for 'Tilda's timely interference.

Breakfast over, Adam became distinctly restless. He couldn't sit still. He asked several times how much fast the clock was, and went to the back door again and again to study the weather, although the old lady in her infallible weather-gauge house had been out for many a day, and showed not the slightest inclination to retire in favour of her husband. At last he brought out his very venerable and carefully-preserved hat, which represented a fashion which had been in and out again several times since Adam purchased it, and began smoothing the nap with his coat-sleeve. And he did this in so distinctly challenging a manner as to almost compel the question he was waiting for. But Matilda would not respond, and was as ostentatious in her indifference as Adam was in his preparations, and it was only when he had actually reached the doorstep that she managed to squeeze out as lackadaisically as possible, "*Naa* wheer art gooin'?"

The question now that it had come shot through Adam like a shock. He seemed in a moment as if he were paralysed, and then glancing down the lane as if meditating flight, and turning to his wife with a quiet desperation in his look, he answered: "'Tilda, Awm goin' to th' chapil." Matilda gave a sharp cry, and rushed forward as if to stop him by main force, but he who usually quailed before her anger moved not.

"If we wur reet at the first," he cried, "we'en putten aarsels i' th' wrung lung sin. An', 'Tilda, my heart's bleedin' fur me dowter an' her little un. Aye, an' fur my owd friends yond. An' it's Kessmas toime, a toime o' peace an' forgiveness, an' Awm goin', chuse wot tha says."

Another minute and Adam was hurrying along the lane, striking his stick upon the hard ground by way of emphasis to his excited thoughts and pressing on rapidly as though he feared his wife was after him to bring him back.

But she wasn't. Standing at the little window at the end of the house, where she could see down the lane, she watched the retreating form of her husband with a strange intentness. And as she gazed the hard lines melted out of her face, her eyes began to shine with very unfamiliar dewiness, and at last she murmured, "God goa wi' the lad! Tha'rt best bit a human nature as iver walks that owd loan. Bless thi; Awm no fit ta tee thi shoon."

Meanwhile, Adam was pressing on towards the village. As he passed Quaking houses he looked out eagerly for a little curly head that never appeared, and presently slackened pace and felt his legs shaking under him as he came in sight of the chapel. Now, the Scowcroft male Methodists, however early they arrived at the gates, never thought of entering the chapel until the preacher arrived. A body of men, therefore, were propping up the railings and standing in various positions about the chapel door as Adam came in sight. One or two remarked, as they caught sight of him, that he'd been failing badly lately; and Jacky o' th' Gap, once Adam's inseparable chum, heaved a little sigh as he thought of happy Christmases of yore, and then remarked, "Aw thowt they didn't hev sarvis at the loft at Kessmas."

But by this time Adam had left the road, and, instead of turning down towards the "loft," had struck across the croft, and was making straight towards them. They stood back in silent astonishment as he came up, and turned to stare at each other in amazement as he passed them by with bowed head and walked right into the building.

The door was open, and a moment later they beheld Adam kneeling in the pulpit, with bent head and shaking with suppressed emotion. In a few moments the great news was taken into the vestry, where the appointed preacher was already selecting his hymns. Surprise and delight struggled together on the faces of all in that little room; and when Tom Crompton came in and said, in a tragic whisper, "Th' owd lad's picking his hymns aat," everybody looked at his neighbour in bewilderment.

"Well, that's th' coppest thing we'en seen i' this chapel for mony a yer," cried Jacky o' th' Gap, and everybody else looked emphatic endorsement.

For a moment the preacher was inclined to resent being thus supplanted; but the rest felt that, if Adam was coming back, they could not stand on trifles, and so, having pacified the dethroned one, they all hastened into the chapel, and Jacky climbed up the narrow stairs into the organ loft, and cried to the man at the instrument, "Thaa munna play that thing this mornin', naa."

By this time the news had got to the villagers, and many who had not intended to come presented themselves for worship.

Presently, in a high, unnatural tone, Adam gave out "Christians, awake"; and when that had been sung with quite unusual fervour he tried to pray. For a time everybody listened breathlessly, but before he had done the scene resembled an old Scowcroft revival meeting, and men and women of hard aspect and unemotional nature were laughing and crying together from pure overjoyfulness. By the time the sermon was reached even the dislodged local had forgotten his grievance, and in every pew men were propping their chins on the pew-tops before them, and eagerly waiting for Adam's discourse.

"Owd frens," he cried, "Aw conna keep away ony lunger." ("Praise the Lord!" from Jacky o' th' Gap.) "But Aw have na come back o' mysel', moind yo'. The Lord's driven me back. He wur maulin' wi' me aw day yesterday, till my hert wur welly brastin'; and last neet He sent me a vision."

One or two looked doubtful as to whether it was not presumptuous for Adam to rank himself with the ancient prophets, but Jacky o' th' Gap, with glowing face, cried out, "Tell us abaat it, lad!"

"Aw will, Jacky," resumed the preacher. "It wur a dream, yo' known. Aw thowt Aw wur i' th' Cinder Hill fields yond, an' lookin' up at th' stars, an' aw ath wunce Aw yerd a great shaat, an' Aw looked up and theer, by th' mon! Aw seed aw th' stars rushin' towart me loike a swarm o' bees. An' then when they geet narer me Aw seed as they worn't stars at aw, but angils. They leeted loike pigeons aw abaat me; an' then wun on 'em blew a trumpit, an' they aw struck up singing! Hay wot singing!—*Aw* ne'er yerd nowt loike it; Aw didn't know th' tune, but it wur that luvly an' meltin' Aw thowt Awd jine in. But the first nooat Aw tried the angil as wur th' leader turnt raand on me and shaated, 'Huish!'"

"Aw stopt fur a minute, thinkin' as Aw must a-bin aat o' tune, bud when they geet to th' chorus Aw dropped in wi' a soart of a hum, yo' known. But he yerd me, and afoor Awd getten three nooats aat he turnt on me ageean and shaated, 'Huish, mon!'"

"Well, Aw wur fair capped wi' th' job, but just then th' music went heigher and heigher an' swelled aat sa grand Aw couldn't howd in, so a brast aat wi' aw me might an' shaated

'Peace on earth, goodwill to men,' at th' top o' my vice. An' aw at wunce th' music stopt, an' aw th' angils started o' staring at me as if they'd ne'er yerd a mon sing afoor.

"'Wot arr yo' stopt fur?' Aw said, an' Aw wur gettin' a bit raspy abaat it, an' th' leading singer angil come up ta me, an' he said, 'A mon as sings wun thing and lives anuther conna sing wi' us.' An' just then Aw wakkened, an' theer Aw wur up a mi bed. Bud Aw could see wot th' angil meant, Aw could see as aw th' Kessmas hymns aw've sung sin Aw used sing 'em i' this owd chapil 'as bin lies—("Ne'er mind, lad," from two or three)—and Aw thowt ta mysel', if Aw conna sing wi' th' angils daan here, Awst ne'er ha' ta sing wi' 'em i' heaven. But Aw munn! Aw munn! An' so Aw've come to mak' peace, owd frens, and goodwill and brotherly love. Aw want ta sing with angils, aye, wi' th' best on 'em."

The Scowcroft Chapel, although small, had a gallery all round, and all the leading lights of the church sat in the front gallery pews, and so those near the preacher could reach him if they wished, and just at that moment there was a clattering sound in the neighbourhood of the organ behind Adam, and a moment later a burly young fellow with red face and wet eyes leaned over the gallery front, and stretching out his hand as far as he could reach, cried eagerly: "Dun yo' meean it, feyther?"

As quick as thought Adam wheeled round, and snatching at the out-stretched hand of his organist son-in-law he replied: "Aw dew, lad, Aw dew," and began to shake hands as if he never intended to leave off.

Then came whole rows of hands from over the gallery front, and then an opening of pew doors below and a swarming of eager men up the pulpit stairs. In the midst of it somebody struck up—

> What, never part again!
> No, never part again.

And they sang it, and sang it, and shook hands with each other, and beamed on Adam with their homely faces all aglow with delight and affection. Nobody ever could properly tell how that service ended; but, at any rate, there was no more sermon, and after standing round the Communion rail and singing—

> Oh, happy day, &c.,

and

> If this our fellowship below, &c.,

someone struck up Adam's favourite hymn in the happy days of old—

> I want to be an angel,

and when that had been sung through several times over, they finally, and with manifest reluctance, began to disperse.

Half-a-dozen of them immediately got into

## ADAM AND THE STARS.

something as near to a dispute as the occasion would permit as to who should have the honour of taking Adam home to dinner, but when Abram Briggs put in his claim everybody else at once withdrew. As the two approached Abram's cottage that excited young man had an inspiration.

"Stop here a minute, feyther," he cried, and thrust the old man behind the trellis-work screen that protected the door, and then, putting on a very serious look, he stepped inside and said, apologetically, "Sayruh, Awm bringing th' preicher ta dinner."

Sarah's face, red and hot with cooking, became redder still as she answered: "Th' preicher? Bud it's nor aar turn."

"Neaw, but Aw thowt thaa'd happen loike him as it's Kessmas day."

"Thaa knew varry weel Aw loiken noabry bud me own o' this day—bud wheer is he?" she broke off, as a peculiar look on Abram's face attracted her attention.

But before Abram could answer the old man, who had heard most of what had been said, came sliding round the porch.

"Hay, feyther! feyther!" cried Sarah. "God bless yore owd face! Well, this is a gradely Kessmas!" And whilst Adam and Sarah were making up for their long separation, by what to Lancashire folk were most extravagant demonstrations of joy, Abram was yoking the pony, and having driven round to pick up Jacky o' th' Gap, they rattled up the old lane to Spindlepoint, and after a long struggle Matilda was induced to come with them, and soon Adam and his wife were so much at home in Abram's house that nobody could possibly have believed that they had never been in before.

As they went home that night Adam told his wife all about the stars, and the part they had played in the transactions of the day, and after Matilda had stood some moments gazing silently up at them, she did what she had not done for many a long year before—she took her husband's face between her hands, and, after looking intently into his eyes for a moment, silently kissed him.

# WILLIAM'S IDOL.

# WILLIAM'S IDOL.

## I.

It had been a wet washing-day, and knowing full well all that that meant to his natty, house-proud little wife, Quiet William had consumed his "baggin" in discreet but highly characteristic silence. He knew by many experiences that this was the one thing that was always too much for his wife's temper, and as he ate he glanced furtively at her from time to time as she went about clearing away with manifest impatience the last signs of the struggle through which she had passed during the day.

It had always been one of William's boasts that he never knew when it was washing-day at his house, and Hannah, or "Tan," as she was always called, though she affected total indifference on the subject, was secretly very proud of this implied compliment, and exceedingly anxious to be always worthy of it.

But when the rain pours down with steady, exasperating persistence *all* the day, and when the "copper" flue positively won't draw, and you have been compelled to use slack because that "gallous wastril" Toffy Joe has not brought the coals though they have been "ordert" nearly a week, and evening has come and the clothes hang about in a clammy fog, is it any wonder if you do feel "a bit nattered"?

Oh! what a relief it would have been if Joe had brought the coals just then. She could have "cooambed his yure for him" with completest satisfaction, and with even a gratifying sense that she was discharging a duty.

But Joe hadn't come, and as for her husband, she might as well try to quarrel with the peggy-stick, as she nearly had done once that day, as attempt to get up a word-battle with him. If he would only say one little word—anything would do—to set her off and open the valve that was confining all this suppressed and accumulated wrath. But William wouldn't. Of course he wouldn't. He never did. There was no satisfaction in a husband like that. He wouldn't even *look* wrongly at her. His face was as blank as a dead wall. Could anything be more aggravating?

By this time William had finished his meal and drawn back his chair into its corner. He knew just how it was with "Tan." He wished in his very heart she wouldn't trouble so much about trifles. What did it matter? He had been thinking about her often during the day, and watching somewhat anxiously through the dirty mill windows for a change in the weather. But it hadn't come, and he had returned home full of sympathy with his wife, but a sympathy not unmixed with apprehension. In this state of mind he quietly glided his hand up the chimney jamb and took down from the mantelpiece a short black pipe, and began to charge it, glancing uneasily round as he did so, as if fearful of having been caught in the act. Then he lighted a "spill" and applied it to the pipe; and then, after certain experimental puffs to make sure that all was right with his comforter, he drew two or three long, satisfying pulls, and quite unconsciously heaved a deep sigh of relief, looking as he did so with a look of complacent contentment at the red-hot spot in the top of the pipe bowl.

It was a little thing, and might ordinarily have passed unnoticed, but to one who was vainly waiting for any sort of provocation it was more than sufficient. Hannah was busy filling the "maiden" with clothes, but the moment her quick ear caught William's sigh she whisked round, and was about to challenge it. But another thought struck her; her resentment deepened, and from irritable complaint she passed in thought to satire, and cried out, ironically, "Th-e-e-r! tha's some cumfort i' th' wold, hasn't tha', poor, ill-used craytur?"

William was startled; he took the pipe slowly out of his mouth, and turning round to look at his wife, he cried in astonishment, "Tan!"

"'Tan'! Aye, it's aw Tan. Aw th' trubble

o' thi loife's cum fro' Tan, hesn't it? Bud ne'er moind, tha's getten thi poipe, tha knows. Thi own woife, as mauls an' slaves fur thi yer in an' yer aat's noawheer wheer thi poipe cums, is hoo?"

William snatched the offending idol out of his mouth, and holding it down behind his hand as if to conceal it, cried in genuine distress, "Dust na loike it, wench?"

"Loike it? Oh, aye, Aw loike it, sure-*li*. Aw conna help bud loike it when him as owt tak' cur on me thinks mooar o' it nur he does o' me."

"Hannah!" cried William in shocked and distressed tones.

"'Hannah'! Dunna 'Hannah' me, mon; tell th' trewth an' say 'Bacca! bacca! Wot's a woife tew a mucky owd poipe?' William Dyson, Aw've towd thi mony o toime thar't a slave tew it. Thar't smookin' thi brains, an' thi temper, and thi soul away. Bud Aw'll say me say if Aw dee fur it."

As this torrent of raillery was being hurled at him William looked more and more amazed. The words used by his overwrought little wife were of no moment to him, but the weary soreness of mind which their employment revealed seriously alarmed him, and he quietly slided the pipe back upon the mantelpiece and sank down into his chair.

For a moment or two he looked earnestly at

his wife, but perceiving that the pent-up fire had now spent itself and that "Tan" was already penitent, he turned and looked musingly into the fire-grate, whilst Hannah, snatching up her basket of clothes, whisked off into the scullery.

She banged the door after her, but the latch did not catch, and so it remained just the least bit open, and William sat up in the attitude of listening, following and interpreting the various sounds and movements going on in the scullery. First he heard the basket banged into two or three different places, as it evidently would not stand properly. Then he heard a noisy rattle amongst the pots, and then a demonstrative scraping out of a porridge pan. Presently there was a pause, and just as the silence was beginning to affect him he heard a sniff, and then another, and then a soft blowing of the nose, followed by a covering cough. Then all was quiet again, and after a minute or two William heard a long sigh. For some time he waited for his wife to come forth, and glanced every now and then toward the scullery door, but the disturbed woman gave no sign. Presently he unclasped and drew off his clogs, removed his coat, looked at his fingers to make sure they were not greasy, and then, groping up the corner of the fireplace, he drew down a carefully preserved but venerable fiddle.

Gently and cautiously, and with many a

glance at the little door, he ran his hand over the strings, and screwed with expressive grimaces at the pegs.

Then he paused again, took a long expostulating sort of look at the obdurate door, and then, lifting the fiddle to his chin, and drawing the bow across the strings gently, he played a few bars, and softly glided off into "Annie Lisle."

This was the first tune William had ever learnt to play, and the one that first won him a smile from the pretty Hannah Grimshaw, in the days of auld lang syne. As he played his eyes glistened and his lips moved; but, however eagerly he watched that green inner door, it would not open. Then he ran off into snatches of old chapel tunes and anniversary anthems; and just as he was waxing warm with the ever green "How beautiful upon the mountains," the door gave way, and Hannah, with a chastened countenance, came forth carrying the porridge pan. She brought it straight to the fireplace and perched it on the front bar. Then she leaned her left arm on the mantelpiece and her head on her arm, and stood looking dreely down into the pan and stirring as for dear life.

Then she paused a moment, and William, with a hungry coaxing look at her, glided off into Hannah's favourite revival tune, and then, as her face suddenly saddened, he blinked his

## WILLIAM'S IDOL.

eyes in the intensity of his earnestness, and bending eagerly over the instrument, and apparently putting all the music of his soul into it, there came trembling forth:

> Though often here we're weary,
> There is sweet rest above, &c., &c.

Great tears swam into Hannah's already red eyes; she dropped back into a rocking-chair, covered her face with her hands, and sobbed unfeignedly, whilst the boiling porridge kept up a sort of bloberty-blob, bloberty-blob, blob, blob accompaniment to the music.

William played on, apparently too absorbed in his occupation to notice his weeping wife. But presently he paused and leaned back in his chair, and began to contemplate the floor-boards above his head, as though trying to think of another tune. But the melody would not come, and so, after waiting a long time, ostentatiously oblivious the while of his wife's presence, he was just about to put the instrument away when Hannah got quietly up, took hold of the pan of porridge, lifted it gently upon the "hob," and then, looking intently down into its depths, she murmured, in a tone in which confession, apology, and caressing were curiously blended, "Hay, lad! ther's nowt loike the owd tunes, is ther?"

And William, who had just found the peg he was groping for, hung the fiddle up, and then, slipping his hand along the mantelpiece to feel for his pipe again, answered gently, "Neaw."

## II.

Now this was by no means the first attack which old Hannah had made on her husband's besetment. She had never really become reconciled to it, or at any rate she would never admit that she had. But somehow William had got the idea that his little wife was not at bottom opposed to smoking, only she liked to have some handy subject for feminine raillery, and this was generally the easiest and most obvious point of attack. And at first William was inclined to think that this was only another, though a somewhat more serious, outbreak of the same feeling, the additional severity of it being of course attributable to the wet washing-day, and his wife's consequent and very excusable irritation. But somehow he didn't forget it as he generally did. As a rule his wife's "bits o' husks," as he called them, were forgotten almost immediately, but for some reason or other this last incident refused to be thus ignored.

Hitherto also his beloved fiddle, though brought in because of its tried influence on the temper of his wife, succeeded generally in dispelling gloom from his own mind and relieving it of all unpleasant recollections. But for once even the fiddle failed. Hannah was certainly kinder than usual after her outburst, so that there was nothing from that source to prevent him forgetting the late incident. And yet for the life of him he couldn't.

All next day, as he went about in the mill, his thoughts reverted with most unusual and distressing frequency to the occurrence of the previous night. What could be the reason of it? Did Hannah really dislike tobacco so much as that, and had she all these years been quietly enduring it with only occasional half-playful protests? And if so, had he become such a callous wretch and so wrapped up in his pipe as never to have noticed what his poor wife was suffering? Was tobacco so blinding and benumbing his perceptions that he could no longer read his wife's feelings, or was he growing so hardened as not to care what she felt? If so, what a hard-hearted monster he was becoming! And if the enslaving pipe was producing such blinding and searing influence on his mind, what must it be doing to his soul!

Once started on this line of thought, William soon recalled a score of little unnoticed circumstances which he now saw were signs of spiritual decay.

Things began to look very serious indeed.

"Tan" had always been much better than he, he well knew. What if she had noticed his spiritual declension, and had been so troubled about it as eventually to lose her temper in warning him? Had anybody in the world such a wife as he had? Oh, what a sinner he must be to have treated her like this!

This kind of torturing self-accusation went on for days, and poor William got no relief. He had not got far enough for the desperate remedy of total abstinence from the weed, but he had got far enough for any indulgence in it to make him miserable, so that the "bacca" didn't taste the same, and he had to admit ruefully to himself, "Aw con noather smook nor leeav it alooan."

And then William was a steadfast believer in Providence. Every unusual occurrence was to him a sign of something, and so when, on the following Sunday, the appointed preacher was not able to attend through sickness, and had sent a "Primitive" to take his place, William regarded it as nothing short of direct interference of Providence when the preacher, taking for his text, "Little children keep yourselves from idols," launched out into a terrible tirade on the use of tobacco, and clinched his argument by relating a thrilling incident about a man who had a dream in which the recording angel stuck to it against all that he could say that his name was not in the Book of Life. And at last, after reading the record through for the fourth time, announced that the name was there, but so hidden under tobacco smoke that it was scarcely decipherable.

This was awful! Whatever doubt William might have had as to the necessity of giving tobacco up was now dispelled, for this remarkable change of preachers, bringing with it such an entirely unexpected but richly-deserved message to him in his benighted idolatry, left not the slightest doubt in his mind that "Providence" was in it all.

He felt sorely in need of advice. But to whom should he go? All his old friends smoked more than he did himself with the exception of Miles, and Miles only abstained because he had tried again and again and couldn't manage smoking. What should he do? He longed to consult "Tan"; but he felt sure she would pretend to like it out of pity for him, and she had already expressed herself in trenchant terms about the sermon that had disturbed him. So that she was clearly prejudiced and her opinion was not to be relied upon.

Whilst he was debating these matters with himself and smoking rather more than usual as an aid to reflection, but with a consciousness of growing depravity, the prospect of help came from an entirely unexpected quarter.

There was in connection with the chapel a Literary and Mutual Improvement Society. It was only active during the winter months, and seemed to hibernate in the summer.

It held fortnightly meetings, and was a sort of rendezvous for all the irresponsible freelances and amateur critics of the village. The majority of the members belonged to the chapel, and consequently the meetings were held in the large back vestry at the rear of that building. But it must not be supposed on this account that the rulers of the synagogue approved of the institution. To them it was anathema. Its very existence presupposed dissent and tacit rebellion, and its continued prosperity was a distinct menace to all proper authority. However promising a young man was in the church he was given up by the leaders immediately it was known that he had joined the "littery." More than once the question had been seriously debated in private whether a "mutualer" could be recognised as a member, and the fact that such wild and treasonable ideas as report said were propagated at the meeting should be spoken on Methodist premises was gall and wormwood to the responsible heads of the church.

But what could they do? When the obnoxious society was first formed, and permission was sought for holding the meetings on Methodist premises, the trustees were horrified, and regarded the suggestion as a deliberate insult. But when it turned out that Adam o' th' Point, who had separated from "th' owd body" some time before and had started an opposition service in "Joany's loft," was offering the new society the use of his tabernacle, and that the reckless spirits at the head of the new movement were so bent on carrying out their purpose that they would go there if not accommodated on their own premises, the trustees felt that they were on the horns of a dilemma, and eventually consented to grant the use of the room, relieving their minds afterwards by denouncing the whole thing as a "Maantibank club."

Ever since then there had been wars and rumours of wars in the chapel without end. Miles Grimshaw expressed his supreme contempt for the intellectual endowments of the members on every conceivable opportunity. Quiet William shook his head and sighed sadly. Jimmy the Scutcher, after drawing out one of the most enthusiastic of the advocates for the new society, and listening with a show of friendly interest to the discussion of various taking titles for the society, made an atrocious pun on the mutual, calling it *mew*tual, and finally suggested that it should be called the "Tom Cat Society," and all its literary productions "pussy cat tails." But a crisis arose when one day a beaming youth, swollen out with a sense

of the importance of his new dignity as
secretary, came into the preacher's vestry and
handed the steward a pulpit notice announcing
the opening *soirée*. Jacky o' th' Gap peremptorily refused to have the paper " geen aat ";
and when the second minister, who happened
to be the preacher for that morning, ventured
to plead for the announcement, Jacky lost all
control of himself, and cried angrily, "Yo moind
yore preiching, and leeav theeas galivanting
bermyeds ta me."

The society was now in its third session, and
was, perhaps, all the more popular with the
rank and file of the chapel-goers because it was
known to be so objectionable to the officials.

One Sunday morning, during William's painful mental struggles about his beloved pipe, the
preacher announced that on the following
Wednesday night an essay would be read at
the Mutual Improvement Society meeting on
" Tobacco," which would be followed by open
discussion.

The essayist on this occasion was to be
Abram Briggs, whom everybody knew as a
violent teetotaler and anti-tobacconist, and so
the whole affair presented itself to William's
mind as another direct providential interference to meet his difficulties and bring him to
repentance. And so he felt bound to swallow
all his scruples and go and hear what could be
said on the subject. That very night his

terrible brother-in-law Miles announced his intention of going to the meeting, too, and "giving them 'Johnny Raw's' belltinker," and as this threat spread rapidly through the village everybody felt that such an occasion was not to be missed, and so the affair promised to be a great success.

Once or twice only had the officials of the church patronised these obnoxious meetings, but on this occasion, feeling that the subject was a direct challenge to them, they all announced their intention of being present, especially after they discovered that Miles the redoubtable would actually enter the arena against the essayist.

This was certainly an opportunity not to be missed, and every man smacked his lips and blinked his eyes in prospective enjoyment of the "bancelling" the hapless essayist would receive.

On Wednesday morning, however, a most disappointing announcement had to be made. Miles was ill, and as he had been working the week before in a house where fever had since broken out, the doctor feared he might have caught the infection, and peremptorily forbade him to leave the house for three days lest he should spread disease.

Poor Miles! It took him quite a quarter of an hour to relieve his mind to the doctor and pour scorn on his regulations. Then he sent a stern message to his brother-in-law William, exhorting him on peril of certain terrible pains and penalties to "Goa an' ston up fur thisel' at th' meeting," and another message was sent to the essayist challenging him to postpone the meeting until Miles was better, and thus secure for himself "th' best letherin' thaa iver hed i' thi loife."

When the meeting came everybody spent the few minutes before the business commenced lamenting the enforced absence of Miles. Presently the essayist was called upon to read his paper, and as he rose to do so Quiet William leaned abstractedly back against the wall under the window, and closed his eyes to listen.

The reader began by stating that tobacco was not a product of civilisation, but a noxious plant used by savages to poison snakes, and introduced to the notice of Europeans by the debased and irreclaimable Indians of the wild West. (Here William began to feel heartily ashamed of himself.) The essential spirit of tobacco, the essayist went on, was a deadly poison called nicotine, one or two drops of which would poison a cat (William winced, and felt that he was beginning to perspire). The reader next gave a list of the diseases which were either originated or developed by the deadly weed, and enlarged eloquently on its benumbing effect on the brain and conscience, and William was conscious of several mysterious pains in the head and stomach, and felt himself a hardened backslider.

Then the essayist gave statistics to show how much money was wasted on "this seductive but deadly plant" every year, with hints of the good that might be done with such money if it were spent on philanthropic objects, and then wound up with a highly rhetorical declamation, in which the man who used tobacco was denounced as "a sensualist, a spendthrift and a slave."

Whilst the essay was being read, Jacky o' th' Gap had followed it by an energetic running comment, which gradually swelled into one final explosive negative, and before the chairman could invite any one to reply, Jacky was on his feet pouring out the vials of his wrath upon both the paper and its bold author. But the members of the society prided themselves on their familiarity with the rules of debate, and several of them at once rose to order. This only made Jacky the wilder and more incoherent, and after lashing out on every side for several minutes he was suddenly called to order by the chairman, and sat abruptly down in a pet, leaving a feeling in the minds of the assembled company that he had certainly not helped his own side.

Then two or three of the young orators of the society took up cudgels in defence of the paper just read, and kept themselves so well within the lines of fair argument that their very moderation created an impression favourable to the essay; and as Jimmy the Scutcher was absent and the redoubtable Miles sick, there was positively nobody bold enough to represent the opposition except poor William, and he hovered between a desire to get up and avow his determination to eschew the wicked weed for ever, and a sneaking inclination, coming, he knew, from the old Adam, to slink out of the room on the very first opportunity.

At this trying moment a long-necked, rather hysterical-looking youth, a big piecer at the mill, got up to make his maiden effort in oratory. He had started with a sentence which was a modified approval of the essay, and was just referring to his notes for the next point amidst profound silence, when bang! bang! came at the window outside, the top half of which was suddenly swung open, and through the aperture thus made came the bristling terrier head of Miles Greenshaw, muffled almost to the eyes in shawls and "comfortables," and a moment later his high, strident voice was heard crying, "Well, hez that meety (mighty) Giant getten his little maase kilt yet? Yo' ninnyhommers, yo'! If yo'd set ta wark a huntin' some o' th' big rooarin' lions o' sins ith' wold atstecad o' freetining a little maase of a sin like bacca, it 'ud leuk o foine seet better on yo'.—Naa, then!

naa then!" He broke off suddenly. "Leme be! leme be, wilta!" And at that moment the shadow of a big female fell on the window, poor Miles suddenly disappeared, and as the cold air came in through the aperture the debaters had mental pictures of a little man being carried off home, kicking and struggling like a rebellious baby, in the arms of his buxom wife. There was no chance of any serious argument after that. The meeting laughed and laughed again, and every attempt to resume the debate was but the signal for a fresh explosion. Then the people, feeling that the entertainment was over, began to disperse, and in a few minutes poor William was going moodily home, confessing to himself that he had got "noa furruder," and fighting with a feeling of relief and unholy satisfaction which he realised to be very wicked indeed.

### III.

Two or three weeks passed away, during which William was slowly relapsing into his old habits and his old contentment therewith.

In fact, as he sat musing by the fire and sucking away at his "comforter" of an evening, it seemed to him somehow that his pipe tasted sweeter than ever, and he was compelled to admit that the mental struggles through which he had recently passed gave an added relish to the enchanting weed. Hannah, too, had never said a single word against his habit since the scene recorded in our first chapter, and had even brought home a new spittoon without the lecture which generally accompanied any such expenditure.

One day, however, William was suddenly and most unexpectedly awakened out of his sinful peace. It occurred at the missionary meeting, always a great institution at Scowcroft.

The deputation—a real live missionary—had made a most eloquent speech, during the deliverance of which William's intentional shilling had gradually grown first to eighteenpence and then to a florin, and when at last the speaker sat down after a most touching appeal for help, William felt that nothing less than half-a-crown would do justice to the occasion.

Before the glow of fervour which the missionary's speech enkindled had had time to cool, the chairman called upon the curate to address the meeting. Now this was an entirely new item in the programme. The curate was new to Scowcroft, and had shown himself so very friendly to the chapel people that Jacky o' th' Gap had taken it upon himself to invite him to the missionary meeting. The vicar, who was regarded as "a dacent chap, bud terrible standoffish," was away, and so Mr. Bransom had nobody to consult, and had cheerfully accepted Jacky's invitation.

To William all this was pure delight, and so when the curate rose he quietly hugged himself with pleasure, and settled himself down in his seat for another good time.

In a moment or two the young priest was speaking on self-sacrifice, and began in what William regarded as quite a Methodist sort of way to show how much people spent on luxuries, and how comparatively little they gave to philanthropic objects.

William felt a cold chill creep down his back, and he looked round with an uneasy glance to see whether everybody was not looking at him as the guilty culprit, whilst a little tin canister and a short brier pipe rose like ghosts before him, and an old brass box containing thick twist deep down in his pocket began to feel very hot, as if even in that snug retreat it was blushing. Somehow the curate had a most awkward way of putting things—no wrapping the thing up at all; and William positively caught him looking straight at him as he was saying some of his most pointed things. This was no sort of missionary speech. It would certainly spoil the collection. Besides, it was so personal. William's indignation was fast getting the better of him. Then his thoughts took another turn. It was strange that the curate should be at this missionary meeting of all others when the vexed question of tobacco or no tobacco was still under debate in William's mind. Stranger still that he should select this particular kind of argument, and talk about giving up little indulgences for the sake of others. It was Providence and nothing else! God was still wrestling with the hardened Ephraim, who was so entirely given up to his idols. Oh, what an extravagant wretch he was! Blowing money into the air that might be the means of saving some poor little black wench. (Somehow, William always thought of the heathen as little black wenches, perhaps because he had once had a little wench of his own; only, instead of being black, she was very fair—too fair, indeed, for health and life.)

The curate was still talking and still appealing for more self-sacrifice. Oh, why didn't he stop, or change the subject? William was nearly beside himself, and when at last the young parson, with just the slightest possible break in his voice, appealed for self-sacrifice "just for the love of Jesus," William had great difficulty in preventing himself "brastin' aat o' shriking," and heaved a sigh and choked back a sob as the speaker resumed his seat.

And now the battle had all to be fought over again, and William regarded himself as roused for the last time from his false peace, and with one final chance before him. How could he be a Christian and cling so to his pipe? It was impossible. It wouldn't bear thinking of, and the big, tender-hearted man went out of the chapel with a terrible load of guilt on his soul.

He did not smoke that night, but sat musing by the fire long after Hannah had gone to bed, and finally he followed her with the great question still unsettled.

Next day William was absent-minded and gloomy all day. When asked his opinion of the missionary meeting he endorsed the universal verdict as to the missionary's address, but found it difficult to speak with unqualified approval of the curate's deliverance. He could not rest in the house that night, and at last got a richly-deserved taste of Hannah's tongue, "trapesin' in an' aat loike a maddlin'."

Then he sat down by the fire, but as he began to fear that "Tan" would notice his distraught air and abstinence from the pipe, he sidled off into the lanes for an uneasy stroll.

For a time he walked up and down muttering to himself and praying, and presently he wandered across the croft and over the bridge into the wooded lanes on the other side of the canal. Then he strolled back, and stood leaning over the parapet of the bridge, and looking into the muddy waters below..

## WILLIAM'S IDOL.

There was a waning moon, and in its light William stood peering down upon the waters in anxious thought.

He heaved a great sigh, and put his hand into his coat-pocket. Then he hesitated, stood staring down the canal at a grimy coal-barge lying alongside the mill engine-house. Then he sighed again, and with a desperate effort thrust his hand into his pocket and drew it out full.

For a moment or two he stood in the moonlight, looking steadily and sadly at the things he held in his hand.

There was the little tin canister, there was the brass tobacco-box, and there was his old and beloved pipe. William laid them carefully on the parapet and stood looking at them intently. Then he looked hastily round to see if there was anybody near, and then glanced up at the moon as if objecting to be so spied upon. In a little while he picked up his pipe, and handling it with great affection he turned it over and over again, examining with strange fondness a crack which he had repaired himself long ago. Then he laid it down carefully on the bridge again, and picking up the little brass box he opened it and took a long relishful sniff at its fragrant contents. Closing the lid presently with a loud snap, he commenced rubbing the box on his thigh to make it shine still more. Then he put it down alongside the pipe and canister, and heaving a deep sigh stood looking wistfully at them.

Presently he sighed again, took another look round as if he would have been glad of an interruption, and then, gathering the treasures once more into his great hand, he held them out over the dim waters below. Then he drew his arm back again and hesitated. "Th' little wenches! Th' little black wenches," he murmured, thickly; "they're sunbry's little Hannahs if they arrna moine. Lord help me! Lord help me!" and as he thus prayed he thrust his arm slowly over the parapet and held his treasures over the water again. Then he shut his eyes very tightly, paused a moment waveringly, sighed again, and slowly opened his hand.

Flop! Flop! went the pipe and box and canister into the canal. William stood for a moment peering through the pale moonlight at the little widening rings on the water, and then, with a sigh that was almost a sob, turned hurriedly towards home.

By the time he reached his own house he had partly recovered himself, and was fast overcoming his regret at parting with his treasures, and he did so the more easily, as he not only began to feel a comfortable sense of moral elation at the sacrifice he had made, but commenced also to be apprehensive as to how he would deal with his wife. She would be sure to notice if he did not take his nightcap pipe, and he was not sure that, in spite of all her recent denunciations of tobacco, she would allow his sudden and complete abstinence to go unchallenged.

He knew also that he would have a very rough handling from his cronies at the chapel; but as he was often in disgrace with them, he felt less concerned about that than otherwise he might have done.

But however unsuspecting Hannah might have been, her husband's manner would have aroused curiosity in the most indifferent mind. He sidled into the house humming a tune with a busy sort of drone in it. Then he took down the violin and began to play, running, however, from one tune to another in a most erratic and confusing sort of way.

Then he started a conversation, but he talked so rapidly and incoherently, and so entirely unlike his own laconic style, that that alone would have been sufficient to excite suspicion in a far duller person than his sharp little wife. Presently he took his clogs off, and made off upstairs to bed in his stocking feet, for slippers were quite uncommon luxuries to Scowcroft males.

When he had got upstairs old Hannah stood listening on the hearthstone at the creaking of the boards over her head under William's enormous weight. She was evidently thinking rather than listening, and in a moment or two she turned with one of her characteristic jerks, and drawing a low stool from under the table she stepped upon it and began exploring the mantelpiece end just where William's smoking materials were kept. They were all gone!

Then she leaned over and searched a little three-cornered shelf in the chimney corner, but nothing satisfactory could she find. Then she got down from her perch, put the stool away in an absent pondering way, stood for a time looking fixedly into the fire, and then with an "Hay mi," "Hay *dear* mi," she proceeded to join her husband. No word or hint did Hannah give of her discovery, but William was kept awake for an hour or two that night with the disturbing certainty that his wife had found him out.

Several days passed, during which William went through all the stages of experience to which those who make such self-sacrifices are subject. At first he was buoyed up by an elevating sense of moral victory. Then he suddenly discovered that this was spiritual pride, a worse sin even than smoking. Then the colour seemed to fade out of his sacrifice, and he felt inclined to despise his own heroic act, and to think cynically of the romantic appearance his actions had for a time assumed in his mind.

Oddly enough, for two or three days he felt

no great desire for the foresworn weed, and was surprised and very inconsistently disappointed at the ease with which he had conquered it after all.

A few days more, he told himself, and he would be entirely free from the appetite, and, strange to say, he did not feel half as elated at the prospect as he knew he ought to be. Then his friends found him out, and the obstinacy aroused by their rough and unsparing chaff carried him over several more days. By this time he felt that the struggle was practically over, and he was greatly surprised, if not disappointed, that he had got through the crisis so easily.

For three or four days now he had had practically no desire at all for his old idol, and was beginning to despise the hold which he had imagined it had obtained over him.

Meanwhile, Hannah was greatly exercised about the matter. Really she did not care a jot whether her husband smoked or not, only she must have something to "read off abaat" occasionally. In fact, she had so long been accustomed to tobacco that she was surprised to find how much she missed it herself. And if she missed it, what must her husband be passing through! Nobody knew better than she how dearly he loved his pipe, and although, of course, she took care not to let him see it, and kept him in his place out of sheer force of habit, yet she loved her big, quiet, tender-hearted husband with intense affection, and was ready to cut her tongue out when she found that its wicked wagging had deprived him of one of his few earthly indulgences. For several days now, therefore, she had been narrowly watching William, and inflicting on herself all sorts of mental castigations. Sixpence per week! she said to herself; that was all he ever spent. What was that if it really did give him the pleasure it seemed to do? And then she went back over all the years of their married life, and recalled the numberless sacrifices, great and small, he had made for her and for their one child now in heaven. She reminded herself also of the many nights on which he had sat up nursing little Hannah during her illness, and the delight which the little angel took in seeing her father puff away at his pipe. Then she compared William to all the other men she knew, and especially to Silas Shaw, for whom she had once nearly given William up in their courting days, but who was now a rough, drunken, canal boatman. Oh, what a wicked woman she had been, and how keenly she watched William during those days of his abstinence!

One day as she was musing on these things the greengrocer came to the door, and Hannah, hastily wiping away a tear with the corner of her apron, went out to make her purchases.

The hawker was a youthful member of the "Mutual," and a violent anti-tobacconist.

"Well, Hannah, is he stickin' yet?" he cried, as she came to the cart side.

"Stickin'! Wot art talkin' abaat?" she demanded, with unusual asperity, although she knew quite well to whom the young fellow was alluding.

"Abaat yore William. He's gan o'er smookin', Aw yer, an Aw whop (hope) he's owdin' aat. The 'Mutuals' dun sum good yo' seen."

"Aw wish th' 'Mutual' an' aw th' bermyeds as goos tew it wur at th' bottom o' th' say, so *theer.*" And Hannah looked fiercer than the hawker had ever seen her do in her life.

"Whey, Hannah," he cried, "wot's up? Aw thowt yo' wanted yore William ta give up."

"Tha thowt wrung then! Awd rayther he smooked till he wur black i' th' face, an' if he doesna tak to'ot ageean, Aw'll—Aw'll start mysel'."

"Bud, Hannah, it's wasteful, yo' known, blowing good brass int' th' urr" (air).

"He nubbut smooked tew aance a wik, tha lumpyed," this with almost blazing indignation.

"Tew aance! Well, that's sixpence a wik, a' sixpence a wik for forty yer cums ta"—but he never finished his arithmetic, for Hannah was back on the doorstep, and, drawing herself up to her very fullest height, which was not very high after all, she delivered her final philippic: " Aw tell thi Aw durn't cur ha' mitch it is; if it gan him as mitch cumfort as it seems ta ha' done, it's abaat th' cheppest mak o' cumfort as Aw've iver yerd on. An' if he doesn't start a' smookin' afore th' wik's aa Aw'll—Aw'll *mak* him!" And retiring as red as a turkey cock, and in imminent danger of sudden tears, she banged the door angrily in the greengrocer's face and left him to himself.

Now the same day William had had a very worrying time at the mill. Everything had gone wrong with him. Early in the morning a loom had broken down, and whilst he was "fettlin" it he turned round and discovered suddenly that there was an enormous " float " on the other loom. And so for hours that day he had only had part of his looms going.

Towards three in the afternoon, however, things began to get right again, and when at last he was able to stand up and stretch himself, he sighed with a big sigh of relief as he glanced down the alley and saw all his looms at work once more. Then all at once there came upon him an intense longing for his pipe. It was very sudden and unexpected, but most unaccountably strong. In five minutes he wanted a pipe worse than he ever remembered to have wanted one in his life. He sent up hastily a little prayer for help, but somehow he found that their was no heart in his petition. He tried to resist the feeling—he couldn't smoke in the mill in any case. He struggled to shake it off and forget it, but there it was. Then he began to look at the clock over the weaving shed door, and tried to think of his pleasant little house, and how nice it would be to rest there when six o'clock came. But into the picture of restful comfort his fancy painted, there somehow floated a little brass tobacco-box and a most tempting little pipe. Oh, what should he do? Tobacco he must have by some means. More than once the impulse came to him to go down the loom alley to Pee Walker and borrow a quid and try to chew; but that he had always held was so much worse than smoking that common consistency compelled him to resist the desire. It was a long, terrible afternoon, and when six o'clock came William went home still struggling with a fierce desire for his old comforter.

Hannah received him with quite unusual kindness, and brought out what was in those days a very rare delicacy, only procurable at the grocer's, and carefully reserved for Sundays—a pot of marmalade; and the helping she gave him made him absolutely certain that something was going to happen.

But, strange to say, the wonderful marmalade was rather insipid for once, and even a little hot fat-cake which Hannah produced out of the oven about half-way through the meal failed to appease the longing of the poor weaver. Indeed, he was glad when the meal was over, and turned away from the table feeling that he ought to be an exceedingly happy and grateful man, and he wasn't. Oh! what a poor, weak thing he must be, and how basely ungrateful.

Then Hannah began to clear away the tea-things, and presently she thrust the little table close to his chair, closer, in fact, than usual, and William leaned his elbow upon it, and sat looking wearily into the fire and fighting with his craving for the weed. Once he thought Hannah was poking about strangely near him, but glancing round with his eyes without moving his head he found that she was just disappearing into the back-scullery.

Then he sighed again and moved his elbow. What was that? Not surely the smell of tobacco to tempt him still further? He sniffed again. It was strangely like it. Yes! there it was, unmistakable this time. He moved his elbow again; it seemed to strike something hard. He sat up and took a good look at the table. Yes, there it was close to him—a tin canister with a pot nob screwed in upon the lid, just like his old one, and full of most tempting dark shag, and there by its side was a new churchwarden pipe.

William positively went cold. He saw through it all in a moment. This was his little wife's way of expressing repentance, and William felt he would like to smoke just to show her that all was well.

But he dare not, and the more he longed for it the more he felt he dare not. And as he sat there, one moment looking longingly at the objects of temptation, and the next turning his back to them and gazing into the fire, Hannah came out of the back kitchen. As she passed towards the fire she glanced sharply at the table and noticed that her gifts had not been touched, and then, leaning forward over the fire, she began to poke it very vigorously, glancing every now and again stealthily at William's unusually perturbed face.

Presently she reached a candle from the mantelpiece, and setting it down near the tobacco she drew her chair up to the table, put on her spectacles, and made a sort of show of darning stockings.

Two or three times she glanced at the tobacco, and then again at her husband; and presently she said in soft, coaxing tones, as if she had not previously noticed his abstinence, "Artna' gooin' furt smook, lad?"

William started from his reverie, flushed a little, rubbed his big fat face, and then said, "Smeokin's sinful, wench."

"Wot?" cried Hannah, sternly, "has *thaa* started o' strainin' at a gnat an' swallerin' a camil? Awm shawmed fur thi!"

William's eyes opened slowly in mystified astonishment.

"Hannah!" he cried, "Aw thowt thaa didn't loike me furt smook?"

"Aye, thart allis thinkin' some lumber. Dust think Aw should a' letten thee smook aw theeas yers if Aw hedn't loiked it? Thaa's smooked lung enuff ta pleeas thisel', tha'll ha' ta smook ta pleeas me naa," and, pushing her hand across the table, she slid the tobacco and pipe towards him.

But William didn't offer to take them. He somehow felt he could not. And so, as he sat there glowering into the fire, Hannah resumed: "Naa, Aw'll tell thi wot. Aw'm gooin' t' have tew aances a wik off Noah, an' if thaa doesn't smook it, Aw'll smook it mysel'.

The mental picture of his fastidious little wife with a churchwarden pipe was too much for William, and he burst into a great laugh. As it subsided, Hannah gave the tobacco canister another push, but William did not heed her.

After that they sat for several minutes in silence, and at length Hannah said, in a soft, restrained voice, "Aar Hannah used loike ta see thi smook didn't hoo, lad?"

William winced, and a vision of a little fairy child who used to climb up on his knees and light his pipe for him, and then ripple off into a merry little laugh, which he would have given worlds to hear again, came before him and his eyes grew dim.

"Dust remember haa hoo browt thi poipe ta cumfort thi that neet thi muther deed?" Hannah went on softly, looking at her work through glasses that were getting very misty.

"Dunna, Hannah, dunna," cried William, putting out his hands.

But Hannah got softly up, and pulling out the stool again reached up to the mantelpiece and brought down a long vase-shaped vessel of brown clay. It was full of pipe-lights, and as she put it on the table she said gently, "Aar Hannah towd me th' wik afoor hoo deed ta allis keep it full o' spills fur her daddy's poipe, an Aw hev done ever sin'. Bud haa con Aw du that if tha' niver smooks?"

There was a long silence, during which William, though he, of course, saw the weakness of his wife's argument, seemed strangely moved, and glanced wistfully at the tobacco.

"Bud smookin' sa wasteful, tha' knows, Tan."

"Wasteful! Them as talks abaat it being wasteful spends twice as mitch up a watch guards an' 'dickies' an' foine clooas." Then she rose and went off into the scullery again, and when she returned William was seated with the churchwarden held out before him, amid clouds of wreathing smoke, with a look of placid satisfaction on his face which even an anchorite could not have begrudged him.

# JACKY'S TROUBLE.

# JACKY'S TROUBLE.

## I.

Miles Grimshaw, dressed in the seedy, black, greasy-at-elbows-and-knees which had in its better days done duty as his semi-clerical Sunday best, came hurrying, with his coat-tails flying, down Cinder Hill Lane and along the croft, with amazement and consternation expressed on every feature of his speaking face.

"Wotiver's ta dew, lad?" cried his big, round wife, coming out of the scullery, with a dish in one hand and a towel in the other, and gazing at him in wonder as he stood panting on the door-mat.

"Ta dew! ivery thing's ta dew! Th' divil's brokken lose, th' Church is disgraced! A good mon's gooan wrung, an' a dacent woman an' her dowters turn't into th' street!" and Miles nearly broke down as he spoke.

"Miles!" cried Mrs. Grimshaw, standing in stern anxiety over her husband, who had dropped into a chair, "tha'll be gooin' *off* i' sum o' them figgaries o' thine, as sewer as Awm a livin' woman. Be quiet wi' thi, an' tell me wot it's aw abaat."

"Abaat! it's abaat starvashun an' ruin, an' disgrace to th' Church! that's wot it's abaat!" And Miles rose to his feet and glared fiercely at his wife, whilst a tear stood on his faded cheek, and his wide mouth worked in pathetic twitches.

Dinah looked very grave by this time, and standing back a little and balancing herself uneasily she demanded: "Miles Grimshaw, arta goin' ta tell me wot's ta dew or tha artna?"

"Wot's ta dew?" and Miles glanced at his wife as if she had been the cause of the great disaster. "Whey, Jacky o' th' Gap's gotten th' *bums* in—that's wot's ta dew." And having at last got rid of his awful news, Miles sank back into his chair, whilst his wife limply dropped into another.

There was silence for a moment or two, during which Dinah sat looking at her husband with a stunned and bewildered expression, but Miles could not bear his wife's sad look.

"Dunna, woman! dunna stur (stare) o' that-unce," he cried, and then rising and walking about excitedly in front of the fire, clasping his hands together and wringing them in acute distress, he wailed: "Oh, Jacky! Mi owd friend! mi owd friend Jacky!" and, groaning like a man in an agony, he stamped on the sanded floor.

But Dinah was Quiet William's sister in

more senses than one, and so after sitting in a dazed, helpless manner in her chair for a few moments, during which she contrived to get out of her husband in a disjointed sort of way some few particulars of the great calamity, she quickly rose, put away her pot and towel, and leaving the washing-up to take care of itself, she put on her outer garments, selecting by some odd sort of instinct her black ones, as if for a funeral, and in a few moments was hurrying, as fast as her ponderous proportions would permit, up the lane towards Cinder Hill Farm, sighing and crying and quietly praying for her friends as she went.

Arrived at the farm Dinah made her way to the back-door. Opening it softly, she crossed the scullery towards the big kitchen. Pushing the door open before her without knocking, she drew back for a moment with a start, for there, seated comfortably by the fire, smoking a short clay pipe, was the smug-faced, bullet-headed Nat Ogden, the bailiff.

Ignoring Nat's offensively familiar nod, and turning her eyes away from him with cold severity, she asked, in a husky voice, "Wheer arr they?"

But before Nat could answer Dinah heard a step and a startled cry behind her, and turning quickly round she caught a tall, worn-looking woman in her arms, and silently hugged her to her breast. They stood there for several minutes without speaking, and then Dinah began to stroke gently the head that was buried in her bosom. "Poor wench! Poor wench!" crooned Dinah, glancing sympathetically down on the sobbing woman, "bud th' Lord knows, wench—th' Lord"—but just then the face on her breast was lifted suddenly, and with hot, flaming cheeks the stricken woman cried out vehemently, "It's nor him, wench; it's no Jacky, Awll tak me decin ooath it's nor him." At that moment there was another wail, and a fair-haired girl with red, swollen eyes and quivering lips came rushing in from somewhere, and seizing Dinah's free arm, cried: "Neaw, Dinah! Neaw! It's no' my fayther. Tell 'em aw soon. Tell aw as knows uz it's nor him. He wodna hurt a maase, Dinah."

"Neaw, wench, he wodna Aw know; he wodna," murmured Dinah, soothingly; and then she stopped, and looking round inquiringly she cried, "Bud wheer is he; wheer is the poor lad?"

"Huish! Huish!" cried both women at once, and dragging her further away, and pointing to a door close to where they had been standing, the younger woman cried: "He's i' th parlour, Dinah, an' he'll noather cum aat, nor speik nor eight (eat). Oh, wot mun we dew, Dinah; wot mun we dew?"

Dinah soothed the distressed woman, who seemed more concerned about the effect of the trouble upon Jacky than anything else, as best she could.

"Yo mun leuk up, bless yo," she said. "God's up aboon, yo known; sooa leuk up. It's allis darkist afoor dayleet. God bless yo booath, an' poor Jacky, tew," and, with another loving, mother-like hug and a long, clinging kiss to each, she left them.

Meanwhile, Miles stood staring, first at the fire and then out of the window, quite unable to keep himself still under the disturbing influence of his own thoughts. But it was not in his nature to remain alone and in silence under such circumstances, and so in a few moments he went out to consult with the only one of his cronies available at that hour of the day—Noah the grocer.

Noah was cutting and weighing thick twist into half-ounces, but when Miles had communicated to him the sad news they adjourned into the little parlour next to the shop, and for the next two hours discussed the painful subject in all its bearings.

As it drew near to six o'clock Miles returned home, and, having drawn from his wife the scanty additional details of the sad event she had to offer, he snarled and grumbled at her because she could tell no more, but seemed greatly disturbed by the information that Jacky would see nobody.

As he mused on these doings, watching impatiently for the mill to stop in order that the question might be discussed in full council, Noah joined him with a long clay pipe and sat down to wait for the approaching consultation.

Quiet William was the first to arrive. He had heard something of the trouble in the mill, and came hastily to get the details. Raising the latch he held the door a little way open, and looked searchingly into the faces of Miles and Noah and, finding there abundant confirmation of his fears, he heaved a heavy sigh, stepped inside softly, closed the door after him, and went and sat down very close to the fire without saying a word. He had scarcely got seated when Jimmy the Scutcher arrived. Before entering, Jimmy had taken a hasty peep over the window curtain, and when he saw the long faces of his friends, his own assumed a most peculiar expression. The side with the expressive eye in it puckered up as if in extreme pain, whilst the other side assumed a portentous length and gravity. Jimmy, too, had heard the news in the factory, and had knocked down the "little sewer" who brought him the intelligence.

For a long time nobody spoke, but at last Noah got up and knocked the ashes out of his pipe, and the others watched the operation with a painful, abstracted sort of curiosity. Then as he refilled it he remarked, slowly,

"Poor Jacky! he wur niver mitch of a manager."

Now Noah, though much better off than the rest of his associates, was never regarded as of very much account, his opinions being mostly very mild reflections of the emphatic ones of Miles, and the sentiment he had just given utterance to had been expressed times without number in bygone days by the excitable tailor, between whom and Jacky no uninitiated one would have guessed there was anything more than ordinary friendship, for they were too much alike to get on well together. But now, though Noah's tone was not in the least censorious, but rather apologetic, Miles jumped to his feet, and, glaring at Noah, cried in bitterest sarcasm, "That's it. Gooa on! The poor felley's daan, sa give him a punce" (kick).

Noah stopped in the midst of lighting his pipe, and looking at Miles in alarm and deprecation, whilst the pipe-light burned its way perilously near to his fingers, he began meekly, "Aw nobbut said——"

"Thaa nobbut said! Neaw; bud if th' poor lad ud a bin here, tha darna a said 'chirp.' He's mooar brains i' his little finger nor sum on uz hez in arr yeds, but just 'cause he conna bring his moind daan to chalking cubburd durs, and keeping Tommy bewks, he conna m-a-n-i-d-g-e," and Miles put unutterable scorn and mockery into his pronunciation of the last word.

Quiet William heaved a great sigh.

In a moment Miles had jerked himself round, and was demanding fiercely, "Wor art *thau* siking at? It 'ud leuk better on thi if tha'd oppen thi maath an' say summat atsteed a snurching and sniftering theer."

Miles's tirade, though it did not appear to affect William in the least, had a moving effect on the mind of Jimmy the Scutcher, and he just seemed to be about to say something when his daughter opened the door, and without looking at him called into the room, "Fayther, yo're ta cum to yo're baggin."

But Jimmy, though still in his greasy mill clothes, loftily and ungraciously waved his hand for the girl to be gone, and in a moment they were alone again and in silence.

Then two or three of the less important of the chapel people came in, and as they had many questions to ask and many remarks to make, conversation soon became general. It was all, however, extremely sympathetic towards Jacky, for the slightest hint of blame was at once pounced upon by Miles, and the person who uttered it had a very bad five minutes.

Presently Jimmy was sent for once more, but again he waved his hand imperiously, and the messenger departed as she came. As the door closed Quiet William lifted his head, and glancing up at the clock over the mantelpiece softly remarked, "It's toime fur t' meetin'."

It was prayer-meeting night, a fact everybody present had until that moment forgotten, and when they were thus reminded nobody heeded. And Miles probably voiced the feelings of the whole company when he said, with a heavy sigh, "Awve na hert fur meetin's ta-neet."

The others sighed in sympathetic endorsement, and just when a stranger would have thought the subject had been dropped—especially considering that neither Jimmy nor William had had tea or were washed and dressed for a meeting—William looked once more fixedly at the clock, and asked in the same low tones as before, "Wot's meetin's fur?"

Nobody replied, and the before-mentioned stranger might have concluded that nobody had heeded William's remark; but in a few moments the big man began to sidle towards the door, and presently disappeared. Nobody seemed to notice his departure, but in a minute or so Jimmy the Scutcher, dirty and "linty" as he was, got up and followed, and nobody needed to be told that he had not gone home to tea. After another brief interval, Noah and the others left one by one, and at last Miles, now entirely alone, looked

9

resignedly round the room, and, picking up his hat, departed to join the rest at the meeting.

Now it was well-nigh impossible to get Quiet William to take any public part in the affairs of the church. Only on very rare occasions had he ever even led the prayer-meeting, but on this sad night, without consulting anybody, he took charge of the proceedings. Everybody present prayed, but nobody made any definite reference to the one thing that lay heavily on their hearts. When he was concluding William seemed suddenly to get "liberty." Whilst only using language of studied generality, it was evident to all that he was thinking chiefly of their friends at Cinder Hill Farm. When he came to "Aw—aw, them that are i' trubbel," his voice faltered; but he got over it, and with uplifted hands and glowing, intense faith he prayed until those who were not entirely overcome by the simple petition listened with the feeling that they were following one inspired. And when the long, impassioned prayer was over, Abram Briggs, as he went out at the door wiping his eyes, turned to the equally affected Noah, and said, earnestly, "Sum rooad aat ull be fun fur Jacky after this, tha'll see." And Noah, turning and looking earnestly at Abram, said in tones of solemn conviction, "If ther isna, ther isna a God, that's aw."

## II.

Later on that night William, Miles and Jimmy might have been seen plodding their way through the mud along Cinder Hill Lane to the Farm. Their purpose was to see Jacky at all costs. But they did not succeed. He would not see anybody, and Mrs. Jacky and her daughter stood before the parlour-door and tearfully entreated the deputation not to persist in its purpose. In a long conversation, during which William did nothing but shake his head, and the rest of the party, including the women, had to exert all their powers to keep Miles from quarrelling with the obnoxious bailiff, they elicited all that was at present known by the women on the subject. It was the bank that had taken such sudden action. The local manager had been dismissed unexpectedly, and for some reason instant action had been commenced against two or three overdrawn debtors, amongst whom was the unfortunate Jacky.

That was all the women had to tell, and even that information had not been obtained from the farmer himself, but from the bailiff and others.

As they were departing, after offering a few clumsy words of consolation to the women, it was noticed that William was missing, and looking round and stepping back into the kitchen they espied William kneeling at the inexorable parlour-door, behind which was the heart-broken Jacky; and before they could speak they heard him repeating, in a loud voice and with his mouth to the keyhole, " When thou passest through the waters I will be with thee, and through the rivers they shall not overflow thee; when thou walkest through the fire thou shalt not be burnt, neither shall the flame kindle upon thee."

For the next two days little was talked about in Scowcroft but Jacky's trouble. Miles and his friends went about with sad faces and bowed heads, and seemed to find their only comfort in getting together in the evenings, and smoking and sighing and saying nothing—for all the world like Job's friends without Job, and without also their obstinate views about the government of God. In their hearts they all feared that Jacky had not been the best of business men, but they were ready to fall upon and rend any incautious person who ventured, however distantly, to hint at such a thing. They knew, also, that there had been a mortgage on the farm when Jacky took it from his father, and though Jacky had never exactly hinted at financial difficulty, and his wife and daughter always held their heads rather high, yet it was an open secret amongst them that their friend's worldly position had never been as easy and secure as appearances would seem to have indicated.

Of course Dame Rumour was busy in these days, and Jacky's companions were hurt and stung every few hours by some fresh and unjustifiable story. It was confidently stated that Jacky had not been solvent for a dozen years, and evil-minded ones added significantly, "An' him preiching loike a bishop aw th' toime."

Miles went in pursuit of his calling to the farm adjoining Jacky's, but when he had got the coat he had to turn taken to pieces, and was sitting cross-legged on the large table under the kitchen window tacking it together, old Garlick, the farmer, came in and at once introduced the topic of the hour. To his surprise Miles, who had generally a very decided opinion on almost any subject that could be introduced to him, and was always ready at any moment to state and defend that opinion, and pour scathing ridicule upon any contrary one for any length of time, was on this occasion simply dumb. Nothing that Garlick could say had any effect in inducing him to talk.

"Well," grunted the farmer, in his wheezy way, as he stood with his back to the fire and his hands behind him, looking uneasily at the tailor, "Awst be sorry ta see Jacky sowd up, that's sartin, and Awm thankful aboon abit as he doesn't belong ta *aar* church."

Now, if the slow-minded Garlick intended

this as a means of making Miles say or do something he succeeded; for the tailor suddenly sent the coat he was stitching flying into the window bottom, and then spinning himself quickly round he jumped from the table, stepped hastily to the door, made a gesture as of a man casting the dust off his feet, and before anybody could stop him he was plunging through the mud in his working slippers towards home. The Garlicks kept Miles's boots in the hope that he would be compelled to go back for them. But though when they finally sent them home they sent also an apologetic message, old Garlick's coat has never been finished turning to this day.

If there was any person in Scowcroft who could be said to derive real satisfaction from the rumours that were going about it was that singular individual Reuben Tonge, the sandman. As has been already hinted in a previous chapter, Reuben had been brought up a Methodist, and at one time bade fair to be a shining light at the chapel. But he had a very proud, imperious temper, and when Annie Clarkson rather lightly jilted him and soon after married one of his companions, Jacky o' th' Gap, he had left the chapel, become a backslider and a keen-tongued scoffer at religion, so that the sudden dishônour of his erstwhile successful rival must be supposed to have been particularly gratifying to him. He heard the news amongst the earliest, and laughed a great, hoarse laugh. And when the person who told him the tidings had left him, he still stood in the back-lane where the communication had been made, looking musingly at the ground, and evidently in deep thought. Presently, he lifted his head, looked round for a moment, gave vent to a queer sound which even the experienced "Pablo" could not quite understand, and then giving his dingy steed a familiar knock with his whip, he said, "Another canting Methody, Pablo! Another canting Methody!" and then lifting his head he sent ringing down the lane, his ancient cry, "Weshing up mugs, stew mugs. Whaite sand an' *rub*bin stoan."

Later in the same Saturday afternoon, it was discovered that Quiet William was not to be found, and it was concluded by his friends that he was making another attempt to see the unhappy Jacky. This turned out to be correct, and about six o'clock he was seen to turn the corner from Cinder Hill Farm, and presently he entered his brother-in-law's house. In a few minutes all the friends had gathered to hear the news.

Yes, William had seen their old friend, and the picture he drew of Jacky's haggard look and hollow, weary eyes brought lumps into their throats and drew heavy sighs from all present.

William brought also brief but authentic particulars of the trouble. In short, it amounted to this, that unless Jacky could find £500 within the next few days he would be sold up and turned into the lane.

Jacky couldn't see where he could get one-tenth of the money, though it was an open secret that he had befriended many an unfortunate acquaintance in similar difficulties, probably to his own hurt. Nat Ogden and his assistants were to commence marking the goods for the sale on the following Monday morning. The big man told his story very slowly, with many sighs and pauses, and when he had done a feeling of helpless dumbness fell on the company, and the smoke poured out of the smokers' lips in thick, jerky volumes.

"Poor felley! Poor, poor felley!" groaned Noah.

"Aye, God help him," responded Abram Briggs.

"An' uz," groaned Noah.

"Aye, an' uz tew," sighed Abram.

Jimmy the Scutcher sat behind a thick cloud of smoke, evidently trying to control his very peculiar countenance. At last, taking his pipe out of his mouth, and speaking in his hardest tones, he remarked, "A penn'orth a help's woth a paand o' pity."

"Pity!" cried Miles, starting as if he had been stung, and almost shrieking in his excitement, "Is ther a mon here as wodna give his last shillin' ta save him?"

Every face in the company looked an emphatic endorsement of Miles's demand, and every eye was turned with a sort of challenge in it upon the Scutcher.

Jimmy was, as usual, entirely unmoved, but in a moment or two, fixing his off eye keenly on Miles, whilst the rest listened intently, he rose to his feet, and striking the table with a mighty thump, cried, "Daan wi' thi brass, then."

Now the idea behind this challenge was so entirely new, that the men who heard Jimmy's words sat looking at him with half-opened mouths and eyes full of astonishment and perplexity; for they were all poor men, and the times were none of the best.

For some time nobody spoke, but presently Miles jumped to his feet, clambered hurriedly up the stairs behind the door, and was immediately heard walking about on the floor above and opening and shutting drawers and boxes. Then he returned, nearly missing his footing as he came down. His eyes shone with excitement as he came into the light again. He was pale, and his tightly-drawn lips twitched with emotion. He had a greasy black book in his hand. It was the pass-book of the Wallbury Penny Bank, and contained entries of the rare and scanty savings of a lifetime. Stepping forward he banged it defiantly down on the table, and looking eagerly at Jimmy, cried, "Ther's forty-wun paand odd theer; naa folla' thi leeader."

Jimmy, who had evidently planned something of the kind and come prepared, put his left hand into his inside coat-pocket and produced a book similar to Miles's, and throwing it carelessly down on the top of Miles's, he said quietly, "Aw theers—sixty-seven mooar."

No painter on earth could have painted Quiet William's face at this moment. Surprise, delight, gratitude and a blending of embarrassment were mingled strangely upon it. But at last, giving way to the tears that couldn't be kept back, he stammered out, "Aw—Aw—hav' na brass ; bud Aw—Aw—Aw—con morgige th' haase."

And this was a trying moment for prudent Noah. He moved uneasily in his chair, coughed nervously, blinked his small eyes with curious rapidity, and then said, "We'er nobbut lannin' (lending) it Aw reacon?"

Miles gave a violent start, a blaze of indignation flashed into his face, and he was just about to explode on the unfortunate Noah, when Jimmy sprang up, and stopped him with an imperious gesture. He knew, as they all did, that Noah was better off than the rest of them, and could help substantially if he would. He was, therefore, a person to be managed in this difficult business, and so, standing in front of the excited Miles, he turned to Noah, and said, "Of course, we'er aw lannin' it. Dust think Jacky ud tak' it off uz ony other rooad?"

"Jacky," cried William, in sudden concern, "Jacky must know nowt abaat it till it's dun."

But Jimmy stopped him with another masterful and impatient wave of his hand, and stood facing Noah, evidently waiting for that worthy's contribution. There was a long pause, during which Miles was fidgetting behind Jimmy, but at last Noah said, hesitatingly, "Well, awst ston me corner?"

The only other person present was Abram Briggs, and as he was notoriously henpecked, nobody was surprised when he announced, "Awst ha' ta see aar Martha abaat it."

Then they fell into a discussion as to how the thing should be managed. They were a long way as yet from the five hundred pounds required, but it was eventually decided to hand the matter over to Noah, who, though he hadn't a banking account, was, after all, a man of business; and when they separated later on, everybody looked as though a great load had been lifted from their minds.

## III.

Meanwhile a very different scene was being enacted at Reuben Tonge's house in Lark Lane. The weather, cold and raw all day, had turned to rain at night, and Reuben, having had his "baggin" and made Pablo comfortable for the night, proceeded to make up a good fire, and clearing his table, pulled out a couple of dirty account-books, and sitting down before them was soon engrossed in their contents. Reuben, though his dress and appearance were mean enough, and his occupation poor, was quite a capitalist in his way. He did a little select and very secret business as a money-lender, confining his operations to places and people outside Scowcroft. He was also virtual owner of two or three of the canal coal-barges, and dabbled a little in mortgages and ground-rents. His recent effort in connection with his daughter and the Scowcroft mill had quite disorganised his arrangements, and he was considerably overdrawn at the bank. It was necessary, therefore, that he should look well after his affairs and pull himself round as quickly as possible. He was, as will have been seen, a man of strong, deep nature, but he had allowed himself to be warped and injured by his early disappointment in love. Jacky o' th' Gap had, he concluded, beaten him in the fight for Annie, because he was supposed to have money, and therefore since that time Reuben had bent all his energies upon the acquirement of wealth. He had neglected himself, allowed his nature to harden and sour, and was now at the end of thirty years, in possession of considerable means, whilst his successful rival was bankrupt, and would in a few days be without so much as a covering for his head. Reuben was thinking of all these things as he balanced his books, and was disappointed to find that he was not happier for the reflection. He had dreamed of this day of triumph for years, and now that it had actually come, he could not honestly say that it gave him much satisfaction. He had stopped for a moment, and, with his face turned to the fire and his pen between his lips, he was looking meditatively at the sputtering coals. Just then a knock came at the door, and Reuben turned his head to listen. The knock was low and timid, and the sandman, after staring hard at the door and listening for a moment, concluded that it must be a beggar, and so resumed his bookkeeping. He had redipped his pen, and was just about to make another entry, when the knock came again, louder than before, but still timid and hesitant. Reuben gave an impatient grunt, and went hastily to see who was there. Throwing back the catch over the "sneck," and opening the door hastily, he bent his head, and with knitted brows peered crossly into the darkness. The visitor was a woman, tall and respectably dressed, and Reuben recognised her at once, and his heart began to beat.

"Whoa is it? What dust want?" he demanded, gruffly, pretending not to recognise her. The woman waited for a moment, evidently expecting that the sandman would see who she was, but as he didn't or wouldn't, she said, faintly, "It's me, Reubin."

"Thee! An' whoa the ferrups art thaa, comin' at this toime at neet?"

But the woman, disappointed and disheartened at not being recognised, and unable to find further language, stood mutely in the dark.

Reuben waited a moment or two, and then, as no response came to his rough question, he bent down, and knitting his brows again, as if vainly attempting to read his visitor's countenance, he cried, more roughly than ever, "Whoa are-ta? Cum in a' show thi'sel if tha wants summat," and, turning round, he led the way to the fire, and the woman shrinkingly followed him.

As the door swung to behind her, she stepped abashed and confused upon a piece of old sacking which served the sandman for a doormat, and stood timidly waiting once more to be identified.

"Oh! It's thee, is it?" cried Reuben, pretending suddenly to recognise her; and a pang went to his heart as he took in the dejected and sorrowful expression of a face that had once been so bright and sweet. But, heeding not his own heart, and dropping into a hard, mocking tone, he went on: "But thar't mistan wench. Tha doesn't want *me*, tha doesn't *know* me tha knows; tha hasn't known me for monny a yer."

The suffering woman shook for a moment with feeling, and dropped her head, whilst shame and resentment struggled within her to overcome an evidently great purpose and defeat her errand. Presently she obtained a little self-mastery, and said, quietly, "Th' Reubin Tonge as Aw knowed, wi' aw is fawts, wur genrus."

Reuben burst into a great laugh.

"Genrus! Oh, aye!" he cried. "Mooar Methody cant. Then thar't beggin' arta?"

Reuben pretended to suppose that his visitor was canvassing for subscriptions; but the woman was overwrought; and, catching at his last words, whilst her brimming cup of bitterness at last overflowed, she burst into a passion of tears, and cried, "Aye, Reubin, Aw'm beggin'."

The sandman was stirred to the depths of his being. He was not usually affected by women's tears, but this woman had never been like the rest of her sex to him. But he would not show his feeling. He laughed again, louder and more harshly than ever, and cried, in feigned astonishment, "Wot! Jacky o' th' Gap woife beggin' off a poor owd sond-knocker! Preichin Jacky woife beggin' of wun o' th' scum?"

But the agitated woman was too desperate now to be influenced by taunts, however cutting, and so she cried, wringing her thin hands, "Aye, Reubin, beggin', weer i' troubbel, Reubin. Weer i' trouble," and, leaning over, the stricken woman dropped her head upon the drawers standing near to her, and began to sob as if her heart would break.

Reuben, greatly disturbed in spite of himself, turned his back on his visitor and began to glower sulkily at the fire. But in a moment the weeping woman was by his side, and whilst the tears rained down her pale cheeks, and disfigured a face that was still very comely, she cried with humility, almost abject, "Help uz, Reubin—help uz, fur sake o'-o'-o'-owd toimes."

But poor Annie had touched the wrong chord this time. "Owd toimes," sneered the sandman, "which owd toimes? Th' toime as tha' left me stonnin' three haars i' th' rain woll thaa wur marlocking wi' Jacky i' yore parlour? Th' toime as thaa sniggered and snurched as thaa druv past me owd sand-cart an' thee peerched up in Jacky's new trap? Th' toime as thaa threaped Jacky's sister daan, as tha' wurna' gooin' wi' me, an' niver hed dun? Is them th' toimes as tha' wants me ta think abaat?" and for the moment Reuben was really bitter.

Mrs. Jacky heaved a great sobbing sigh, and was just about to reply when Reuben resumed, almost savagely: "Thaa'd a' hed me if ther hedna' a' been ony Jacky abaat; bud a sondmon wur noawheer wheer a farmer cum. Well, tha wanted thi farmer and tha's getten thi farmer. Tha's made thi bed; tha mun shift ta lie on it sum rooad."

This was all very cruel, and the suffering woman shivered as the hard words fell on her like so many blows. She felt if she spoke just then she would ruin her case, so her hand dropped to her side again and she stood quietly crying. And her silence and his own sudden remorse irritated Reuben more than her words had done, and so, with a curl of his masterful lip, he went on scornfully: "A Methbody with bums in, an' a preicher, tew, if he'd a' stopped a' whoam an' moinded his wark atstead o' gaddin' abaat ——."

"Reubin!" screamed the goaded woman, turning fiercely round with anger and defiance blazing through her tears, "Dunna *darr* ta say a wo'd ageean Jacky. Sithi Aw'll say it naa, ith' wo'st trubble Awve ever hed. Ther' isn't a mon in Scowcroft parish as can howd a candle tew him. Theer'!" and here the maddened woman drew herself up in passionate disdain. "Thee! tha artna fit ta woipe his shoon an' niver wur. If Aw hed to dew it ageean Awd tak' him if he hadna' a rag ta his back—bless him!" and breaking down with sudden tears, she gave the man near her a push, and suddenly rushing to the door was gone before he could prevent her.

---

## IV.

When Mrs. Jacky left him on that dismal Saturday night Reuben stood on the hearth-rug for a long time like a man in a dream. He had had the revenge he had waited for for years, and the taste of it was positively bitter to him. All that was good in him commended Annie for what she had said and done, and this made him bitterly angry with himself. He never imagined that Jacky's wife would have taken his words as she had done. Least of all did he expect she would have left him with her errand unaccomplished, and the sandman actually caught himself sighing. He moved about the house absently for some time, and then sat down to his accounts again. But he could not give his mind to them. The haggard, tearful face of the woman he had once loved with all the strength of his deep nature haunted him, and blurred the figures as he looked at them. These books had diverted his mind and given him relief and pleasure many a time before, but now their charm was entirely gone, and he presently shut them up with a petulant snap, and putting them hastily away went and stood in the doorway, listening to the dripping of the rain.

Where was she?—that pale, sad woman he had so ruthlessly driven from his door? Then he moved uneasily, and presently went out into the broken-down old stable to see that Pablo was comfortable for the night. Somehow the silent presence of his old companion soothed him, so he lingered over his work, pausing every now and again to listen to the rain and wonder where Annie was. Then he stroked and patted his pony until that sagacious animal looked round inquiringly as if wondering what this unwonted gentleness would lead to. Presently, moving his hand from Pablo's back, where he had been tenderly examining a raw place, Reuben began to pat his ragged neck, and then, as he turned to go, he said, "Pablo, thee an' me durnt breik th' Sabbath mitch, but weest ha ta dew it tamorn, Awm thinkin'," and then as he moved to the door, he added, "if it *is* breikin' it."

Next day about noon, though, the weather was still threatening, Reuben, in a shaky-looking old trap, not much more respectable than his sand-cart, left home on a journey, apparently to Wallbury. But, after making a call there, he travelled onward to other places, and when they returned, late that evening, though the pony looked tired, Reuben had a much more cheerful air than when he left in the earlier part of the day.

Pablo did not even then seem to have quite recovered his astonishment at being taken out on a Sunday, but his surprise was still greater when he found himself, in spite of an almost unalterable precedent to the contrary, actually making his way to Wallbury again early on Monday morning.

They put up as usual at the "Black Lad," and whilst Pablo munched his corn, his master rapidly made his way down Coalgate to the bank.

The Town Hall clock chimed a quarter to ten as he went along, and, discovering that he was somewhat early, Reuben checked himself, and dropped into a quiet saunter. As he turned the corner of the street and came in sight of the bank, he suddenly pulled up, and gave a low whistle of astonishment, for there, right under the gas lamp opposite the bank door, stood Miles, William and Noah, evidently waiting for the bank to open. Reuben looked for the moment annoyed and disappointed, but another thought seemed to strike him, and the next moment he had dodged into a convenient passage, and from this vantage-point he stood looking at his acquaintances with a puzzled, and not too amiable expression on his strong, rough face.

Now the circumstance which interfered with Reuben's procedure requires some little explanation. The fact was that the friends had discovered that after all they could do £300 was the very utmost they could raise in this emergency. Quiet William had then proposed that Noah should go over to Wallbury and see if the bank manager could be induced to accept a smaller sum, and the grocer had agreed. But by Sunday night his courage had failed him, and he had conceived a most unaccountable dread of the manager. And so, as a last resource, Miles and William had undertaken to accompany him and see what could be done.

They were none of them much acquainted with the ways of banks, and so, being all exceedingly uneasy and impatient, they had left Scowcroft by seven o'clock in the morning, and had reached the bank before nine, only to discover that they were an hour too early. There was nothing for it, therefore, but to wait, and so they had been standing under the lamp for the last hour.

At last, just as the clock struck ten, a sprightly young clerk flung open the doors, and the three Scowcrofters, intimidated by the clerk's manner and overawed by the grandeur of the place, stepped nervously in, and falteringly asked to see the manager.

He had not arrived, but would be there in a few minutes, and the clerk showed them into a private room, and shut the door upon them. Then the friends took their hats off—they were all dressed in their Sunday best—and seated themselves on the very outer edge of their chairs. Miles gazed round with undisguised curiosity and wonder. Noah sat looking earnestly into his hat as he held it in his hand, and Quiet William sighed deeply, and moved his lips in silent prayer.

They all started as if caught in some dishonourable act when the door suddenly opened and the manager entered. Then they all rose from their seats in embarrassment and bade the official a curt and awkward "good morning."

"Well, gentlemen, what can I do for you?" said the manager, putting away his umbrella, and hanging his hat up, as if this dreadful business of theirs was the commonest thing on earth. And then William looked at Noah, and Miles did the same, and added an energetic nod; but Noah seemed tongue-tied, and looked helplessly at William. Miles could hold in no longer, and so stepping forward and putting a shaky hand on the manager's table he said, "We're comin' abaat that bother o' Jacky o' th' Gap's."

"Jacky o' th' Gap," murmured the bank official in perplexity. "Oh, ah! the Cinder Hill Farm affair, I suppose?"

"Aye! that's it," cried Miles, now fairly at liberty. "Yo'n made a mistak', mestur; yo'n sent trubbel to wun o' th' dacentest chaps i' Lancyshire," and Miles made the manager's pens jump on the inkstand as he brought his fist down on the table with an emphatic thump.

"No doubt! No doubt!" said the manager, a little startled by the tailor's energetic manner. "But unfortunately that won't pay the bank's claims; will it, gentlemen?"

"Wot will then?" demanded Miles, now quite courageous; "if it's ony good tew yo' ther's wun or tew on uz here as 'ull foind three hunderd paand," and the way Miles quoted the figure ought to have filled the bank man's mind with visions of untold gold.

But somehow it did not. He gave a slightly impatient gesture, and trying to keep a contemptuous look out of his face he shook his head and said, "No use whatever, gentlemen—no use at all."

Quiet William groaned audibly and sighed under his breath, "Lord help us!" Noah glanced up at Miles with an "I-told-you-so" sort of look, and Miles, goaded by a sense of failure, was just about to make an indignant reply, when the door opened and in stepped Reuben Tonge.

"Hello!" he cried, affecting extreme astonishment at the sight of them, "wot's yo' chaps doin' here?"

None of them replied. Reuben Tonge was the sworn enemy of the chapel and had been for many years. Moreover, he was specially bitter against "Preiching Jacky," as he sneeringly called their friend, and had been ever since Jacky's marriage.

This was certainly not the man to be taken into their confidences, and, in fact, his sudden appearance was regarded by each of them as a bad omen, and they realised keenly how he must be gloating over Jacky's ruin and their own great trouble.

So nobody spoke, and Reuben, after looking anxiously from one to the other, asked, " Aw reacon you cum'n abaat Jacky han yo?"

And whilst Miles glared sullen defiance at the sandman, and Noah hung his head shyly, Quiet William, who had more exact knowledge of Reuben, and especially of some of his recent acts than the others, proceeded to tell him their business. And as William in his gentle way told the story of their sorrowful sympathy with Jacky, their anxiety for the honour of the church, and their proposed sacrifice of all their little savings, the manager's eyes grew misty, and even hard Reuben had to turn his shoulder to the speaker and gaze steadily at the frosted window.

When William had finished and fallen back into his seat, Reuben turned again, and looking them over calculatingly for a moment, said,

"Well, it's a rum un, this is; Aw've come on th' same busniss mysel'."

The three men looked at him with fresh astonishment, and so he proceeded: "It's reet. Aw've come abaat nowt else"; and then, going over and touching Miles on the buttonhole, he said, "Naa leuk here. Aw dew a bit o' businiss wi' theeas fowk. Gooa yo're ways whoam, an' leeave it ta me."

The three friends hesitated; but on the manager assuring them that the affair would not suffer in the hands of their odd neighbour, they reluctantly departed.

It was a melancholy walk home for this disappointed deputation. Miles was full of hope one moment and full of fear the next; Noah maintained an unalterable tone of despondency; but William seemed quietly, but immovably, hopeful.

Reuben had told them he would see them later in the day, and so they kept together and lingered at Miles's in most restless impatience. About three o'clock Reuben drove up to the door in his jingling old conveyance, and by his side sat a clerk from the bank—a sign which William regarded as most distinctly hopeful.

"Naa, then," cried Reuben, brusquely, "jump in, an' come on to the farm."

Pablo never had a heavier load in the old trap in all his memory, and he puffed and panted up the Cinder Hill in anything but an amiable mood.

When they arrived Reuben bade the clerk go first into the house, and when a moment or two later he returned bringing Nat Ogden with him, Reuben, who had never been in the house for over thirty years, led the way into the kitchen. But the sudden and unexpected removal of the bailiff had caused excitement within, and when they entered the kitchen they found Jacky standing on the hearthrug, and his wife and daughter clinging to his arms and crying for relief and joy.

"Thar't a bonny mon!" cried Reuben in assumed indignation, as soon as he put eyes on Jacky.

"Reuben!" cried Mrs. Jacky, suddenly stepping between her husband and the sandman, "tha munna say a word! Aw'll darr thi t' say it!"

Miles was stepping forward, but before he could speak Reuben turned fiercely on Mrs. Jacky, and, pointing at her husband, cried, "Dust know wot he's dun?"

"Aw durnt cur *wot* he's dun! He's dun nowt! Nowt! Aw tell thi."

"Dust know haa he's getten inta this lumber?"

"Neaw, nor Aw durnt cur! He's dun nowt wrong Aw'm sartin."

"He's getten i' this mess wi' being bun (bound) fur that foine cousin o' thine az run away last Wissun Day. An' 'cause he gan his wod, he'd nooa mooar sense nor pay, the foo him!" And Reuben turned and looked at Jacky with a look in which scornful reproach seemed to be struggling with something very like admiration.

So that was the explanation of the unexpected distraint—Jacky, to save his wife's family pride, had, unknown to her, and, of course, to the rest of his friends, been bound for a cousin of hers—a showy, plausible, but untrustworthy farmer at Sniggleton—and when he disappeared suddenly, as the other bonds could not pay, Jacky had overdrawn an already unsatisfactory account at the bank. Things had gone badly with him since, and then when the old bank manager was found to be defaulting and was suddenly replaced, Jacky's account proved on examination to be so unsatisfactory that summary proceedings had at once been commenced. The scene that followed is quite beyond the descriptive powers of the present chronicler, and so we leave the rejoicing friends to their gladness. Reuben Tonge, it appeared, had spent Sunday afternoon in getting at the facts in his own peculiar way, as to the original cause of Jacky's trouble, sorely disturbing the mind of the new bank manager by interviewing him on the Sabbath Day, and the sandman greatly enjoyed the grimace with which the mercurial Miles received this last item of information. Still everybody expressed great gratitude to Reuben for his help, and especially for the fact that Jacky's character and the church's honour had been saved.

"Pablo," said Reuben that night, as he foddered his pony and mused over the events of the day, " wun or tew moaar things loike we'en hed ta-day an' them Methodys 'ull convart thy old mestur."

And Pablo looked as if he had not the slightest objection.

# BILLY'S BLUNDER.

# BILLY'S BLUNDER.

## I.

SCOWCROFT to all its other claims to distinction could add the great honour of possessing the most remarkable musical genius for miles round. To look at, Billy Wardle was anything but prepossessing. His large long head and longer features, and his tremendous arms caused him, when sitting, to look tall, but when he stood up it was seen that he had never been much above middle height, and a slight stoop made him appear even less than he was. He had mild-looking, almost soft blue eyes, a wide but weak mouth, and a few long and neglected hairs at each side of his face, and under his chin were evidently the best that Billy was capable of in the way of hirsute adornment.

Nobody ever looked less like a man of mark than did Billy as he sat in his place on a Sunday, waiting for the minister to give out the hymn. But when the number had been announced, and the instruments, or in later days the organ, had played the tune over, and the minister had read the first verse, you were startled by a sudden and terrific vocal explosion, and glancing upwards, you beheld a sickly-looking man with a hymn-book, held as far away from him as possible in one hand, whilst with the other he was wildly beating time, and his head, when it was not turned round to admonish some laggardly singer, was held at such an acute angle and so far away from the hymn-book, that your surprise at the music was soon forgotten in fear that the singer would overbalance himself and fall.

Billy could not read music at all, but he knew every tune in the tune-books in use at the chapel, could play any instrument introduced to him, and could reproduce almost any tune he had once heard. It was no use any mischievously-disposed preacher sending up to the singing gallery a list of peculiar metres in the hope of puzzling Billy. The only result was a twisting, twirling, many-runned tune, which woke up the old folk to vociferous ecstacy, and caused the younger ones to stand still in bewildered and helpless dumbness. Billy could only read very indifferently, but he knew most of the hymns by heart, and could fill up any forgotten lines with most artistic pom poms, interspersed with emphatic and jerky instructions to his assistants.

  And sing with all the—pom-po-pom-po-pom,
  And sing with—nay, wenches, bell aat,
  And sing with all the—ler 'em hev it, lads,
  The hendless song a-bo-o-o-ove,
  The pom pom song abuv.

Billy was the author of several very popular local tunes, and at least one most astonishing anthem, and was often absent during the earlier part of the summer conducting the music at adjacent village anniversaries.

But of late Billy's throne had been a somewhat uneasy seat. Some of the younger people in the choir could read music a little, and one of the tenors had learnt the wonderful new tonic sol-fa. Besides which, young Abram Briggs, who played the organ, had a standing grievance against his conductor in the fact that he was never consulted in the selection of tunes, and though he and other juniors in the singing pew knew several grand new tunes, they were compelled, Sunday after Sunday, to sing the very oldest of the old, and were sternly snubbed both by their leader and by the authorities of the chapel if they made anything approaching to a complaint.

But of late the young people had received considerable support from outsiders. The junior minister had on two recent occasions asked for particular tunes to certain hymns, and on being informed on the second of these occasions that "We sing noa new-fangled balderdash here," he had shrugged his shoulders and elevated his eyebrows in a manner more expressive than any possible words.

And then it was plainly hinted, though with bated breath by those few degenerate souls who had so far forgotten themselves as to attend the parody of an anniversary held recently by the Methodist Adullamites in "Joany's loft," that the music on that occasion was better than that at the Scowcroft Chapel, "sarmons" and "mooar moderner," and this, in spite of several long and heated arguments in his defence, had done more to injure Billy's prestige than anything else.

What made matters worse was that most of the young people at the chapel were ardent teetotalers, and though they had no particular fault to find with Billy on that score, save that he would neither sign the pledge nor attend their meetings, yet his two sons were notorious in the village for drunkenness, pigeon-flying, and every species of riotous living, whilst his wife, who by the way was the sister of Jimmy the Scutcher, was not only a fierce-tongued and brawling neighbour, but was more than suspected of drinking habits as well. And the virtuous young Temperance advocates of Scowcroft, many of whom were in the singing pew, protested that it wasn't "dacent" for the husband and father of such a disreputable set to be leading the worship of the chief sanctuary.

And as luck would have it, just at this time a new bookkeeper came to the mill. He turned out to be a Methodist, and as bookkeepers were regarded as persons a little above the common run, the chapel people received him with open arms, and congratulated themselves on having bagged a great prize. Judge, therefore, of the consternation of the one party and the triumphant pride of the other when, after attending the services one whole Sunday, the bookkeeper actually postponed his selection of a pew, on the ground that he was not sure he could " cast in his lot " with them because the music was really so very old-fashioned and slow that it made him " fair crill " to hear it, and entirely destroyed any chance of profitable worship. This was serious. The bookkeeper was, of course, an educated man, and a great catch for the chapel; his opinion, therefore, as a mere ordinary worshipper was of great weight, and to allow him to go to church, or to that disreputable " Joany's loft," would be an everlasting disgrace. But when it was discovered that the new-comer had been harmoniumist and choirmaster at a small Independent chapel in Manchester, the young people at once realised that Providence had sent them, not only a powerful leader in their opposition to Billy, but also an efficient and up-to-date successor to that worthy's position. And now from mere spasmodic skirmishing the struggle suddenly passed to serious conflict. The bookkeeper was suave and insinuating, and excessively friendly. He invited the young folk to his house in relays of three or four, and gave them evidence of his skill and knowledge of music, deftly expressing his surprise at the musical quality of some of their voices, if only they were properly trained. Then he related stories of some of his own musical triumphs, and alluded in a familiar, almost patronising, way to some of the leading musicians of the day. This was the man. They would *have* some music at Scowcroft if only they could get " Mestur Ryle " (Royle) to lead them. " Owd Billy " was a " blethering owd Bluffinyed." He had a " vice loike a corncrake," and was " that ignorant——"

And the more vociferous and vehement the opposition became the more stubborn and immovable were Billy's defenders. The heads of the church were unanimously and enthusiastically on his side. He was an old friend. His taste in tunes was exactly theirs, and they had so long regarded him with pride as one of the chief glories of the place that all attacks upon him seemed to them to be so many challenges to proper authority, and threatened the very foundations of order and government. If Billy went some of them would speedily have to follow, and the instinct of self-preservation made them obdurate. Never did those masters of strong language, Miles and Jacky o' the Gap, perform such feats of denunciation. Never was the terrible Jimmy so cutting in his satires and so prolific of caustic, biting jokes. Even the peaceable Noah the grocer waxed argumentative, and Quiet William was be-

## BILLY'S BLUNDER.

trayed into language very unlike his name and character.

"Aw wur axin' the beuk-keeper abaat yond pew this morning," said Noah, slowly, as they sat round Miles's fire early one Saturday evening.

"Tha niver did, thaa lumpyed! Aw'd see him at Dixey afur Aw'd ax him ageean," cried Jacky, indignantly.

"Well, wot said he?" demanded Miles, with threatening looks.

"He said as he hadna' made up his moind yet. He wur thinkin' o' tryin' Adam's shop (Joany's loft) ta morn."

"Let him tak' his papper dicky an' fancy moustache wheer hee's a moind. We can dew baat him, Aw con tell thi."

"He said as Billy's vice remoined him of a crow as 'ud getten the chin-cough."

"The impident hupstart!" shouted Miles. "Billy were singin' i' that chapel afoor he wur born! Chin-cough, hay! Ther's mooar music i' Billy's clugs nor i' aw his brazzened body!"

"Dust remember haa he used sing 'Thaa Shepherd ov Hisrael an' moine' ta owd Ransom? It used mak' me fair whacker wi' jye. Aw used feel as if Aw wur i' heaven," said Quiet William, softly.

"Heaven! Tha'll ne'er yer nowt loike it ageean till tha *gets* theer, that's sartin!" cried Jacky, with a tear in the corner of his eye.

"He's sung 'Rock of Ages' at mooar deeath-beds nor ony mon i' Lancashire," said Noah, with conviction.

"Aye, an' Aw whop as he'll sing it at moine, tew," cried Jacky, with a suspicious sniff.

"An' moine, tew," responded William and Noah.

"We mun ston up for him, chaps. We mun feight! We munna hev that blessed owd chapil turnt into a music-hall. It's bin th' gate o' heaven tew uz mony a toime, an aar faythers afoor uz. We mun feight fer it! We mun feight!" and Miles pursed out his lips and projected his chin and struck his fist with a desperate and yet pathetic resolution.

"If iver Billy goes off his peirch i' that singing pew it ull no be his fawt, it ull be *aars*," and Jimmy the Scutcher looked steadily at Dinah's paper-covered special occasion copper kettle hanging on the joists above Miles's head, and drew out the "*aars*" to a most expressive and emphatic length.

"He'll neer goo off that peirch till he's carried off feet furmost," cried Miles. "He's owd and he's welly blind, bud—bless his owd pow (head)——Wot the ferrups is that?" and Miles whisked round and stared hard at the closed outer door, whilst the rest rose hastily to their feet and did the same.

And they might well stare, for as Miles was about to pronounce a fervid and for him tender

## BILLY'S BLUNDER. 167

eulogium on the absent choirmaster, a most outrageous noise was heard outside. It sounded like a wild Indian war-whoop, and was followed by the shrill laughter of a number of youthful voices.

All those assembled round Miles's warm fire stood still and held their breath. Not a sound was heard save the crunching of sand under their clog irons, and all at once there smote on their ears the words of an old Methodist tune sung as only Billy Wardle could sing it.

> I'm a pilgrim and a stranger,
> Rough and thorny is the road.

"Wot the heck is he up tew?" shouted Miles, looking round at his friends in wonder and indignation. Nobody replied, and so as the singing proceeded and had a very eccentric and irreverent sound about it, Miles stepped to the door and flung it open.

The rest stood still on the sanded floor intently listening.

In a moment they heard an angry exclamation from Miles, and then the singing stopped and the laughter recommenced, and was louder than ever.

Then they heard the singer give a wild and most ungodly yell, and then strike off into another tune. It was a most strange proceeding. What could it mean? But at that moment the door closed abruptly, and Miles, white and trembling, stepped back into the house, and standing in the middle of the floor and looking round on his friends, in a voice of cruel dismay he cried, "Chaps, it's Billy! An' he's drunk—ay, drunk as a foo'!"

And with another cry that was almost a sob, he dropped into his chair and buried his head in his hands.

The rest gave vent to various sounds in which wonder, fear and distress were blended. Then they stood and gazed at each other with looks of stupefied horror, and then by sudden consent they rushed to the door, and standing in the entrance beheld the following humiliating spectacle.

There in the middle of the croft, nearly opposite to the chapel, stood Billy. He still had on his dirty workaday clothes, which ought to have been changed hours ago. He was without hat, and had only one clog. Around him was a ring of boys and girls, with piggy sticks and cricket bats in their hands, jeering and laughing, and evidently wickedly enjoying the sad sight. All down the row fronting the croft every door was occupied by a spectator, and those who had been already in the croft when Billy appeared had left their various occupations, and were standing in groups and watching the scene, half in shame and half in amusement. Yes, Billy was drunk, mad drunk, and standing there, in the midst of an ironical but applauding audience, he was running from one dear old tune to another, and bawling and gesticulating until the more serious of the spectators shuddered at the profanity of it.

And as the friends stood there enduring torments of mortification and shame a finishing touch was given to the disgraceful scene by the sudden appearance of Billy's wife. She came running across the croft, angrily shaking her fist at her husband, and then when she reached him she seized him by the back of his coat-neck, gave him several energetic shakes, called him names we cannot write, and then transferring her grip from his coat to the back of his arms, she got behind him, and giving him a starting push, ran him before her homewards.

And as if this were not humiliation enough, just at this moment a well-known yellow pony came slowly round Lark Lane corner. A great scornful laugh smote on their ears, and the mocking face of Reuben Tonge turned sneeringly towards them, whilst his harsh voice was heard crying, "Anuther canting Methody, Pablo! Anuther canting Methody! Wayshin'-up mugs, stew mugs, whaite sand and *rubbin* stoan!"

## II.

When the vociferating and gesticulating Billy and his termagant wife disappeared round Cinder Hill Corner, Miles and his friends slunk back into the house with feelings it would be impossible adequately to describe. Amazement, shame, and mortification struggled together in their minds. They were humiliated, but above all they were defeated. For the scene they had just witnessed was all that was needed to complete the triumph of Billy's enemies. Even his friends could not help him now, and just when they were making a last desperate stand in his defence, Billy himself had played into their opponents' hands and settled the matter.

For a time no one spoke. Most of them remained standing, and those who had dropped into chairs squirmed about in them and groaned until their seats creaked in melancholy sympathy.

"Lord help uz," sighed Jacky o' th' Gap, with a most lugubrious countenance.

"Aye, Lord help uz," responded Noah, and then they were silent again, whilst each was busy with his own mortifying thoughts.

"It's happen a sunstrooak," ventured Quiet William at last.

And this was just the little touch that

Miles's pent-up feelings required in order to explode, and so he whipped round, and glaring at his unfortunate brother-in-law, he cried in outraged indignation: "S-u-n-s-t-r-o-o-a-k, thaa lumpyed. Hast ony een (eyes) i' thi yed? Sunstrooak, mon! it's drink strooak; it's Red Cat strooak; it's ale strooak! We're byetten (beaten), mon! We're floored! and we're disgraced in at th' bargin."

"Aye, it's aw up wi' uz naa," sighed Jacky, wearily shaking his head.

"An' th' bewk-keeper 'ull ger in," groaned Noah.

There was another long, melancholy silence, and then Quiet William got up and went out, and nobody needed to ask where he had gone.

"An' it's th' Trust sarmons ta morn," said Noah at length, sadly.

"Aye, goa on wi' thi! Mak' it wur nur it is, thaa sniftering Joaab's comforter, thaa," snapped the irascible Miles, and then, glaring round resentfully at the rest, he cried, sarcastically, "Hez ony on yo' else owt noice ta say?"

"He'll be on his peirch ageean i' th' morn yo'll see," said the Scutcher, with conviction.

"On his peirch!" shouted the goaded Miles; "bud he winna! He shanna!"

"Wot's th' use meythering?" added Jacky, "he'll ne'er goa i' that singin' box ageean as lung as he lives."

The others, Jimmy excepted, looked a sorrowful admission, but just then William returned, and walked with a crestfallen and dejected air to his seat. As he ventured no information, Miles, after waiting impatiently for some time, whisked round sharply and demanded, "Well?"

But William did not reply.

"Speik, mon! Wot's he say?" demanded the tailor, fiercely.

"Nowt."

Miles looked at William as though he would like to put him under torture to compel him to be more communicative, and Jimmy the Scutcher asked cautiously, "Wot's *hoo* say?"

"Nowt."

As a matter of fact, Billy's wife had banged the door in the big man's face, and told him from behind it that when she wanted any of the chapel people she would send for them; and the men sitting round the fire remembered, as an additional difficulty, that Rachel and her good-for-nothing sons had done their best for years to wean Billy of his attachment to the chapel.

The friends lingered at Miles's all the evening, partly in the hope that some one would be able to devise some means of escape for them, and partly out of fear of the criticisms they knew they would encounter if they went abroad.

## BILLY'S BLUNDER.

One thing, however, was agreed upon. Billy must be prevented at all costs from taking his place in the singing-pew on the following day, and as nobody cared to face Billy's wife Quiet William and Jacky o' th' Gap were deputed to waylay the erring choirmaster if he attempted to enter the chapel, and thus prevent him making things worse.

The next morning proved very wet, and Jacky was somewhat late at his post. William, however, was there, and he stood very dejectedly propping up the railings outside the chapel when Jacky arrived.

"Hast seen owt on him?" asked Jacky as he came up, out of breath with hurrying.

"Neaw."

They waited a while, but Billy did not appear.

The congregation began to gather, but no Billy. The preacher arrived, but still no Billy.

"He's no' comin'," said Jacky at length. "Pooer lad, he conna face it."

William looked very hard at the Mill chimney, and after blinking his eyes rapidly and trying to swallow something, he said, "Pooer felley! Pooer owd lad!"

Just then the organ began to play, and the two watchers turned and nodded at each other in mutual confirmation of their previously expressed conviction that Billy was not coming.

Then, without speaking, they entered the porch, and as they did so they turned and stared at each other in surprise and consternation, for the singing had commenced, and above every other sound they could hear Billy's loud, harsh tones ringing through the chapel as if nothing had occurred.

Before they could speak the red inner door opened, and out stepped the bookkeeper with outraged righteousness written on his smug face. After him came several of his supporters, and glancing upwards they saw the members of the choir, evidently by pre-arranged agreement, picking up their books and disappearing down the narrow back-stairs, making all the noise possible, presumably as a protest against Billy's scandalous presence.

The two discomfited watchers walked sadly up the stairs to their seats in the gallery, but when Jacky reached his pew and glanced round William was just disappearing downstairs again. As the hymn went on the singing-pew gradually emptied, until when it ceased Billy was absolutely alone.

Very little heed was given that morning to the prayer, and the quiet of the service was disturbed again and again by the banging of pew-doors, as several righteously indignant worshippers, who felt they could not stay to countenance the offending presence of the choirmaster, left the chapel.

# BILLY'S BLUNDER.

When

> Come, Holy Ghost, our hearts inspire,

which was the perpetual chant at Scowcroft, was started, Billy was still alone, but hearing the deep bass tones of a second voice suddenly blending with the leader's, the worshippers glanced up and beheld Quiet William standing as close as ever he could get to Billy, and singing away with all his might, as if he would fain take the place of all those who had left, and in apparent unconsciousness of the many astonished eyes that were fixed upon him.

When the service was over every man with any semblance of right to do so made for the vestry, and when the preacher entered he found it full of indignant and protesting men who were shouting out in the excess of their excitement their various opinions on the crisis which had thus sadly arisen.

Somebody suggested that Billy be sent for, but the messenger who went in search of him announced that he had already disappeared. In the course of a long and noisy wrangle the friends of the bookkeeper made it abundantly clear that no compromise was possible, and the looks of virtuous indignation which they cast upon Miles and his party made those worthies feel as though they were in some way responsible for what had taken place.

At last, after a long and heated discussion

the authorities undertook that Billy should be kept out of the singing-pew pending a future settlement of the case, and all were preparing to disperse when some one rashly suggested that the bookkeeper should be asked to take Billy's place, at any rate until something definite could be arranged.

Miles and his friends suddenly stiffened, and looked sour and defiant, but as the bookkeeper's advocates protested that they only meant this as a temporary arrangement, without any prejudice to the final appointment, the old men were constrained, though much against their feelings, to give way, and all seemed settled for the time, when, to everybody's astonishment, Quiet William suddenly turned obstinate.

"Aw'll tak cur as Billy does na goo in, an yo mun keep th' bewkkeeper aat, tew," he said, with quiet firmness; and so, though victory seemed to be thus slipping from their grasp in the very moment of success, the friends of the new man were compelled to be content, for though William was gentleness and conciliation itself as a rule, they had learnt long ago that when he did take a stand it was more than useless to try to move him.

Several Sunday dinners were spoilt in Scowcroft that day, for when the party in the vestry broke up it was only to split into two sections, the larger one standing in the croft and debating afresh the various points of the situation, and the smaller one adjourning to Miles's to decide how to deal with Billy.

It was a melancholy business. One moment they were anathematising the bookkeeper and all his ways, and the next they were expressing their mortification at the conduct of their old friend Billy.

How were they to proceed?

William could not be induced to visit the offending choirmaster's house again at any price. Jimmy the Scutcher had not been on speaking terms with his sister for years, and the rest plainly dare not face her at all. Someone suggested the extreme expedient of a note, but Billy could not read writing, and his better educated sons were too worthless and wicked to be approached, even if they were at home and sober, which was exceedingly doubtful. It was evident that Billy was avoiding them, for Quiet William reported that when he rose from his knees after the benediction Billy had already disappeared. Nobody seemed able to make any very useful suggestion, and so William and Jacky were deputed once more to waylay the offender and prevent him taking his place in the singing-pew.

And this time they would be early enough. Soon after five o'clock they posted themselves, one at the gate to intercept Billy as he went in, and the other near a clothes-post in the croft to watch for his approach. They watched and watched, but Billy never appeared. Then Tom Crompton, the chapel-keeper, came to unlock the doors, but still no Billy. A number of boys began to assemble round the doors, but no Billy. Then the congregation commenced to arrive, and Jacky came from his position at the clothes-post to consult with William.

Just then a red-haired lad came clambering down the gallery steps, and leaning over the "banister," he stood looking for a moment at the two in consultation, and then cried in a loud whisper, " Heigh, William, dun yo want Billy?"

Jacky, who stood with his back to the entrance, suddenly wheeled round and replied, "Aye! wheer is he?"

"He's i' th' singin'-pew."

The two outwitted watchers turned and gazed at each other in bewilderment, and then, as Jacky's face grew longer and longer, a sneaking smile flickered for a moment on William's broad face, and he cried, under his breath, "Well dun, Billy!"

Just then Miles, who was steward that year, came rushing down the narrow entry on the south side of the chapel, and with his thin hair flying, and his face all awork with nervous agitation, burst upon them, crying indignantly: "Wot arr yo dooin' theer, yo gawping lumpyeds! He's i' th' chapil! He's i' th' singin'-pew, Aw tell yo."

At this moment a number of young people were approaching the entrance. They caught Miles's words instantly, and in a minute or two they were standing in the croft outside the railings absolutely refusing to enter until the objectionable choirmaster had been removed.

Then they were joined by others, then more still, until the front of the chapel was almost blocked with people all talking in restrained tones, not so much about Billy's fall as about his shameless and hardened persistence. By degrees, and after much coaxing, some of them were induced to enter the chapel, where the service had already commenced, but the greater number strolled off in small parties to adjacent cottages to discuss matters.

The heads of the church took no part in the service that evening. Most of them, in fact, never entered the main building at all, and those who did simply stole up the front stairs to satisfy themselves by actual sight that Billy was in his place, and immediately came down again.

Things were becoming desperate, and after a long, low-toned discussion in the vestry it was determined to waylay Billy as he came down the back stairs and carry him off bodily, if he resisted, to Miles's house, and try to bring him to reason.

And by this time a kind of suspicion had

arisen against William, and so Jimmy and Abram Briggs were deputed to carry out the arrangement.

As soon as the collection had been made the two stationed themselves in the passage at the foot of the singing gallery stairs, and waited. The last hymn was sung, and Billy's strident voice was heard up to the very last notes of it. Then there was a short pause, and then a shuffling of feet and a banging of pew doors, and the thudding of feet going down the front staircase, but nobody came down the back stairs. Billy had escaped before by being first man out of the building, but he was certainly in no hurry this time. Then the organ stopped, and young Abram Briggs, the organist, came stumbling down the narrow stairs.

"Is he comin'?" demanded Abram's father.

"Is whoa comin'?"

"Billy."

"Billy! He gooan lung sin; he strade o'er th' partition an' went alung the gallery an' aat at the front dur!"

Something very like anathemas broke from the lips of the cheated liers-in-wait, and they turned sulkily round and made for Miles's, where their coming was impatiently awaited.

Their appearance empty-handed and discouraged brought forth more cries of discomfiture, and when Miles arrived just behind them, the reproaches to which he had subjected Jacky and William for their failure were as nothing to those he heaped on the hapless heads of Jimmy and Abram.

Then he discovered that Quiet William was not present, and demanded to know where "that shaffling sawftyed" was. Nobody knew, whereupon the irate tailor asked them fiercely "what they used their een for," and then including both them and the absent William in one general sweep of condemnation as "dateliss, numyeds," he put his hands under his semi-clerical coat-tails and stood glowering around, whilst the rest, with gloomy and abashed faces, slowly charged their pipes.

A few minutes later a scuffling of feet was heard outside. The door was flung noisily open, and the offending choirmaster came staggering into the room as if he had been pushed from behind, followed by Quiet William looking somewhat "checked" and out of breath.

Billy had a crestfallen and almost frightened look, and as he fell into a chair, and sitting sideways, leaned his arms on the chair-back and buried his head in them, the onlookers thought that they never saw him look so utterly miserable.

For several minutes nobody spoke. Miles looked down again and again at the unhappy Billy as if about to address him, and fidgeted about uneasily as if scarcely knowing how to commence.

"Thar't a bonny mon, artna?" he said, looking Billy over from head to foot.

But the culprit neither moved nor spoke, and William gave a long, sympathetic sigh as if to reassure the suffering man.

It was quite enough, however, for the peppery Miles.

"Wot's up wi' *thee?*" he demanded with a snarl.

William paused a while, softly hissed a fragment of a tune between his teeth, and then answered slowly, "Nay, Aw wur nobbut thinkin' abaat Him as talked abaat throwin' th' fost stooan."

"Stooan! It's nor a stooan az hez come daan upon aar chapel to-day; it's a—a—havalanche!" and Miles, whose zeal for the honour of the church was blended, at the moment, with ungodly pride at having so appositely hit upon a long expressive word, glared defiantly around on the company.

The accused man uttered a deep groan, but gave no other sign.

Miles waited for some time to give Billy an opportunity of replying, but as he did not do so he cried at last, "A Methody leeadin' singer lewks weel guzzlin' i' th' Red Cat, doesn't he?"

The culprit hastily lifted his head as if about to speak, and then, closing his eyes as if in

## BILLY'S BLUNDER.

pain, and groaning more deeply than ever, he dropped his head again upon his chair-propped arms.

"He's no' bin i' th' Red Cat fur twenty yer," remarked William, quietly.

"Red Cat! Neaw! He's bin wi' them wastril lads ov his ta Kitty Codger's, Aw reacon!"

"He's neer bin i' Kitty's sin he wur born."

"Then wheer the ferrups did he get it? He geet plenty on it sumwheer, that's sartin."

William shook his head slowly, as if that were the point that specially puzzled him.

Then there was another pause, and at last Miles resumed, "Well, ther's wun thing sartin: he goos inta that singing-pew no moaar, chuse haa?"

Billy gave a start, moved uneasily in his seat, and then, lifting a haggard face, he cried piteously: "Dunna, lad! Dunna!"

Miles was touched. A sudden film seemed to pass over his vision; but seeing that the rest were in similar plight he obstinately choked back his emotion, and said, "Aw see nowt else fur it. Tha'll ha ta goo aat."

Billy jumped to his feet, a wild, desperate look in his eyes, and his face all wet with tears.

"But Aw *winna* goo! Aw *conna!* Dun yo want ta kill me?"

"But tha *mun* goo!"

"But Aw *winna* goo!"

There was a dead silence. A man who actually would not resign when bidden was a novelty, and the assembled authorities looked at each other in perplexity.

At last Jimmy the Scutcher raised his head, and with a sad face and sadder voice said, " Tha'll ha ta goo, lad! "

Billy, now fairly at bay, turned upon Jimmy, and cried in pleading, protesting tones, " Aw tell thi Aw winna goo! Aw've set i' that pew forty yer. It's the ony bit o' heaven ther is i' my loife. Wod yo tak' *that* off me ? " And with another wild cry he shook his fist in passionate desperation, and reiterating " Aw winna goo! Aw winna goo! " he made a sudden dash at the door, and before any one could stop him was gone.

## III.

In the moody and fitful conversation that followed Billy's sudden exit, it became clear to Miles that if he wished to carry his point he would have to proceed with great care. For it was very evident that William and Jimmy only needed a very little to drive them into open defence of the choirmaster at all cost and against all comers. Jacky, too, was by no means decided in his mind, and Miles felt himself very shaky on the point. William and Jimmy would not hear of Billy's place being filled, either by the bookkeeper or any one else, and when Miles demanded if they thought it right that a "druffen felley" should lead the singing they simply sighed and said nothing, and the utmost he could get them to consent to was that for the present Billy should be kept out of the singing-pew. And the week that followed brought no relief to the situation. The young people and the more advanced of the older ones were unanimous in demanding Billy's instant dismissal, and even threatened that if there were any more "dilly-dallying" they would carry the matter straight to the super. And young Abram Briggs, the organist, who was the only person in the village who could play the instrument, and had been especially trained at the expense of the trustees, stoutly declared that it was a teetotal organ, and there would have to be a teetotal leader if it continued to be played at all.

Billy was the mill cop-carrier, and in that capacity came into constant contact with the hands. They had therefore many opportunities of speaking with him, but he now adopted a stand-off and gruffly taciturn manner that kept everybody at a distance, so that the generally genial and loquacious old man compelled everybody to leave him alone.

Saturday afternoon came round again, and, in spite of the numerous discussions, reluctantly commenced and painfully prolonged, no settlement of the case had been arrived at. Everybody agreed that Billy must be kept out of the singing-pew for the following Sunday, and several others at any rate, but the cop-carrier's manner left in the minds of the authorities an uneasy feeling that Billy himself might have quite other views of the matter.

It was decided on Saturday evening at Miles's that the chapel should be watched from earliest morn, so that if the offender tried to enter surreptitiously he could be prevented. This was accordingly arranged for, Abram senior and Noah watched from daybreak to prayer-meeting time, and were then relieved by Quiet William and Jimmy. Half-past nine arrived and no sign of Billy. At a quarter to ten the chapel-keeper came to open the doors and attend to his duties. Still no sign of Billy, and the watchers were just coming to the conclusion that their old friend had thought better of the matter when the chapel-keeper came clambering noisily down the back stairs crying, as soon as he saw his friends, "Whey, chaps, he's *theer!*"

"Theer! Wheer?"

"On his peirch i' th' singin'-pew!"

The two watchers turned and looked stupidly at each other for a moment, and then, rushing

## BILLY'S BLUNDER.

indoors, climbed up the narrow staircase and saw for themselves.

Yes, there was Billy. He had a rumpled, dishevelled sort of look about him, and his seedy Sunday clothes were creased all over, indicating only too clearly that he had slept in them, and must therefore have entered the chapel the night before.

He did not move or turn round as the astonished men gave vent to various characteristic exclamations, but sat steadily looking into his own old hymn-book with a look of dull desperation on his face.

"He's getten in through th' vestry winda!" shouted the chapel-keeper in a loud whisper from the bottom of the staircase. Quiet William stood looking down on the obstinate choirmaster with a face in which sympathy and amusement were struggling for the mastery, and then, without a word or a sign of what he was about to do, he stepped carefully down towards Billy, stooped, and threw his great arms suddenly round him, lifted him to his feet, and whilst Billy kicked and struggled, and almost shrieked in protestation, carried him down the stairs through the yard, and along a narrow back lane to his own little cottage in Lark Lane. And that was the last that was seen publicly of Billy that day.

Now Jimmy the Scutcher had from the beginning of this unfortunate business been strangely quiet about it, though evidently deeply and anxiously concerned. The fact was, he looked at the subject from a standpoint of his own. Billy had married Jimmy's sister, and the Scutcher had good reason to suspect that Billy's wife gave him a very uncomfortable time of it. For the first few years of their married life there had been constant storms; rumour darkly hinted even at blows. But after a while these seem to have ceased; but Billy lost his old sprightly look, and jocose garrulous manner and looked habitually pensive and dejected. It was commonly supposed that he was "i' th' club" (henpecked), a suggestion which Billy always resented with quite unnecessary heat. For years now no particular notice had been taken of the family, and whilst Billy had grown more and more attached to the chapel, and especially to his own department in it, his sons had become notorious drunkards and gamblers, whilst his wife was more than suspected of being inclined to drink.

But Billy would not have it so. The misdemeanours of his sons were too numerous and too flagrant to conceal, but any hint, however distant, at misconduct on the part of his wife, he resented with the utmost heat.

Some years before the circumstances we are narrating took place, Jimmy the Scutcher had found reason to remonstrate with his sister on her conduct towards her husband, but though Jimmy was a terror to all ordinary people in debate, he was no match for his fiery sister, and after a long noisy interview he had poured a last fierce volley of reproach and threatening upon her and had left the house, and since then the two had never spoken.

But this disgrace of his brother-in-law's troubled him a great deal more than he showed. He could not help thinking that Billy's wife had had something to do with his fall, and strongly suspected that some more than usually distressing circumstance had driven the unhappy choirmaster to take to drinking.

The preacher that morning therefore need have had no fear of the great critic had he known it, for truth to tell Jimmy heard next to nothing of the sermon, his mind being occupied altogether with painful thoughts about his poor friend who had just been forcibly removed from the chapel.

In the quietest part of the same afternoon, therefore, Jimmy sauntered into Quiet William's cottage. "Wheer is he?" he asked, as he sat down on the long-settle and carelessly threw one leg upon it whilst he drew a long clay pipe from up his coat-sleeve.

William jerked his thumb upwards to indicate that Billy was in bed upstairs, and went on smoking.

After several minutes of silence, during which William was evidently preparing to speak, he leaned forward, tapped Jimmy significantly on the knee, and said, "Aw'll tell thi wot it is: ther's summat mysteerious abaat aw this."

Jimmy put on a complicated look of secrecy, nodded slowly, and then waited for William to proceed.

"Aw've fun aat az he's neer bin in ony alehaase within tew moile of here, an' he hedna toime furt goo furrer."

Jimmy nodded again comprehendingly, and then said, "It's my belief aar Rachil gan it him aat o' pure divilment."

"Nay, hoo'd no goo that fur, sure*li*," said William.

"Aw tell thi hoo'd dew it ta spoite th' chapil an' haggrivate me."

William looked as if he were very loath to believe any such thing, but Jimmy went on with a sudden accession of resolution: "*Thaa* con dew as tha's a moind, but if *he* goos *Aw* goo, that's aw."

William was evidently of much the same mind, but contented himself with leaning back, sighing heavily, and remarking, "Th' chapil winna be th' chapil baat Billy."

Then they lapsed into silence, and as the boards over their heads began to creak, and it was evident that Billy was getting up, William hastened upstairs to attend to him, and presently returned followed by the disgraced singer, looking very sheepish and crestfallen, but all the better for his rest.

Nobody spoke, and Billy shrank shyly into a chair in the opposite corner of the fireplace to William. Then Mrs. William brought in the tea, and they all drew up to the table. Billy tried to eat, but could not; his food seemed to be choking him; and at last, putting down an untasted cup of tea, he burst into a great sob, and cried in quivering tones, "Hay, bud yo arr koind ta me."

"Huish! mon, huish!" cried William, scarcely less agitated than his visitor. "Ha sum crumpets, wi' thi?" And he thrust a piled-up plate of the delectable Sunday tea confection close under Billy's nose.

But Billy was thinking of things far more serious than crumpets.

"Aw've disgraced you aw'. Aw've shawmed yo'. Aw wuish Aw'd a-deed afoor Aw'd dun it," he wailed, with a burst of hot tears.

"Huish, lad! Dunna tak' on! Tha con live it daan, tha knows."

"Live!" he almost screamed; "Aw conna live at aw! Dun yo' think Aw con live baat the *chapil?*" and then he paused and sobbed again, crying presently, "Aw'll niver dew it ageean. Niver! Niver!"

Nobody wanted any tea after that, and so, after giving Billy a moment or two to recover himself, William asked gently, "Wot did t' dew it fur? Hed yore Rachil bin agate on thi?"

A sudden change came over poor Billy. A look of alarm and suspicion shot into his red eyes, and he cried earnestly, "Aar Rachil? Neaw! Hay, hoo's a good un, Rachil is; hoo made me a fat cake last neet."

"Aw thowt tha'd happen getten drunk 'cause hoo'd been fratchin' wi' thi;—sum felleys does."

"Neaw!—hay, neaw! Aar Rachil had nowt ta dew wi' it," and the look of suspicion on Billy's face deepened.

All this time Jimmy had been listening intently and narrowly watching his brother-in-law, and as William paused, evidently by no means satisfied, Jimmy rose to his feet, and putting on a most fearful scowl he tapped Billy on the shoulder and said sternly, "Billy, thar't lyin'."

"Naa, then, thee let me alooan," cried Billy, more frightened than ever.

"Aw tell thi' thar't lyin'. Yore Rachil's bin agate on thi."

"Nay, hoo hasna—no—no mitch."

"Naa, come! aat wi' it." But neither sternness, nor threats, nor coaxing could induce Billy to say anything against his wife, and so at last, though still very suspicious, his two friends turned the conversation to other phases of the subject.

Greatly relieved to get away from what he

evidently regarded as dangerous ground, the cop-carrier became exceedingly pliable on all other points.

He consented after a struggle to abandon his intention of resuming his seat in the singing-pew, and then, as it was thought wise that everybody should know as soon as possible of his change of mind, he also agreed to go to the chapel and sit somewhere else.

Having gone so far, Billy went further and announced his intention of going to the penitent form after the service, and it was with some difficulty that he was dissuaded. So far all was well. Billy went and sat with Quiet William in the front pew of the gallery. The singing-pew being thus empty, the organ led the singing alone, and Billy stood up by the side of his friend, hanging his head down, and every now and again wiping his eyes. After service William took Billy with him to Miles's, and the company assembled there did its best to make the poor fellow feel at home. Late in the evening, however, a note was brought to Miles. It was from the super. He had been preaching at Cockey Lane in the afternoon, and had there met the bookkeeper, who, as they walked home together towards Wallbury, told him the story of Billy's fall and the agitated condition of the society, and the note was a brief request to Miles to call a special leaders' meeting for the following night. Now the bookkeeper could not have taken a course more certain to defeat his own ends than the one he had resorted to, for when the super's note had been read there was not a man present but was heartily, almost fiercely, on Billy's side.

"Oh! he thinks he'll manidge it that rooad, does he?" cried Miles, indignantly. "Well, them as lives th' lungest 'ull see th' mooast, that's aw," and the rest looked eloquent endorsements of Miles's words.

The rest of the evening, Billy having departed, was spent in raking up and reciting all the good things the choirmaster had done, and the sacrifices he had made for the Scowcroft chapel and congregation.

Next night the super arrived to find the vestry lighted up and prepared for the meeting, but quite empty. He waited a while, but nobody came. He began to pace up and down the room impatiently, looking every moment or two at his watch, but nobody arrived. A quarter of an hour passed and he was still alone. He hunted up the chapel-keeper and made a few inquiries.

But that officer knew nothing, or, at any rate, would tell nothing, and at last the super made his way to Miles's.

When he opened the door he could scarcely see for tobacco smoke. As it had cleared a little he glanced round and discovered that the room was inconveniently full, every man whom he expected to have seen at the vestry being present, Jimmy the Scutcher alone excepted.

"Gentlemen, have you forgotten the meeting?" he asked, in not too gracious tones.

"Neaw," answered Miles, with a rising inflection of his voice which was ominous had the super known it.

"But we must not stay here. I have come over purposely. We must go and hold the meeting."

Miles leaned as far back as he could in his chair and said, with a studious indifference as he contemplated the shank end of a ham that was hanging on the joists near the door, "Yo con goa if yo'on a moind."

"But, gentlemen," began the super, amazed and a little nettled, "we must really——" But just then the door opened and in stepped Jimmy the Scutcher, still greasy, and covered with lint and dirt, having evidently not yet been home since he left the mill. He appeared not to have seen the super, but stepping eagerly across the floor and standing over Quiet William, he fixed upon him that terrible eye of his, and glancing slyly at the super out of the other, he cried, "Didn't Aw tell thi he wur lyin'?"

William looked up eagerly and demanded "Haa dust know?"

"Aw've fund it out. Aw've bin maulin' wi'

yond owd—owd huzzy iver sin' the shop (mill) losed."

"Well?"

"Aw could get nowt aat of her fur a great while, the brazzened besom; bud at the lung last Aw've fun' this aat," and Jimmy paused for the question he knew would follow.

"Wot?"

"*He wurna drunk of his own accord*," and having delivered his master stroke, Jimmy stepped back to watch its effect on the rest.

There was a long pause. "Yes, but nobody can make a man drink if he doesn't want to, you know," said the minister dubiously.

"Conna they? Hay, mestur, yo' dunna know iverything, an' yo' dunna know aar Rachil."

The minister seemed disposed to argue the point, but he soon found that every man present believed with Jimmy, and that it would be impossible to get anything like an impartial discussion of the case. He soon learnt also that Billy had retired from his post, and as this was the main point of anxiety with him just then, he was fain to leave the rest for the present, and in a short time he took his departure.

The next Sunday the singers were all back in their places, and Billy sat once more with his old friend Quiet William.

In a week or two efforts were made to get

## BILLY'S BLUNDER. 197

the bookkeeper appointed choirmaster, but on that question the elders were quite immovable and the singers had to be content for the time with such guidance as Abram the organist could give them, the bookkeeper meanwhile transferring his patronage to " Joany's loft."

For the next few weeks nothing worth recording in connection with this story occurred, except that our friends noticed that Billy was gradually getting very thin and sickly-looking, and that even when the choir, repenting of their harshness, sang a tune which Billy always regarded as his greatest triumph in original composition, he never put in a note.

And just then a diversion occurred. One of those exciting and yet morally and spiritually fruitful revivals broke out at the chapel, and for a time Billy and his fall were forgotten in the overwhelming interests thus excited.

The effects of this visitation manifested themselves, as they often do, in somewhat singular forms, and one day a deputation of the choir, made up entirely of teetotalers, waylaid Billy after a week-evening service, and formally invited him to return to his place in the choir. Very sadly, and yet with a firmness strange to him, Billy declined, and the elders of the church, though greatly disappointed, admitted that they liked him all the better for it.

One evening, just at the commencement of a

special revival service, who should walk into the chapel but Rachel Wardle. Billy was sitting upstairs, and did not see her, but as soon as the prayer-meeting commenced, Rachel, without a word of invitation, walked straight up to the Communion rail and fell on her knees. Then Billy saw her, and a cry that was almost a scream, broke from him, and he hurried downstairs, and in a moment or two was kneeling and praying at her side.

One or two, as was the custom, went to speak to her, and were somewhat nonplussed by the candour and naïveté of her descriptions of her feelings and desires.

Presently she rose to her feet, and turning her back on those who were counselling her and facing the congregation, she cried, "Fowks, Aw conna get saved till Aw get summat off my crop." Billy, still kneeling at the communion rail, gave a little startled cry at the sound of his wife's voice, and rose hastily to his feet as if to interrupt her.

But she waved him back with her left hand, and said, "Aw've bin a weary bad un fur a decal o' years naa," and then she paused to wipe her streaming eyes. "Bud Aw should 'a' bin a foine seet wur if Aw hedn't a-hed a husband as wur a hangil aat o' heaven."

"Huish, woman! huish! Sit thi daan," cried Billy, in eager and yet somewhat suspicious excitement.

"Aw winna huish! Aw'll speak chuse wot tha says."

Then Billy turned with distress in his eyes to the congregation, and cried, "Yo munna believe her, fowks. Her's wandthering." Rachel stood quietly still for a moment with more dignity than seemed possible to her, and then she went on, "Aye, Aw've bin wandthering ta lung, bud Aw've come to my senses at last."

"Bless the Lord," rang out all over the chapel.

"Fowk," she continued, "Aw want ta tell yo' abaat aar Billy being drunk."

The responses and "Amens" instantly ceased, and there was a deathly stillness all in a moment, whilst Billy jumped to his feet and was about to interrupt again, when Quiet William, who had stolen up behind him, took him by the arm and pulled him back, at the same time covering Billy's mouth with his great hand. "Fowk, he didna tak it hissel; it wur teemed daan his throttle bi his nowty lads an' his nowtier woife." "God forgive her."

"Hallelujah!" shouted several through choking throats.

Rachel seemed about to say more, and had opened her mouth for the purpose, but suddenly breaking down she turned and rushed at her husband, and seizing him by the neck and passionately kissing him, she cried, "Bless thi owd face! Bless thi!"

The scene that followed must be left to the imagination of the reader. Only when the excitement had somewhat sudsided somebody suggested a hymn, and Billy, starting forward and raising his voice, burst out in one of the very oldest of the old Scowcroft tunes—

> God moves in a mysterious way
> His wonders to perform.

And next Sunday Billy resumed his place in the singing-pew.

# A SILENT SERMON.

# A SILENT SERMON.

## I.

THE long row of cottages facing the croft at Scowcroft was broken in two places, the first by the chapel and the second by Noah's grocer's shop. This, the chief place of business in the village, stood back a little from the rest of the houses, and was a squat, wide-windowed stone structure, which belonged to the period when Scowcroft was a quiet agricultural hamlet, undisturbed and undisfigured by canals, mills and mill-people. In those days it had been a small farmhouse, with a neat garden and wooden palings in front; but now the fence had vanished, the garden had been trodden hard, and there was nothing but an open space littered with old soap-boxes, butter-tubs, and the like. The low, wide, dusty window had a thin layer of nuts on the bottom, upon which stood imitation Chinese bowls of green coffee berries, whilst a tall, fly-blown cone of loaf-sugar occupied the place of honour in the centre. These were backed up by once-gorgeous show cards, which had held their positions longer than most of the customers could remember. The shop itself had a broken, flagged floor, and a ceiling hidden from view by innumerable bundles of candles of all counts, strings of onions, brushes, breakfast-cans, clogs, pattens, and blue-and-white pint-jugs, interspersed here and there with hams and sides of bacon. The counter was L-shaped, and at the end nearest the window there was a small desk hidden behind a pile of mustard and Epsom salts boxes. In the inner wall was a small window, which commanded a view of the counter and the desk at the end of it, and which was screened on the inside by a curtain. This curtain was a very dainty one, for however untidy and greasy the shop where Noah and his assistant Peter reigned, everything was as neat as a new pin in the house, and these two worthies had to be on their very best behaviour when they ventured across its threshold.

Late one windy afternoon in the middle of the week, when business was slack and customers few, Peter was standing at the desk apparently deeply engrossed in booking, but really engaged in a very much higher kind of literary labour. He was of medium height, but his long neck and short trousers made him look taller than he was. He had a narrow, receding forehead and a long weak chin, prominent teeth, dark, sunken eyes, and a helpless sort of mouth which always had a pathetic curve about the corners. There were signs that he ought to have had a slight moustache, but such adornments were not considered quite religious, and so his lip was always carefully shaved whenever it seemed to him to require it, which, to tell the truth, was not very often. He had long black hair, which was thick and bristly, and would have stood up and made him look quite fierce, only it was copiously hair-oiled and carefully combed back to make its owner look poetical. Not that Peter aspired to be a maker of rhymes; his ambition soared far higher than that. It was the dream of his life to be a preacher and thrill the crowds at anniversaries, only nobody had any idea of it but himself, and his most partial friends would have laughed at his aspiration had they known of it. And nobody knew this better than Peter himself, and so he kept it to himself and brooded over it and nursed it, and dreamed beautiful dreams of the great day coming when those who scorned him now would listen with wondering ears and gaping mouths to his enthralling eloquence. Meanwhile he was preparing himself, as he thought, and making sermons; yes, and preaching them, too, only as yet he had found no audience but the boxes in the shop, or the gooseberry bushes in his aunt's garden up Cinder Hill Lane.

At the moment we are introduced to him he is revising and rehearsing one of these wonderful discourses. It is laid on the little desk before him, and he is reading it half aloud to himself. Presently he warms to his work and begins to move his right arm about very earnestly, then he raises it above his head in tragic emphasis, then he suddenly shoots it out as if giving some imaginary adversary a knock-down blow, and then as he evidently approaches a grand climax he wildly throws both his long arms into the air and brings them down with an emphatic thump upon the desk, making the stumpy pens dance again and the brass weights on the counter jingle in their scales.

And all this time some one is watching him. The curtain of the little window above described is turned back just the least trifle, and a fair sunny face, with laughing grey eyes, is peeping at him in evident enjoyment of his caperings.

Unconscious of the amusement he was providing, Peter was still standing with his hands on the desk glaring with head thrown back and pursed-out lips at the bacon and candles and pint-jugs hanging from the low roof above his head, when the cracked door bell was suddenly set ringing, the little white curtain at the window was hastily dropped, and in stepped a very brisk-looking young fellow some three years Peter's senior. He was altogether a striking contrast to the young grocer—smart, good-looking, and well-dressed, with a bright, lively air about him which made him popular wherever he went. By profession he was an accountant; that is, he collected rents and debts and club-money, and canvassed for orders for furniture on the weekly payment system, and so was very well known in the neighbourhood. Besides this he was a local preacher, a taking teetotal advocate, and a very popular Lancashire dialect reciter. Altogether, in fact, Squire Fogg was about the best known and most popular young fellow in the neighbourhood, a great favourite with the young men, and a perfect Adonis amongst the "wenches."

"Hello! Pe, lad," he cried, as he came fussily up to the counter, "heaw goes it?" But though his tones were very cordial his manner showed little interest, and his eyes wandered eagerly towards the little window and the inner door at its side.

"Oh, Awm reet enuff," replied Peter, slipping a piece of butter-paper over his manuscript, and coming shyly out from behind the desk. "It's windy, isn't it?" and he put his hands into his pockets under his apron, and leaning against the fixtures behind him, assumed an appearance of ease he was far from feeling.

"Aye," answered Squire, absently; and then, suddenly changing his manner, he raised his eyebrows, dropped his voice, and, jerking his thumb in the direction of the inner room, he asked, eagerly, "Th' owd chap in?"

"Neaw," answered Peter, in slow, hesitant tones, for he was thinking rapidly, and a great idea had suddenly entered his head.

"Aw say, Squire, that wur a grand sarmon tha preiched a fortnit sin."

"Oh, aye, aye!" replied Squire, with careless impatience; and then, lowering his voice again, he said earnestly, "Pe, is hoo bi hersel'?"

But Peter was thinking on quite different lines to those of his visitor, and so ignoring, if he had really heard, the question, he inquired, "Is it yezzy ta mak sarmons, Squire?"

"Oh, aye, aye," answered Squire, impatiently. "Is hoo in, mon—is hoo in?"

"Aye; a-a-a - - - n-e-a-w—dust feel narvous when thaa preiches, Squire?"

"Preichin' be hanged!" cried Squire, angrily, but just then a new thought flashed into his quick mind, and pulling himself up sharply, he demanded, "Wot art meythering abaat preiching fur?"

Peter went white to the lips, changed his position nervously, and then answered slowly, "Nay, nowt."

"Naa then, dunna start o' lyin'; tha's getten summat i' thi noddle; aat wi' it, mon," and Squire glared impatiently at the aforesaid noddle as if he would very much like to have knocked it against the fixtures.

Peter twisted his clog heel about uneasily in

## A SILENT SERMON. 209

the sand, glanced up shyly at a string of picking-hooks above Squire's head, and at last forced himself to say, "Nay, Aw wur nobbut thinkin' Aw met try ta preich mysel'."

"Thee!" cried Squire, and with all the effort he made he did not succeed in keeping surprise and contempt out either of his face or his voice.

There was a pause, during which Peter was feeling that he could have crawled into the proverbial mouse-hole, whilst Squire was slowly conquering his astonishment and collecting his thoughts. Presently he said, leaning over the counter and speaking in tones of coaxing confidence, "Pe, thee an' me's allis bin thick."

"Aye! oh, aye," cried Peter, in eager tones.

"Well, if thaa'll help me, Aw'll help thee."

"Wilta? Wilta, lad?" and Peter's sallow face beamed with eager delight.

"Sithi, Pe, if thaa's ony preiching in thi thaas't preich."

"Shall Aw? Hey, shall Aw?"

"An' if thaa wants ta goa on th' plan thaas't goo on th' plan."

"Shall Aw? Hey, shall Aw?"

"Thaa shall, lad, thaa shall; bud tit fur tat, thaa knows."

"Oh, aye, aye! Sithi Aw'll read thi a bit o' this," and Peter was stepping up to the desk to produce his precious manuscript, when Squire laid his hand on his arm, and, checking him, said hastily, "Owd on; thaa mun dew summat fur me fost."

"Aw reet, wot dust want?"

Squire paused, glanced stealthily round, gripped Peter's arm tightly, and, scowling with a look of intense mystery, earnestly said, "Pe, Aw want get thick wi' Dolly, an' thaa mun help me."

All the eager light faded out of poor Peter's face; he went pale to the lips, which trembled as he helplessly licked them.

But Squire, although he was staring hard at the young grocer, never noticed the change; he was too intent on his own thoughts and aims to trouble about Peter's feelings.

"Thaa mun talk tew her abaat me, an' tell me wot hoo says."

But Peter only licked his lips and stared helplessly before him.

"An' thaa mun tell her az aw th' wenches i' th' village wants me."

Still Peter never spoke.

"An' thaa mun tell her az Aw'm makkin tew paand a wik, an' mooar."

Peter heaved a great sigh, and Squire could not help noticing now that something was wrong with his friend. "Pe! Pe! wot's up wi' thi?" he cried, with more of impatience than sympathy in his voice.

"A-a-ax me summat else," stammered Peter, in choking tones.

"Summat else! ger aat wi' thi! Aw want thi ta dew this. Th' owd chap's daan on me an hoo's az fawse az a foomart, bud Aw'll hev her! Therr's nowt loike her abaat here, an' Aw'll hev her, if Aw dee fur it."

Peter looked at his interviewer with gathering fear and distress, and pressed against the fixtures as if he would have shrunk through them if he had been able. "Bud Aw conna——"

"Thaa conna! Thaa con if thaa's a moind, Sithi; thee keep thi blinkers oppen, an' th' fost toime az th' owd chap goes aat at neet thee whip raand ta aar haase, an' then leeave it ta me, an' Sithi, Pe, th' fost neet az Aw get her bi herself i' that parlour, thaas't goo tak my appintment."

But just then the cracked door-bell rang again, and in stepped old Noah. Squire looked confused for a moment, and then putting on a bold face he greeted the grocer effusively, and cracked a clumsy joke about Noah looking "as smart as a snig." But Noah really looked very stern and glum, and stood still, evidently waiting for Squire to finish his business and be gone; and so, after a few rather stammering words and a significant look at poor Peter, he hastily departed.

"Wot's yon mon want?" demanded the grocer when the door had closed.

"Nay nowt; we wur nobbut talkin'.

"An' dew Aw keep a big bluffin-yed loike thee furt talk ta wastrils loike yond?"

"Aw wur nobbut——"

"Thaa wur nobbut—well, if Aw catch yo at it agean Aw'll chuck him aat o' th' shop an' thee efther him, soa Aw'll tell thi!" And with a fierce, threatening look Noah walked forward into the house, and poor Peter was once more alone.

## II.

For the next five minutes or so Peter bustled noisily about the shop, presumably with a view of convincing his master that he was busy. Then a customer came in, and he talked to her in an unnecessarily loud voice for the same purpose; but although she only wanted three articles, Peter made so many mistakes in serving her that she asked him if he was in love, and appeared by her face to have a fear that something even worse than that was the matter with him.

When she had gone Peter, heedless evidently of the banter he had just provoked, stood gazing absently at the dusty old ink-pot on the desk with thoughts that were clearly very distressing. As he thought his chin dropped, the

## A SILENT SERMON. 213

corners of his mouth began to droop pathetically, and turning half-round he looked earnestly at the shelf against the window jamb, and appealing as if for sympathy to the hair-oil and castor-oil bottles before him, he moaned, "Awm in a bonny pickle naa."

Then his eyes wandered pleadingly around the shop, as if looking in vain for pity and comfort, and finally they came slowly back to the manuscript on the desk. His brow cleared a little, he stepped up to the paper and began slowly to scan the writing. Suddenly, whoever, he started, sprang back, and stood glaring wildly at the document. Then he dashed forward again, seized the paper and crushed it in his hands; then he threw it upon the floor in tragic disgust, and putting his clog upon it, stamped it down on the sanded flags. For some time he stood looking down on the once cherished manuscript, and presently the fierce look on his face began to fade before one of tender concern, the leg holding down the paper grew limp, and then moved just enough to release it. He stood gazing thus for a full minute or more, and ultimately he stooped down and rescued the document, and placing it once more on the desk he carefully straightened it out and brushed off the adhering sand.

"Hey, wot a pickle Awm in," he groaned again, and began to move aimlessly about the shop, as if to divert his painful thoughts by active employment. But Peter did very little real work that night, he groaned deeply every few minutes, made all sorts of absurd mistakes, and at regular intervals groaned out again, "Hey, wot a pickle Awm in! Hey, wot a pickle Awm in!"

When the shop closed that night Peter seemed very reluctant to go home. He loitered about doing odd jobs for the wilful little lady who ruled in the grocery parlour, until Noah lost his temper and inquired if he was intending to sleep there, upon which Peter affected great haste and departed, but forgot his haste as soon as he got clear of the house and dropped, though the wind was still high, into the slowest saunter.

Presently he approached the cottage in Cinder Hill Lane where he resided with his only relative, a rather gruff and hasty-tempered aunt.

"Naa then, Gawmliss, dust see wot a puther thaar't makkin'?" cried Aunt Jemima, who was fat and squat, with a broad masculine face and a distinct moustache, as Peter opened the door and let in a rough gust of wind.

The young grocer quietly closed the door after him and proceeded to hang his greasy cap on a peg behind it.

As he did so he sighed, and then sidled quietly to a seat already set for him at the table where a large empty basin was waiting his use.

Jemima, still grumbling, brought the porridge pan from the hob and emptied part of its contents upon the plate, and then brought forth from the pantry a jug of milk, and with a discontented "Theer" set it before her nephew.

Then she retired to a little low seat near the fire, and commenced to work upon a partly-finished hearthrug.

And as she worked she watched the unusually gloomy youth at the table. Two or three times she seemed about to speak but did not. At last, rising to her feet and going over to the other side of the fire, where she had a better view of Peter, she asked, brusquely, "Wot's up wi' thi?"

"Me! nowt!" exclaimed he, with feebly affected surprise.

Jemima stepped up to her nephew, and giving his shoulder a push so that she could see his face more distinctly she demanded, sternly, "Wot's up, Aw tell thi."

Peter moved uneasily in his chair, and then, shaking off the hand on his shoulder, he murmured, "Dunno meyther me."

"Arr ta gooin' ta tell me," and Jemima lifted her hand, which for so short a person was a very broad one, and holding it out as if prepared to box his ears demanded once more and with increased sternness, "Wot's up wi' thi?"

Peter wriggled still more uneasily in his chair, and then answered in an injured tone, "Squire says he'll larn me t'preich."

"Well! that's wot tha wants, isn't it? An' a bonny mess tha'll mak on it, tew."

"Bud he wants me ta dew summat fur him."

"Well! wun gooid turn desarves anuther, sure*li*. Wots he want thi ta dew?"

"He wants me ta help him ta get thick wi' Dolly."

"Is that aw? He met a wanted *me* bi th' way thaa talks."

Miserable as he was Peter couldn't help smiling at the grotesque idea suggested by his aunt, but the smile soon died away, and he sighed again and looked more wretched than ever.

"Well," demanded Aunt Jemima, still standing over him, and evidently waiting for more explicit information, "that's yezzy enough, wot's ta hinder thi?"

But Peter only shook his head and sighed.

"Naa then, if he helps thee whey conna thaa help him, Aw should loike furt know?"

Peter threw his head back and shut his eyes tightly, and turning his face to the ceiling he cried piteously, "Aw conna, Aw conna!"

Jemima, who under all her roughness loved

this nephew of hers as much as mother ever
loved her son, was now genuinely alarmed, but
as according to her philosophy she might do
anything under the sun rather than show it,
she only looked the more grim and uncompromising as his distress increased, and so in a
moment she demanded, "Wot the ferrups dust
want, thaa lump-yed? If hoo wants him tha'll
ha nowt ta dew, an' if hoo doesn't want him
tha'll ha nowt ta dew; wot art meythering
abaat?"

"Yo' dunna know, Aunt, yo' dunna know."

"Wot dunner Aw know?"

"Aw want Dolly mysel'."

## III.

To say that Aunt Jemima was astonished by
the statement with which the last chapter
closed would be an altogether inadequate
manner of describing her condition. She was
simply dumbfounded. It was the very last
thing under the sun she would have expected
to hear. And then it was so very distressing.
She knew Peter, and in her fond eyes he had
no equal. But her strong Lancashire common
sense made it impossible to be deluded about

him, and she had only too much reason to know his many limitations. She had to admit —to herself, at any rate—that he was not bright, and she was perfectly well aware that her neighbours regarded him as scarcely *compos mentis*. She knew also how the villagers would laugh at the idea of Peter " puttin' up " for the dainty Dolly Ward, and how much their chaff would irritate her excitable nephew. She had only too much cause to remember also how prone her poor charge was to these ridiculous infatuations how excited he was about them whilst they possessed him, and how ill and miserable he became when he had to abandon them. For years now she had been haunted with a feeling that one day he would have an infatuation that he would not get over, and she felt as she stood looking at him now that if that fatal delusion was to come, this was it. His craze about preaching was bad enough, but this was infinitely worse.

Peter had always been very delicate. She told people yet, in confidential moments, that she should never "rear" him. He had had about every complaint that a child could have, and it is only doing her the barest justice to say that but for her slavish devotion to him he would not now have been alive. Any great strain, she felt sure, would be fatal to him. This, therefore, was the time for a supreme effort, and she made it. For fully half-an-hour she exerted her very considerable powers of argument to their utmost; rough raillery, vigorous abuse, biting ridicule and coaxing cajolery were all tried, and when these made no impression she at last fell back on a weapon very seldom used by her, and sat down and softly cried. This last argument certainly did seem to affect Peter. He was startled, ashamed, and deeply distressed. He fidgeted about until the chair creaked under him; then he got up and began to pace about the room. At last he stopped and seemed about to speak, but just then a new idea seems to have entered Jemima's head, for she raised her head, sat staring at her nephew for a moment or two, and then said, abruptly, "Peter."

"Wot?"

"Artna thaa starting o' preichin?"

"Aye, wot be that?"

"Bud tha'll nobbut be a Local, Aw reacon?"

Now this was the first time that his aunt had admitted the possibility of his being able to preach at all; she was letting the cat out of the bag. She *did* believe in him. She evidently thought that he might even be thinking of something more than mere lay preaching. Well, if she thought so, why not? This had been beyond his wildest dreams. But if he could preach at all, why not altogether? He had caught his aunt this time, and would make the most of his opportunity.

"Bud Aw mun be a Local fost; th' plan fost, an' th' ministry efther."

"Bud if thaa goos i' th' ministry thaa conna' be wed fur a great while. Thaa munna meyther wi' wenches, mon."

"Bud, aunty, Squire 'ull get her."

"Squire me leg! Dust think hoo'll bother wi' Squire if hoo sees a chonce of a minister?"

Peter's face was a study. Delight and wonderment struggled together upon it. He stood gazing at his aunt in a sort of ecstasy, and at last he rushed at her, and, slapping her heartily on the back, he cried, "By gum, aunt, yo' *arr* a stunner!" and Jemima was afraid for a moment that the lad was going to kiss her, but that was a form of caressing they had not indulged in for years.

And whilst Peter was pacing excitedly about the floor, and talking in broken snatches about his great future, poor Jemima turned her face to the wall, and murmured under her breath: "God forgi' me for lyin'. He's aw Aw hev i' th' wold."

For a full hour after this poor Peter walked about the house and talked and dreamed of his coming pulpit glory, and Aunt Jemima, with many sharp pangs of remorse, encouraged him, and finally sent him off happy and contented to bed. Then she had a bad half-hour with herself on the hearthstone before retiring, and on her way to rest she paused to listen at Peter's

## A SILENT SERMON.

half-open bedroom door. Then, assured by his heavy breathing that he was asleep, she stepped softly into the room and approached his bedside.

She began to cry again as she stood watching him, and presently she murmured through her tears, "Bless thi lad, tha's preiching enew i' thi heart if tha's noan i' thi yed," and wiping her wet eyes with the corner of her working brat, she glided softly away to repent of her fibbing and accuse herself of much other wickedness, but not to sleep.

Next morning Peter was at his work betimes, and was in a tolerably comfortable frame of mind. But just as he was finishing lighting the fire, which was his first task every morning, a soft voice was heard humming a tune upstairs, and a moment later Dolly came down. Poor Peter! all his aunt's labours of the previous night were undone in a moment. There was nothing remarkable in Dolly's features; many a factory girl in Scowcroft could have given her points in that respect. But not one of them had such a radiant skin, or such bright sunny eyes, and her hair, such a mass of fluffy golden glory was it, that that alone would have made her beautiful. Peter felt his heart jump, and her gay "Mornin', Pe Lad," sent such a thrill through him that he was glad to escape into the shop. And here, as he dusted the counter and polished the scales, he was fighting his battle over again. How could he give her up even in pretence and only for a time? Besides, if she was to wait for him to become a minister, she must know that he was intending to be one, and for the life of him he dared not tell her. Moreover, wouldn't his aunt's wonderful plan involve deceit and treachery towards his friend Squire? How could anything prosper if there was falsehood in it? He must find some other way of working the details of his plan, or rather his aunt must, for she had to do all the scheming for both of them. At any rate, for the present he would do what he had promised to Squire, and God would bring it all right, with the help of his aunt. A moment later a bright voice from the house called him to breakfast.

"Pe," cried Miss Dolly, as he drew up to the table, "thaa lewks bonny an' peart this mornin'; wot's up wi' thi?"

Peter's heart nearly came into his mouth. Now for it! But he would do what he had promised.

"Nay, nowt," he answered, with a tell-tale quaver in his voice. "Aw wur thinking abaat yo'."

"Me! Naa, Pe, noan o' thi bother! Wot abaat me?"

"Aw know sumbry as loikes yo' terble."

"Aye, it's thee, Aw reacon."

Oh, what a tumult of struggling feelings rolled over poor Peter's heart all in a moment.

## A SILENT SERMON. 223

Dolly would have been blind indeed if she had not seen long ago the idolatrous love with which he regarded her, but she never dreamed of it as the love that leads to marriage, and felt at liberty to joke about it, as, in fact, she often had done. It had been one of Peter's difficulties that she always received his attentions in this spirit.

"Nay, it's no me—no this time."

"Then tha's gan o'er likin' me, has ta?" and this naughty pussy, playing thus tormentingly with her poor suffering mouse, arched her brows and showed her small white teeth and laughed, whilst her victim went white as the tablecloth, and felt very much like crying.

It was some time before Peter could speak, but at last he found power to say, "It's sumbry bet-ter tin me—a foine seet."

And Dolly, who somehow began to suspect that she was giving unintentional pain, answered gently, as she bent over him and pulled at the tuft of hair which even oil could not keep in its place on Peter's forehead, "Nay, ther's noabry loikes me better tin thee, is ther, Pe lad? Bud whoar is it?"

And the question at the end of the sentence just saved Peter. He paused, choked down a sob, and at last blurted out, "It's Squire—Squire Fogg."

"Him!" cried Dolly, in disdainful surprise, and she tossed her golden head and looked scornful; but even Peter was able to perceive that her scorn was not very real, and that a gleam of sharp curiosity and pleasure shot into those bewitching eyes.

"Hay bur he *does* loike yo, Dolly—he's i' luv wi' yo."

Dolly had stepped back a little, but she now came forward again, and putting her hand on the crown of Peter's head she tilted it back until she could look right into his eyes, and then she asked, very deliberately, "Haa does thaa know, Pe?"

Peter blinked his eyes and tried to turn his head, but there was no escape from those great grey orbs that were gazing so searchingly into his, and so at last he stammered, "He towd me sa hissel."

"Did he! It's loike his impidence!" And then she released her hold upon Peter, and stepping back, surveyed him critically from head to foot, and at last continued: "He's a consated, stuck-up gawby. Whoa'd hev him, dust think?"

"Hev him! Whey, Dolly, aw th' wenches i' th' village is efther him."

"An' did he tell thee that tew?"

But Peter found he had got into another tight place, and was just beginning to wriggle uncomfortably in his chair when Dolly's father came downstairs, and Peter made his escape into the shop.

## IV.

BEFORE the day was out, however, Dolly had pumped poor Peter dry, and by the spirits she seemed to be in and the way she sang about the house he was compelled to conclude that the information pleased her, and he was at liberty to proceed to the next step in the negotiations.

After tea he noticed, as he expected, that Squire was hovering about the shop outside, and so, taking his cue, though with a heavy sigh, he slipped out at the back door, having previously given Squire the arranged sign. When he returned, having stayed away as long as he deemed it prudent, he found Squire leaning over the counter and talking earnestly to Dolly, who was propped against the fixtures as far away from her wooer as she could get, and looking very demure, though Peter could see instantly that the two were already on very friendly terms.

Next night Squire came again, and stayed even longer, and on the third visit, when Peter returned to the shop, the two, instead of parting, adjourned to the house, and the lover stayed quite a long time.

This sort of thing went on for about a fortnight, and Peter began to wonder when his instructions in the art of sermonising would commence.

One night, however, when Squire, after staying longer than usual, came out of the inner room he looked more than usually elated, and turning back, he came up to the counter where the young grocer was engaged, and gripping him tightly by the arm, he cried, excitedly, "Awve getten her, lad! Awve getten her! Hay, Pe, hoo is a clipper! hoo is, fur shure."

Peter, to whom the news came like a death-knell, was just opening his mouth to mention the subject of sermonising, when a deep, struggling cough was heard outside, and as they both knew that this was the sign that Noah was returning from his usual chat at Miles Grimshaw's, Squire, pulling himself together, made for the door, and meeting Dolly's father with an airy "Good neet, Noah," he hastened away, leaving Peter to bear the brunt of Noah's wrath for keeping the shop open so much after time.

And now our young friend began to be tortured with most painful self-accusations for deceiving his employer. Noah had taken him when the doctor had said that he was not fit to work any longer in the mill, and it seemed to poor Peter to be the very basest deceit to conceal from him what was going on in his absence. On the other hand, it would not do to get Dolly into trouble, and after all this seemed to be the only way open to the great goal of his hopes, so he smothered down his feelings and heartily wished the business was at an end.

Now the formality of asking the young lady's father was not generally observed in Scowcroft; the parents being left, as a rule, to find these things out for themselves. And in this case Squire, though a most ardent lover, seemed to be, for some reason, exceedingly anxious that the thing should be kept from Noah, at least for the present. And to tell the whole truth, Dolly found that the secrecy of her courtship added so much spice to it that she was almost as anxious as her lover to keep the thing a secret for a little while. During these occurrences, therefore, she was unusually kind to Peter, on whom they both to some extent depended for protection, and that youth was expecting that every time he came Squire would make some proposition about the preaching lessons, and so was more content to be kept at the shop as a cover for the courters than he otherwise might have been. All the same he grew very impatient, and at last one night when Squire was departing he found Peter dressed ready to go home, and was a little surprised when he joined him at the door, and made as if he would walk along with him. Squire didn't like it, but there seemed no help for it, and besides Peter was such a simple fellow that it would be easy enough to shake him off whenever he wanted.

As they walked along Peter seemed at a loss for something to say. He mentioned that it was "a sloppy neet," a second, and then a moment or two after a third time. He seemed to be about to say something two or three times and then changed his mind, and at last as they drew near to Squire's door he stopped suddenly in the middle of the path, and with a nervous, anxious face he managed to squeeze out, "Squire, when arr ta goin' furt tak me wi' thi ta preich?"

"Preich!" and then he suddenly remembered and went on, "Oh aye, Aw'll tak thi some day, lad. Good neet!" and leaving Peter standing in the lane, he disappeared hastily into the house. Peter got no sleep that night, but next evening he joined his friend again and reminded him of his promise, only to be rebuffed more rudely than before. Then Squire took to avoiding the would-be preacher by going out at the back door of the grocery, although he of course gave Dolly some other reason for so doing. This went on for about a week, Peter meanwhile suffering untold agonies of anxiety and fear. On the following Monday night, however, he resolved to be "up sides wi' Squire," and so leaving the shop at the usual time, he lingered about the entrance of the back-yard until Squire should appear.

He had not to wait long, for Noah had grown suspicious of late that all was not as it ought to be at the shop, and so he returned earlier than usual. Squire, taken somewhat by surprise and greatly disappointed, was compelled to make a sudden bolt for it, and in doing so, ran straight into the arms of Peter.

"Naa then, lump-yed, ger aat o' me road, wilta," he cried, as he pulled up and discovered with whom he had collided.

"Squire, Squire," began Peter, "tha promised, tha knows."

"Promised! whoa promised? Wot did Aw promise?" shouted the angry lover.

"Ta tak me ta try furt preich."

"Thee preich! thaa great cawf-yed! ger aat o' me seet!" and giving the too-confiding Peter an angry push that sent him staggering into a filthy ditch, he disappeared into the darkness.

Peter, all wet and muddy, scrambled out of the water, and stood looking in a dazed and woe-begone manner in the direction Squire had taken. It was all over now; even to his dull wits the truth came home that Squire had never really intended to help him in his great ambition. Slowly and sadly he began to move towards home. Before coming into Aunt Jemima's presence, however, it was necessary to decide upon his course of action, and it seemed to him, when he was sufficiently recovered to be able to think, that it would be best for the present to say nothing to her. She was very violent when really roused, and might make matters worse by letting out Dolly's secret, which seemed to him to be a sacred thing to be hidden in his heart until the proper time to reveal it came. Whatever else he must be faithful to Dolly.

Contriving, therefore, though with considerable difficulty, to get into the cottage and upstairs without revealing his condition, he hastily removed his wet garments, and then waited until he heard his aunt go into her own bedroom, when he slipped down into the little back scullery and washed himself, and was quite comfortable before Jemima reappeared.

For two or three days Peter went about scarcely knowing where he was. For besides the ill-treatment he had received he was nearly heart-broken at the thought that his grand dream of being a preacher had been destroyed, and he had nothing in life to think about.

And every day he seemed to feel his disappointment more and more. It took away his appetite and exposed him to constant and very awkward questions both from his aunt and Dolly. His faith in his fellow-men had received a rude shock, and he felt lonely and miserable. But to have to give up the idea of preaching! that was the bitterest thought of all.

But before long his thoughts were turned

into a different channel, and his own sufferings were forgotten in his concern for his beloved Dolly. Every Thursday he had to go to an adjoining village to take parcels of groceries, and was often somewhat late in getting back. On this particular week he was later than usual owing to an accident to the little cart he drove. As he was returning, sitting in his trap and musing on the topic which was with him night and day, he observed a couple of courters a little way on before him. There was nothing very remarkable in that, to be sure, but Peter thought that the female looked rather like his mistress Dolly, and just as he got up to them the moon, which had been for a moment behind a cloud, came out again and shone straight down on the man. It was Squire Fogg, and therefore the young woman with him must be Dolly, as she was of about the same height and figure.

It had got to that then. They were "walking out" in the regular fashion, and as the young lady clung very close indeed to her companion he could only conclude that she liked this even better than indoor courtship. And now Peter felt his own deep love for Dolly suddenly awakening. Oh! how sweet it would be to have her walking by his side and leaning on his arm like that. But that was now for ever impossible—somebody else had got her, and got her with his assistance and as the result of a mean trick. Peter could scarcely sit in his seat. He longed to go and tear his young mistress out of the arms that were now encircling her. But did she know what a mean liar and deceiver the man she was learning to love was? Ought he to let her marry without telling her? If she married and was unhappy he felt as if he should go mad. Oh! what a predicament for a poor lad to be in. Just then the pony turned into the croft, and a moment later pulled up at the grocery. Peter had a bundle from the dressmaker's for the mistress, and so taking it out of the cart he carried it through the shop into the house. But as he opened the door he came to a sudden stand, and the bundle dropped from his nerveless grasp, for there, sitting cosily by the fire, was Dolly.

"Dolly!" he gasped, and then, what with one thing and what with another, Peter had a sudden and awful sense of overwhelming pressure and slipped down on the mat in a dead swoon.

## V.

When Peter came to himself he found that he was reclining on the big long-settle under the little window that looked into the shop. Somebody was evidently propping him up, and feeling

## A SILENT SERMON. 233

something warm beating behind his ear he glanced up and discovered that he was leaning on Dolly's breast, and that her soft left arm was encircling him.

"Arr ta badly, Pe?" murmured a low, sympathetic voice close to his ear.

"Hey, neaw—Awm bet-ter naa," and in confirmation of this statement he immediately fainted away again.

When he recovered Dolly's arm was still round him, and a warm, wet little cheek was being pressed against his. "Poor lad," she murmured. "Poor Pe! Arr ta bet-ter?" and she bent down and kissed him.

Better! Peter didn't want to be better if that was being ill. He was in heaven, and the kiss was like the kiss of an angel. Then he opened his eyes and saw the grocer standing looking at him on the door-mat.

Noah lingered about a few minutes asking Peter every moment or two how he "felt hissel'," and then went off into the yard to put up the pony.

And by this time Peter had somewhat recovered, and was sitting up and leaning against the end of the "settle," whilst Dolly fussed and crooned about him until the delighted lad began to feel quite spoilt.

Then she brought a cup of hot tea with a little whisky in it and compelled him to drink it. He felt better after this, and began to try to comprehend the situation and decide upon some course of action.

"Haa lung is it sin Squire left?" he asked, cautiously, as the maiden took the empty cup from him.

"Left?—he's no bin here ta neet; wot fur?"

Peter paused a moment before answering, and then he said, looking earnestly into the face still bent over him, "H-a-y, Dolly, yo dew loike him, dudna yo?"

"Naa, Pe, ger aat wi' thi; Aw loike thee a foine seet bet-ter."

Peter felt his head beginning to swim again. Oh, why was she so cruelly kind? He knew she didn't mean it—not in the sense he desired, at any rate. Oh, what was he to do? He might be able to give her up himself; he would do that whatever it cost him. He knew that he was in no sense the kind of fellow Dolly would fancy. But then he loved her with all the power that he possessed, and he could not see her giving herself away to a man who was already deceiving her. The woman he saw with Squire could not possibly have been Dolly; there could be no doubt whatever that the two he saw in the lane were on the most loving terms with each other. Was his darling mistress, who was fit to be the bride of a duke, to be a mere second string to a base man's bow! It was not to be thought of for an instant. Poor Peter was not very quick as a rule, but in this case love made him keen, and he racked his poor brain, as he sat looking at the glowing fire, to try and decide what was the right thing to do under the circumstances.

He decided to do nothing for the present. He would go home and think about it and perhaps, if that seemed the best course, consult his aunt.

He sat thinking and resting on the end of the long settle for some time, and at last, announcing that he felt " Aw reet naa,' he got up to go home. Dolly wanted him to wait until her father came in that he might help him on the road, but Peter, declaring again that he felt " Aw reet," went off by himself. The air outside was very refreshing, and he felt himself improving every step he took. He would not go indoors yet, he would walk about a little and think.

" Hello, Pe! is that thee, lad ? Aw wur just seeching thee."

"The voice sent a thrill through Peter's frame—it was the voice of Squire. Not a word could Peter get out. He turned round to face his enemy, but only stared at him with a dazed and terrified look.

" Awm planned at Baalamb Fowt o' Sunday ; wilt come and thry ? "

But Peter was beyond all that now. The desire to preach was as strong within him as ever, but even if he could have trusted this plausible tempter, his own interests were not to be considered for a moment where the happiness of sweet mistress Dolly came. "Neaw, Aw winna," he answered, with peremptory fierceness, and glared at Squire as though he would have liked to fly at his throat.

"Hello! thart huffed, arta? Christians should furgive an' furget, tha knows; it's a noice little place ta start at is th' fowt."

"Awst no goo! Awst niver goo wi' thee, thaa lyin' wastril thaa."

And though Squire disregarded Peter's offensive tone, and argued and coaxed for several minutes, he only made Peter more resolute and abusive.

And now Peter wanted to get away, and turned in the direction of home.

"Pe! Pe! here, lad, dunna goo yet! A-a-hast towd Dolly wot tha seed ta neet?"

"Towd her! Neaw! bur Aw will dew if Aw live till th' morn."

For fully ten minutes the embarrassed lover argued with Dolly's champion to bring him to a different mind, but without the slightest success. Peter, in fact, only grew the angrier, and said the more provoking things as Squire became more and more oily and persuasive. At last his patience seemed to become exhausted, and as another idea suddenly struck him he put on a look of fierce anger, and shaking his fist in

## A SILENT SERMON. 237

Peter's flushed face he cried, "Sithi! if tha does tell her Aw'll, I—Aw'll knock thi brains aat."

"Knock 'em aat then, Awst tell her."

No sooner said than done. In a moment the hard fist of the infuriated Squire flew into Peter's face, and he went staggering into the hedge, whilst his now terrified assailant rushed frantically from the spot. Half an hour later, as Reuben Tonge, the sandman, was returning from one of his rounds, he thought he heard a moan in the hedge bottom, and glancing down he could make out indistinctly something very like a human form. He stopped the never too eager pony and got out, only to discover the prostrate and partly conscious Peter. In a few minutes the wounded youth had been gently laid in the cart bottom, and Pablo was being led along at a pace that exactly suited his tastes, but was not very often possible with so energetic a master. Now there happened to be a heap of stones lying just where Peter had fallen, and as he was found with half his face upon the heap, Reuben concluded that he had fainted and fallen upon them. And what Dolly told, immediately she knew of the affair, of Peter fainting in their house, seemed so exactly to fit in with the idea that when Peter came to full consciousness next morning he found that view of the case so generally accepted that it was a

## A SILENT SERMON.

relief to him in his feeble condition to allow the explanation to stand until such times as he was fit to think and decide upon a course of action. Alas! it was many a day before he reached that state, and when he did so he found that Squire, who was one of the first to hear this version, and took courage from it, had already got very much further on with his ardent courtship, and that Noah had discovered it and had raised no more serious objection than a sulky grumble. Poor Peter! he was now in a worse fix than ever. When Dolly really liked anybody she did like them, and was their uncompromising and almost intolerant defender. Squire was just the man to make the most of his opportunities, and had such a way with women that Peter felt certain that by this time she was head over ears in love with her suitor.

What was he to do? He had allowed the popular version to go uncontradicted so long that he couldn't very well bring forth any other now. And yet he could not warn Dolly without giving some reason, and if he began his tale he knew that he would be compelled to finish it.

Meanwhile Squire was making the most of his chance. He was very uneasy and very apprehensive as to what Peter might do or say. He determined therefore to, if possible, anticipate any trouble by inducing Dolly to think less highly of her champion. He began, one night, to drop hints as to

Peter's soundness of mind, and was surprised to find how quietly Dolly took it, although he did not quite like or in fact understand, the look she gave him as he was speaking. Then he ventured further, and was just about to make his first serious point, when Dolly suddenly flamed up, and for the next five minutes he could not believe his own ears. She stood up to it; she clenched her little fist, she stamped, and before she had done there was not a doubt left in his mind as to the place poor Peter held in his lady-love's affections. It was clear to him, therefore, that he would have to make his peace with Peter by some means, though by what was not at all apparent. Upon his next visit to Dolly, however, an unexpected opportunity presented itself. He had begun to inquire very earnestly about Peter's health, when he suddenly noticed a tear rise into her grey eyes, and her face became very grave. On inquiry he found that the doctor had expressed some doubts as to his patient's ultimate recovery, and had recommended a prolonged rest and change of air. A horrible fear took possession of him. What if he should find himself charged with Peter's death? Recovering himself, however, he realised that this was his opportunity. If Peter could be got out of the way until the marriage was over he could take care of himself afterwards. Besides, what a fine opportunity was presented for getting into Dolly's favour by playing the generous patron to Peter. That was the plan! Having once seen his chance, Squire was not long in making use of it. The very next forenoon, when he knew that Aunt Jemima would be at the mill, he made his way to Peter's residence.

"Art in, Pe?" he asked, as he opened the door.

"Aye, Aw'm in, and Aw want *thee*." And Peter, white to the lips and trembling all over, stood up to receive his visitor.

"Thaa wants me? Wot dust want?" And though the tone was low and wheedling, the expression on the speaker's face was one of keen anxiety.

"Wot 'ud Dolly say if hoo knew wot Aw know?"

"Naa, Pe; come, lad! Sithi——"

And then, after appealing very earnestly to the generosity and good nature of his friend, he unfolded the scheme that meant so much to his own future prospects. Peter listened so attentively to Squire's plausible plan that he thought he was going to succeed right away, especially as it was offered with an expression of sorrow and as some atonement for the injury done. But when he had finished Peter paused a moment, and then said, quietly, "Squire, Aw'll agree ta aw as thaa says, if thaa'll gi' Dolly up."

"Give her up! Aw'll dee fost!"

"An Aw'll dee afoor thaa's t' hev her."

## VI.

AND there the two stood, white and excited, and glaring at each other in fierce defiance. Squire looked as if he could have torn the frail figure before him to pieces, but as this was not his cue for the moment he dropped his eyes, relaxed his clenched fist, and then commenced to coax again. But Peter was not to be moved; the more Squire talked the more obdurate he became. Then the desperate man suddenly changed his tactics. Turning from his rival, he dropped into a chair with a gesture of impatience, and commenced to glower at the fire. Presently he began to look very sorrowful, then he sighed, and, leaning back in his chair, closed his eyes and seemed in deep and very troubled thought. Then he sighed again, and more heavily; and at last, bursting into tears, he gripped Peter's arm tightly, and cried in apparently deep distress, "Pe, Aw've dun wrung—wrung ta thee, wrung ta Dolly, an' wrung ta iverybody! Aw'm a wastril! Pe, Aw'm a sinner! Aw'm nowt else!"

Peter was visibly relenting.

"Oh, Pe, wot mun Aw dew? Aw'm a sinner! Aw'm a wastril! Lord ha' massy on me."

"Happen God 'ull forgi thi, lad," stammered Peter, his eyes swimming with tears.

"He winna! He *conna!* Aw'm ta bad; bud Aw did it aw fur luv o' Dolly."

That was sufficient. Peter felt that a man might be forgiven for almost anything he might do for his dear mistress's sake, and so, with quivering lips and streaming eyes, he cried, eagerly, "Yi! He will, lad! He'll forgi thi just naa, a—a—an' soa will Aw."

"Wilta, Pe—wilta? God bless thi, lad!" and seizing the limp hand of the poor fellow he was deceiving, he shook it fervidly, and blessed him again and again.

It was soon settled after that they were to be fast friends henceforth, and Peter was to help him to get Dolly as soon as possible.

But Peter had forgotten for the moment Squire's second sweetheart, and when he suddenly remembered her he turned stubborn again. But Squire had a very easy explanation of that. She was a girl who had "meythered his life aat," and he was free to admit that he had been "a bit sawft wi' her." But it was all over. The night Peter saw them together was the last time he had seen her, and he only visited her then to finally break with her. "Clippin"? Yes, they were "clippin"—at

## A SILENT SERMON.

least, she was, and he had put up with it as best he could because it was the last time.

And so the two were reconciled, and Peter, though he still declined Squire's offer of a holiday at Southport, expressed himself as very grateful. As Squire was departing he turned back.

"An', Pe, lad, thaa'll put a good word in fur me when thaa sees Dolly?"

"Aw will, lad—Aw will"; and Peter beamed upon his penitent friend with a look of trustful confidence and pleasure.

But the crafty hypocrisy he practised upon Peter availed its author nothing, for, a few days later, a young woman about Dolly's age and height called at the grocery. Before she left she had established a claim upon the deceitful Squire that satisfied his *fiancée*, and filled her with an indignation that was almost terrible to behold. Happily, she found that her affection was not so deeply engaged as might have been expected. She possessed quite her share of that dislike of "bounce" so characteristic of the people of her county, and had never been as entirely satisfied with her lover as he, in his vanity, had imagined.

It was almost a relief to her to have done with the business; but that did not prevent her making Squire's punishment as severe as she could.

When her visitor had gone and she had had

time to recover herself, she sent for her father out of the shop, and then sent for her lover.

He came eagerly enough, but after listening to his angry sweetheart for ten minutes he was only too glad to depart, and Noah was so delighted with the way his daughter had "combed his yure fur him" that he slapped her heartily on the back, and then went off to tell his cronies at Miles's.

The next night Squire was "planned" to conduct the week-night service, and Jacky o' th' Gap prophesied that he "wouldn't face up." The others, however, were of a different mind, and so it was left to Jimmy the Scutcher to "heckle" him if he did.

Now it happened that Peter did not hear of what had transpired that night, and came down to the grocery next day unconscious of any change. When he asked his young mistress what was the matter—for Dolly had got over her first indignation and had just been having a quiet little cry when he arrived—she tossed her head, and answered somewhat tartly, "It's that wastril of a chap tha fun me." And then she told him all that had happened, and Peter, in his indignation, blurted out something that awakened Dolly's suspicions, and in a few minutes she had compelled him to tell her everything. Dolly's anger was wonderful to see; she actually shed tears of indignation as

## A SILENT SERMON.

he detailed Squire's many deceptions. She was like a mother hearing the story of some wrong done to her child, and her little body quivered with scornful resentment. Noah, when he learnt about the matter, was almost worse than his daughter, and waylaid Jimmy on his way from the mill to post him up with these additional particulars.

Jimmy, who had for years shown an unaccountable prejudice against Squire, received the information with manifest satisfaction, and prepared himself for a good innings. When Squire arrived at the chapel vestry he was somewhat taken aback to see that apartment quite full of men. His heart misgave him, but having no idea that Peter had rounded on him, he prepared to brave it out.

"W-e-l-l, Pe, lad," began Jimmy, in his very blandest tones, "arta i' good fettle?"

"Aw'm reet enough; wheer's th' hymn-bewk?"

Jimmy was sitting on the hymn-book; but without moving he followed Squire with his protuberant eye as he hung up his hat, and, then, disregarding his inquiry, he dropped into an, if possible, oilier tone, and asked, "Wot's it goin' ta be ta-neet?"

But Squire was not relieved; Jimmy was never so dangerous as when he adopted this tone, and the others had looks on their faces which confirmed his worst suspicions, and so he answered, sulkily: "Tha'll yer it sewn enuff—wheer's th' hymn-bewk?"

"Aye, Aw reacon sa; Squire con ta preich off *ony* text—reet off, tha knows?" and Jimmy really looked so very innocent that Squire began to wonder whether there really was any reason to feel as much alarmed as he actually was. But the presence of so large a company, and the mysterious absence of the hymn-book were not reassuring, and so, at a loss to know what to think, he answered: "Awm no goin' t' dew ta neet—whoas getten th' hymn-bewk?"

As he spoke the uneasy preacher lifted his head and glanced at the faces of the men who were seated around the room, and meeting in every eye stern and menacing looks he quailed visibly and began to think it time to beat a retreat. "Well yo' con *tak* th' bewk an' th' sarviss, tew!" he cried, angrily, and turned to the door. But as he did so Quiet William rose from his seat and placed his big body against the entrance in a manner that was unmistakable.

"Nay! Nay! dunno goa, lad," drawled Jimmy, in mock expostulation; we want t' yer thi preich. Ween getten a text fur thee, tew."

Squire was now fairly at bay. He was also beginning to be very frightened, and so his one desire was to get out of the room by some means or other; dissembling, therefore, he answered, "Well, wot is it?"

## A SILENT SERMON. 247

But Jimmy was enjoying himself too much to be in any hurry, and so, looking beamingly upon his victim, he said, "Hay, it's a grand text! If ther's awmbry i' this wold con preich off it, *thaa* con!"

"Wot is it?"

"It's sumwheer i' th' Saams—Jacky, just reich me that theer Bible."

With slow and painful deliberation the tormentor turned over the leaves of the sacred book, pausing every now and again as if to recollect where the text he was seeking was. Meanwhile, Squire had glanced more than once towards the door again, but William was there still, and looked too stern to encourage the idea of a rush.

"Oh, it's here," cried the tantalising Jimmy at length. "Hay, it's a topper; thaa could preich aw neet off it, Squire."

"Wot is it, mon? Wot is it?"

"Saam a hundred an' wun, voss seven—just lend me thy specs, Jacky."

Jimmy took the glasses, laboriously breathed upon them, carefully wiped them with his pocket handkerchief, and then read out:

"*He that worketh deceit shall not dwell within My house; he that telleth lies shall not tarry in My sight.*"

There was a deadly stillness in the room for a moment, during which Jimmy was still bent over his book, evidently musing deeply. All at once he rose to his feet, and snatching off the ill-fitting glasses he lifted his head and looked at the wretched Squire as though he would wither him with his glance.

"Thaa lyin' slotch! thaa brazened tew-faced hypocryte, thaa! ger aat o' God's haase."

But Squire could stand it no longer. With a cry like an enraged beast he sprang at his tormentor, and would doubtless have done him serious mischief. But just then Quiet William's great arms were thrown around him, and he was dragged, foaming at the mouth, into the croft, and then flung out into the darkness. And from that time Scowcroft knew Squire no more.

When the details of the gay deceiver's treatment of Peter became known in the village the sick youth found himself astonishingly and delightfully popular, his friends vying with each other in showing him all sorts of little kindnesses. This notwithstanding, Peter grew visibly weaker under their eyes, and Miles Grimshaw went about prophesying all the dreadful doom that awaited Squire if "Owt happens yond pooer lad."

But the doctor removed all danger of that by declaring that, although the blow he had received had been a shock to him, yet he was far gone before that, and nothing could long postpone the end. This deepened the sympathy shown to the sufferer, and gave great

## A SILENT SERMON.

distress to Aunt Jemima and Dolly. Every day now Noah was dispatched early in the forenoon to bring Peter down to the grocery, and he stayed there until his aunt fetched him home. These were happy days. Dolly fed and coddled and talked to her charge until the time flew by with amazing rapidity, and Peter was always surprised and sometimes even a little disappointed when the evening came. Dolly knew more than anybody else about his great ambition to be a preacher, and drew him out as often as possible on his favourite topic. One day she beguiled him into reading that precious manuscript of his, and discovered to her astonishment that instead of being the feeble, cooing, gentle thing she expected from such an author, it was a terrible denunciation of sin and sinners, and contained lurid and most realistic descriptions of the miseries of the lost. She never asked for a second edition.

Now Peter was constantly exercised in his mind as to whether Dolly was not secretly mourning for Squire after all, though her language was definite enough to satisfy any one. Every now and again, therefore, he brought the conversation round to this subject, and Dolly, to gratify him, talked pretty freely about the matter. One day, when they had become unusually confidential, even for them, Peter, after a longer pause than common, said, "Dolly, wot sooart of a felley wilt hev when tha does get merrit?" and Dolly, who was standing on the hearthrug and hanging clean clothes upon a long rack over her head, and whose only thought was to say something that would please him, answered, "Summat loike thee."

"Dolly!"

But she appeared not to notice his amazed exclamation, and went on as though she were talking to herself, "Bud ther's nooan sa monny loike thee, lad," and then, as a sudden choking came into her throat, she murmured to herself, "An' when ther is God taks 'em."

There was silence for a moment, and Dolly moved to the other end of the rack, and so came close to her companion. Presently she felt a trembling hand laying hold of her apron, and a husky voice asked, "Dolly, does ta loike me—a *that* way?" And Dolly turned and put her hand on the sallow brow of her wooer, and answered, "Wot else?"

Peter was some time before he could speak. His words seemed to be choking him, but at last he asked, in eager, wondering tones, "Bud tha wodn't merry me if Aw wur weel, Dolly?"

And a great gush of feeling came into poor Dolly's heart as she remembered that he never could get well, and, reckless of everything but his pleasure, she replied, stoutly, though with shaking voice, "Wod'nt Aw? Thee be sharp and get weel and tha'll see."

## A SILENT SERMON.

If anything on earth could have saved poor Peter this would have done; but it was not to be. He lingered all through the winter, and one day in the early spring he passed quietly away in his sleep, and they laid him in the old churchyard beside his mother. Dolly insisted on joining Aunt Jemima as chief mourners, and when the last sacred office had been performed, and the mourners—of whom there was a great company—were turning away from the grave, Aunt Jemima, leaning over the side and looking down upon the plain coffin below, sobbed out, "Bless him! He'd some grand sarmons in his hert."

"Aye, if nobbut he could a preiched 'em," sighed Dolly.

"Them soart o' sarmons doesna need preichin'," said a voice behind them, and Quiet William walked away wiping his eyes.

# THE SUPERINTENDENT.

# THE SUPERINTENDENT.

## I.

MILES GRIMSHAW was in the very worst of humours. Before dinner he had been quite amiable; twice during the forenoon he had called the long-suffering Dinah "owd chicken," which was the most certain of signs that all was well with him, and was also a form of endearment he only permitted himself to use on very rare occasions. And now ever since about eleven o'clock he had been snapping and snarling at everthing and everybody. Abram Briggs, junior, who had called about his new Sunday coat, was "fair taken to" when, upon offering a very mild and hesitating criticism of its fit, he was called an "awkered, cross-cornered, crow-boggart as noabry c'ad fit"; and "Tay-wayter Martha," who had called to impart to Dinah a piece of most interesting gossip, went away without ever getting her story told, as Miles fell upon her immediately she entered the house, about her irregular attendance at class. Dinah, seeing how things were, had taken quite unusual pains with the dinner, but they were apparently all wasted, for the one bacon collop was "brunt tew a coak" (cinder) and the other was "red-raw," whilst potatoes and oat-cake and small beer were all deficient in some way. And when the irascible tailor resumed his work things were no better; when he couldn't find his wax it was of course because Dinah had mislaid it; the "smoothin' iron" was cold and the fire never could heat it properly—it was always so full of "ess" (ashes).

As for the new plan that had just come in, and was in reality the cause of all this perturbation, Miles snorted at it, gave vent—as he sat cross-legged on the table, looking at it—to short, sarcastic little laughs, and at last crushed the offending sheet up in his hands and flung it scornfully into the window-bottom, amongst the clippings.

"For shawm o' thisel, Miles, wot's up wi' th' plan," and Dinah, as she finished putting the dinner-pots away in the side-cupboard, leaned her portly form over the table and rescued the disgraced document.

"Oh, nowt! Nowt! It's a topper!" and Miles laughed—a loud, sardonic laugh.

"It's reet enuff fur owt Aw see."

"Reet enuff!" And Miles spun round on his seat and down upon the floor, and snatching the plan from Dinah's hands he spread it carefully out on the table.

"Dust caw that reet? an that?" he cried

## THE SUPERINTENDENT. 257

excitedly, pointing at first one number opposite the name of Scowcroft, and then another, " Tew hexorters an three on-trials and awth windbags ith circuit." "Reet is it," and Miles burst into another mirthless laugh.

And Dinah looked as she was commanded, but not at the Scowcroft appointments at all. She ran her eye over the numbers opposite the circuit chapel, and then those for " Rehoboth," the second chapel, which was in the suburbs of Wallbury, and when she had satisfied herself that No. 7 was not appointed at either of these important places she understood all about her husband's anger, for No. 7 on the circuit plan was Miles Grimshaw.

She sighed a little, and Miles was just about to explode upon her when the door opened and in walked Miles's particular crony, Jacky o' th' Gap.

The farmer's coat was open, his scarf hung loose, and his hat was tilted back on his head, whilst his lips were compressed and his eyes rolled about restlessly, all of which were signs that his mind was not at rest.

" Tha's getten it Aw see," he remarked, standing with his hands behind him and his back to the fire.

"Getten it! aye! an a bonny thing it is," and Miles threw up his chin in disdain, and went sulkily on with his stitching.

" He owt niver ta mak anuther plan wo'll his

wik," and Jacky's lips tightened with grim emphasis, and then glancing round into the right-hand corner of the fire-place he reached out a small bundle of long clays, took down the tobacco-pot from the mantel-piece, and sinking into the nearest seat he commenced to charge, upon which Miles whisked away the garment he was making, and descending to the floor, and standing agressively before his companion asked, fiercely, "Wot did Aw tell thi th' fost time Aw iver clapped een on him?"

Jacky evidently did not all at once remember, and threw himself back in his chair, puffing out a huge volume of smoke and looking meditatively at the joists above him, but Miles could not wait, and so he went on. "Aw towd thee i' yond vestry as yond chap' Ud ha wovven his cut i' twelve munth, didn't Aw?"

"Tha did, lad," replied the farmer, nodding his head in confirmatory recollection.

Now, these two men were popular local preachers. Their sermons were expressed in a sort of modified vernacular, and what their utterances lacked in literary grace or grammatical correctness they made up in racy point and idiomatic force. This being so, they were often more welcome in local pulpits than more polished, but less interesting preachers, and were always much in request. But the new superintendent, who had only been on the ground since last Conference, now some four months past, had judged them by what he had seen of them in their own village, and in their private capacities, and had only appointed them at the smaller places. And this was the real grievance, and for the next hour or so the minister's ears must have burnt most distressingly, for not only his plan-making but every prominent act of his administration since he had been in the circuit was canvassed, and he was roundly condemned as a bungler and a failure.

Not a single allusion was made, of course, to their own appointments, it was the weak and corrupt favouritism which had given three more "Ministerial" appointments to Mill-houses than to Scowcroft that was stigmatised, and the outrageous folly of sending 'Hexorters' like Harry Nobby and Fat Rafe " (Ralph) to so important a place as the one they worshipped at, and the thoughtlessness of sending 'Owd Dottle " all the way to Greenhalgh Fold in the winter quarter, and the appointment of Dobson at the circuit chapel just because he was a mill-owner and circuit steward.

"Aw dunnot know ha yo tew con fur shame o' yer faces," cried Aunt Dinah, out of all patience at last. "Yo'n nowt to dew bud lewk at his face ta see wot he is."

"Wot's thaa know abaat it?" cried Miles, with an impatient fling of his head.

"Aye! they sen as th' chap as wur hung at

th' New Bailey t'other day hed a face loike a cherrybim," laughed Jacky, a little uneasily, and they tried to resume their talk, but somehow Dinah's remark had made an impression, and in a few minutes Jacky took his departure.

Miles couldn't settle to work any more, however, for even though his mind was somewhat relieved by the conversation they had just finished, he already began to feel another disturbing influence. The super whom they had been so energetically denouncing was coming to tea that day, or, at any rate, he was expected to do so. It was the week-night service night, and, besides that, it was the day for holding the annual Leaders' meeting— always an important event at Scowcroft. As has been explained in a previous chapter, official affairs were conducted on somewhat original principles in this village. The "Grave and reverend seigniours" settled everything in their informal councils, either at Miles's house, or when lingering behind in the vestry. The supers were not supposed to know this, of course, but they must have been guileless men indeed if the very perfunctory and expeditious manner in which business was got through did not awaken their suspicions. By the time, however, that the good men had found out how they were manipulated they had also generally conceived considerable respect for and confidence in those who thus hoodwinked them, and were content to let well alone. But there was always an element of uncertainty about the first official meeting held by a new chief, and the arrangements for his regulation had to be made with special care. It is necessary to explain also that there was a very rigidly preserved official ring at Scowcroft, and the chief positions of honour rotated upon a well-understood and jealously preserved plan, from which no departure could be made. On the occasion of which we are speaking the outgoing officials were Miles and Abram Briggs, and it had been arranged according to precedent that Jimmy the Scutcher and Noah were to succeed them, and it was Miles's duty to get the absolute necessity of these appointments, and no other, fixed in the minister's mind during the time that they were drinking tea together. Miles, therefore, got himself washed and dressed in his meeting coat, and sat down before the fire to await the arrival of his spiritual superior, whilst Dinah made ready a quite wonderful tea. Things that had not seen the light of day for months were brought out of the cupboard, for only the very best that they had was to be given to the minister, even though he was, as far as they could see, a somewhat unsatisfactory character.

But the minister did not come; the tea hour arrived, but still no super. Miles was indignant; it was just like him! He had never expected anything else. He was no more fit to manage a circuit than he was fit to fly. Super or no super he would have his tea. Half an hour passed, Miles filling up the time with long and scathing denunciations of the new preacher and all his ways. Then he insisted on having his tea, "Parson a or noa parson," and before he had concluded that very unsatisfying meal the rest of the church officers began to arrive, for it was part of the "Plan of campaign" that these should drop in before service time, in order to reinforce their spokesman, if haply any misguided super should prove untractable.

Each man as he arrived raised his eyebrows in surprise when he discovered that the expected cleric had not arrived, but they all found Miles so exceedingly touchy that they settled down in their places and said little or nothing.

"He's happen not sa weel," said Quiet William at last in musing tones, and looking straight before him at nothing in particular.

"He will be when he's getten' th' length o' my tungue, Aw con tell thi'!" And Miles turned and glared at the speaker as if he were to blame for the missing man's absence.

"Huish!" cried Dinah, suddenly; and almost before she could stop her irate spouse the minister stood on the door-mat. He was a tall, rather stately-looking man, with a thin, intellectual-looking face and pensive expression.

## THE SUPERINTENDENT. 263

As he stood looking round on the company he sighed a little, raised his eyes, which had a wearied and sorrowful look in them, and then said, with a slight bow, "I am afraid I've kept you waiting, Mrs. Grims——"

But just at this point Miles rose hastily to his feet, and, avoiding the minister's eye, he said, roughly, "It's toime furt goo to th' chapel, mestur."

The minister, who seemed somewhat preoccupied, lifted his eyes again at these brusque words, and was silently leading the way into the open air, when Quiet William sidled up to him, and, after glancing somewhat anxiously at his face, said softly as they walked along, "Hay yo did cumfurt me wi' that last sarmon o' yores, mestur."

A ray of light seemed suddenly to light up the minister's face, and he slipped his arm into William's, and murmured softly, "Thank you, brother, thank you."

Arrived at the vestry, the discontented officials seated themselves on the benches around the sides of the walls, but further away from the preacher than usual. Upon observing which, William placed his big body right under the minister's nose, and throughout the service kept up a most appreciative and stimulating succession of nods, smiles and low ejaculations, in significant contrast to the stony and quite unusual silence of the others. The discourse was briefer than usual—"A pup off an owd Sunday sarmon," as Miles declared afterwards. Then the congregation dispersed and the official meeting commenced. At the super's suggestion, William moved a comprehensive vote of thanks to the retiring stewards, and after an awkward pause it was seconded and carried very perfunctorily.

"And now, gentlemen, some of you have borne the burden and the heat of the day a very long time, and there are a number of very interesting young people in the church who are doing nothing, suppose we introduce a little new blood into the meeting." William shot an apprehensive look at the chairman, Miles gave vent to an angry snort, Jimmy the scutcher's expressive eye began to bulge out ominously, and the rest holding their heads back against the white-washed wall shot sidelong telegraphic glances at each other. The super was going far beyond Miles's very worst predictions. "There's Brother Entwistle and Brother Greaves and our young friend Barlow," went on the minister, as nobody spoke. Miles and Jacky uttered exclamations of amazement, the others tilted back their heads against the whitewash at still acuter angles and smiled at the ceiling, whilst even William was not able to keep a look of pained surprise out of his face, for the young fellow last named was a bumptious, long-tongued, aggressive fellow, who was secretary of the improvement society, and the willing tool of the mischief-making new bookkeeper.

The minister was not very observant evidently, for after waiting a moment or two for someone to speak he went on, "Suppose I nominate, then, our excellent Poor-stewards to be the new Society stewards; those who agree please to show in the usual way."

This appointment was, of course, in harmony with the decisions already arrived at, and so every one present voted at once.

"And now, which of these young men will you have? They are all good fellows—but you know them better than I do; somebody please make a selection." There was a long and awkward pause, and at last the chairman said, "Come, let us get on? What do you think, Brother Grimshaw?"

"Me! Nay, no me! Aw no nowt! Oh, neaw "—and Miles laughed, a bitterly sarcastic laugh.

The minister began to suspect that there was something wrong, but as nobody spoke he proceeded, "Well, then, I will nominate Brother Entwistle and Brother Barlow to be our Poor-stewards"—and then he paused again. Nobody replied, and so, after hesitating and looking round, he said, "Those who approve, please vote." Not a hand went up; even William, though looking very uncomfortable, kept his hands clasped on his knee before him. The chairman looked astonished. He was accustomed to have to deal with all sorts of people in all sorts of meetings, but this was a new experience. "You don't vote, gentlemen! What is the matter?"

Nobody replied, and Quiet William was just about to relieve the tension by making a conciliatory remark when he heard a peculiar but well-known cough behind him, and glancing apprehensively around, he observed Jimmy just in the act of rising to speak. William winced and glanced pityingly at the man in the chair.

"Mestur shuper," began Jimmy, in his most dry and delusive drawl, "haa lung an yo bin i' this circuit?"

"Oh, never mind that," replied the minister. "Let us get on with the business."

"Abaat five munth, isn't it?"

"Never mind, never mind! Speak to the point, please."

"Dun yo know haa lung wee'n bin here?"

"Well, well, sir, never mind! Let us proceed."

"Ivery mon i' this place ta-neet wur born i' Scowcrof."

The super fell back in his chair with a little gesture of despair, and Quiet William sighed heavily.

"An' wee'st be here when yo're gone."

William was about to interrupt, but the

minister restrained him with another little wave of the hand, and Jimmy growing, if possible, more deliberate every word, proceeded: "If Aw wur yo, mester shuper, Aw'd let weel alooan, an' stick to th' owd uns."

Thereupon Jimmy slowly resumed his seat, and throwing back his head he joined the others in an earnest contemplation of the ceiling.

There was that in Jimmy's tone which indicated that he was face to face with quiet and yet obstinate resistance, and so the "super" decided that he must have more light before he took further action; he somewhat hastily, therefore, adjourned the meeting until he could make up his mind what was the right thing to do.

When he had gone Miles, standing in the midst of his friends and fellow-conspirators, projected his great broad chin, and shaking his fist emphatically, said, "Yond chap 'ull ha ta shunt at th' yer end, moind that naa!"

And William astonished everybody by replying "Aye! He's ta gooid fur uz—pooer felley."

## II.

For some days the obstructive Scowcroft officials were in some doubt as to how the super would act in the matter, and spent their time speculating on the next move, and encouraging each other to resist any encroachment upon what they regarded as their rights. William seemed like deserting them, and shook his head and sighed whenever anything stronger than usual was said. But he never could be relied upon when it came to crises like these, and the most that could be expected of him was that he would do nothing to interfere with their chances of success.

A fortnight passed away, and the service night came round again. This time it was the third or junior minister who was appointed, and the stewards had received a note from the super stating that "his excellent colleague" would hold the adjourned meeting and finish the business left over. This was another offence; the annual meeting could only be held by the super himself, and this was really only part of the former meeting. Besides, the young minister was very popular in Scowcroft, and nobody wished to seem to be opposing him. The super was "duffing," he dar'nt come and fight the matter out himself. Besides, Jimmy the Scutcher had serious doubts as to whether it was legal for an unordained minister to hold the meeting, and he spent what little time he had before the service in searching through "Grindrod's Compendium" in search of the law on the subject. "Will the leaders kindly stay behind a few minutes at the close of the meeting?" said the preacher just before he pronounced the benediction. As the worshippers rose to their feet, however, Jimmy glanced round upon his colleagues and jerked his head doorwards; and they, obeying his signal, sidled out of the room, leaving the young cleric with no supporters except Quiet William and two leaders who were nobodies. A quarter of an hour later news was brought to the house that the meeting had been duly held, and that "th' yung mon" had announced to those who met him that he was instructed by his super to nominate two of the old officials, which he then proceeded to do and immediately closed the meeting.

Yes, the super had given in, and they had won the day. They ought, therefore, to have been satisfied, but they were not. Now they pretended to despise the super for his cowardice; he had "noa spunk in him." He "hedn't th' pluck of a maase," and his attempt to shelter himself behind his young and popular colleague, and draw them into a quarrel with that delightful young man, was denounced in unmeasured terms.

The next Sunday evening the super closed the service without holding a prayer-meeting—an unheard of thing at Scowcroft; and, as if that were not enough, he excused himself from going to supper at the appointed place, which happened to be Jimmy's, and then walked off to take his coffee at the new bookkeeper's. Even Quiet William seemed disappointed at this, and allowed his friends to rail at the offender all the evening without a single word of protest. The next time the super was appointed at Scowcroft on the week-night he sent a supply.

"Wots thaa want?" demanded Miles in his fiercest tones, as the young man entered the vestry.

"The super has been called away to Manchester to attend an important committee," was the reply. Not another word was spoken to the stranger until the service was over, and it seemed as if he were about to get away without further trouble; but just as he was leaving the vestry door Jimmy sauntered up, and eyeing him over very deliberately said, "It's th' fost toime as that tha's bin here, isn't it?"

"Yes, I only knew a few hours ago and was not very well prepared," said the stranger, apologetically.

"Oh! tha wornt, wornt thaa," drawled the terrible critic, whose fame had long been known to the preacher. "Well, tha con tell th' super az he can goa ta Manchester as oft as he's a moind if he'll send thee," and with a sniff that was peculiar to him after he had said anything intended to be final he turned away and left the relieved substitute to make his way home.

The next time the super came to Scowcroft he discoursed on the character of Judas Iscariot, and in the course of his opening remarks described him as an interesting psychological study. Jimmy, whose face up to this moment had worn a look of ostentatious endurance, at once began to show interest, and when, a moment later, the preacher alluded to one of the traitor's "idiosyncrasies" his eloquent eye began to stand out ominously; but when, just as he was concluding, he added a remark which he called a "corollary" Jimmy shut up his open Bible with a vicious bang and turned his head towards the gallery door in a manner which even a dull man could have understood at once. Next Saturday night Jimmy came home with a huge dictionary, which was tied up in a big red bundle handkerchief, and which he had purchased at a second-hand book-stall in the Wallbury Market, and the following Sunday the faded tome was added to his already formidable-looking collection in the pew.

But Jimmy's greatest objection to the new super's preaching was on account of its excessive deliberateness; the Scowcroft standard of pulpit eloquence demanded energy and emphasis and gave the palm to voluble perorations, whilst the super was quiet and slow. "Caw that preichin'," cried Jimmy, sitting in his usual chair at Miles's after the unhappy Judas sermon, "Aw caw it ackering an' hawmpling (hesitating and limping). Flowin' language," he went on scornfully, in answer to a criticism of the super which had been imported from Wallbury, " it niver flows at aw, it comes aat on him a drop at a toime loike alicar (vinegar) aat ov a tripe-staw bottle," and this brilliant simile was so much to the taste of those who heard it that the poor parson was often afterwards denominated " Owd Alicar bottle."

About this time, also, Miles and Jacky discovered, or thought they discovered, signs of discontent with the new super in one or two of the villages they visited on preaching excursions. These complaints they listened to very eagerly, and then they retailed a long list of the grievances, which Scowcroft had against the same unlucky individual. When they reached their general meeting-place at Miles's house they, of course, gave full and particular, not to exaggerated, accounts of what they had heard, thus strengthening, both in their own minds and in the minds of those who listened to them, resentful feelings against the offending minister.

Long before the March quarterly meeting—at which the annual invitation is given to ministers to continue in the circuit—came, our friends had resolved that they would take the very extreme step of not voting for the super, and even, if necessary, voting against him. Quiet William did his utmost to prevent them, and might even have succeeded, but, unfortunately for his good intentions, just on the eve of the great event, the super committed another and even less excusable transgression. He complained from the pulpit that Scowcroft did not contribute its proper share to the Worn-Out Preachers' Fund, and in the vestry after the service he hinted pretty plainly that, in his judgment, the blame lay with the "leaders." That settled it! There must be no " shafflin' wark naa." William was abused without measure or mercy after the preacher had gone, and when the day of the Quarterly Meeting came Jimmy actually got off work for half-a-day in order to attend that fateful gathering.

As the four leaders of rebellion were passing up Lark Lane they were somewhat disconcerted to find William standing at his cottage door and evidently waiting for them. He also had got off work, and the others felt that they could have done very well without him, for he was so peace-loving that he was certain to put a "Scotch" in their wheel somehow; and then he was so very sly when he was "up ta owt" that his presence was nothing short of suspicious. When they reached the school-room door at Wallbury, however, William said he had "a bit of a arrand," and left them; and the super, going home, disturbed and sad, a few hours later, found a small parcel lying on the study table, which on opening he discovered contained a half-pound of tobacco, accompanied by a small slip of paper on which was written in a rough scrawling hand, "From a lovin' frend." When the financial statement came to be read, the senior steward paused at the name of Scowcroft and called the attention of the meeting to the fact that the contribution from that place was some fifteen shillings below what was usual, and as there was an awkward silence many eyes were turned to the back bench where our friends were sitting. William ducked his head and groaned apprehensively; and well he might, for a moment later the meeting was startled by the rasping voice of Jimmy the Scutcher crying out, "Bet-ter preichin', bet-ter pay." Scowling faces were turned angrily upon the daring Scutcher, and William was just rising to his feet when the steward very wisely resumed his reading of the accounts. Presently the time for giving the invitations came, and the official upon whom that duty devolved commenced a very sincere and glowing eulogium upon the super. There were shufflings of feet and certain very peculiar gruntings from the place where the Scowcrofters were seated; all smothered instantly, however, by a stentorian "Yer! yer!" from William.

Then several others followed in the same eulogistic vein, including one at least of those upon whom the leaders of rebellion had been depending for support. Then the vote was put to the meeting, and the anger of the Scowcrofters gave way to quick feelings of shame and surprise as they saw every hand in the meeting held up except theirs, William in fact standing to vote, and extending both hands as far as he could stretch them.

"On the contrary" was called, and those close enough to see were greatly edified to behold the four malcontents suddenly drop their heads into their hands, whilst Quiet William stood menancingly over them with an expression on his face which boded ill indeed to any one who might dare to exercise his rights.

The rest of the meeting's proceedings were of little interest to our friends, although they did make a clumsy attempt to redeem themselves by a boisterous demonstration when their favourite third minister's name was submitted. But the meeting received their effort very coldly, and when the gathering broke up the four abashed and humiliated conspirators were the first to depart. After shaking the super's hand in his own mighty paw until that good man winced again, William hurried away after his friends. Nobody would speak to him, and for some distance they did not even address each other. At last, just as they were striking the Scowcroft road, Miles exploded upon his big brother-in-law; the ice having thus been broken, they were soon all talking together, and William was having a very warm time of it indeed. Miles was so excited that he stopped in the road to thunder out his threats, and was so engrossed in this occupation that neither he nor any one else had heard a rattling cart come down the road after them. At this moment the cart stopped, and the rough voice of Reuben Tonge was heard calling out, "Naa, then, ger in if yo wanten."

At another time our friends would have been surprised at so civil an offer coming from their old enemy, but now they were so engrossed in their angry discussion that they did not think of the peculiarity of it, and sulkily climbed into the cart from behind, still continuing their debate. Reuben sat quietly in the front of the vehicle eagerly listening, but giving no sign; and when they reached his house and, curtly thanking him, departed, still absorbed in fretful debate, the sand man stood watching them as they went down the lane, and at last, as they were just disappearing, he pointed after them with his whip, and as his strong upper lip curled he said, "Pablo! see how these Christians love." And Pablo seemed so impressed with this revelation of the weakness of good people that he stood staring down the road in deep meditation, and had to be actually led into his own stable.

## III.

Now the Superintendent had not caught the very disloyal remark that fell from the redoubtable Jimmy at the Quarterly Meeting; neither had he noticed that the Scowcroft contingent did not vote; in fact, he did not feel that he ought to observe how anybody voted. And the applause that followed the carrying of the resolution was so unanimous and hearty that he could not doubt that his ministry was acceptable to the great majority, and that was all he felt he could fairly expect. Still, he noticed that there was something unusual in the affair, and, being a highly sensitive man, he was somewhat troubled, and tried to get some information from his colleagues. But these good men only laughed; it was some characteristic eccentricity on the part of the Scowcrofters, and that was all they would tell him. All the same, the super allowed the matter to trouble him, and went home in a somewhat depressed and anxious frame of mind. At home, however, he had other things to occupy his thoughts, for his only son was sinking fast into the grave under the baneful influence of consumption, and as he was the only one left of all his children the good man was in deepest sorrow about it. The next day the servant announced that a queer, rough-looking man with a sand-cart had called and left two cock chickens and a basket of new-laid eggs. A few days later he came again, and kept Barbara talking quite a long time at the back door whilst he plied her with a number of very pointed and inquisitive questions about "Th' mestur." The super gave orders that if he called again he was to be detained until he could get to the door to speak to him, but when the day but one after the man made his third visit and was asked to wait to speak to the master, he answered very gruffly, and when the minister had been called and appeared at the kitchen-door, it was only to see a stout unkempt man with a dirty yellow pony just disappearing at the other end of the back lane.

Meanwhile Miles and his friends were only recovering somewhat slowly from their discomfiture at the Quarterly Meeting. The fact was they had begun to feel heartily ashamed of the part they had played at that gathering, and were very uneasy about the super's next visit. Latterly they had fallen to blaming each other for what had taken place, and it was all that Quiet William could do to keep the peace amongst them.

On the morning of the super's next appointment at the village William, contrary to custom, went a little way to meet the preacher.

"Good mornin', mestur shuper. H-a-y, Aw

am fain ta see yo'. Wee'st hev a grand toime this mornin'."

"Thank you, Mister William. I hope so; but everybody——"

"Aye, iverybody! We Aw loiken yo' i' Scowcrof' ther'll be a slappin' congrigation, yo'll see."

"Thank you! Thank you! But I'm afraid —the Quarterly Meeting, you know."

"Quarterly Meetin'! Hay, Aye, it wur a gradely good vooate, wornt it? Aw wur welly skrikin' when Aw seed 'em stick ther hons up."

The minister was touched and yet uneasy, for William was rather overdoing his part.

"Yes, but everybody is not like you, my dear friend; your brother-in-law, for instance——"

"Him! Hay, mester, yo' dunna know aar Miles yet. He allis talks collywest to wot he thinks. Bud he knows when he yers a gradely good sarmon, Aw con tell yo."

By this time they had reached the chapel, and William fussed about the minister in the vestry until his very eagerness to make things pleasant increased the "super's" suspicions. Then Miles came in with a curt "Mornin'," followed immediately by Jimmy, who did not speak at all.

But William proved to be right: there was a quite exceptional congregation that morning, for William had canvassed for it, and the super preached with more than usual vigour, whilst our quiet friend kept up a running fire of ejaculations which manifestly stimulated the man in the pulpit. Whilst the congregation was singing the last hymn Miles and Noah were having an animated discussion in the vestry. There was a half-crown in the collection, and this was so entirely unprecedented a sum to be given at an ordinary service that these two worthies were discussing what must be done. It was a mistake, of course, and Miles was urging Noah to go into the pulpit and ask the minister to announce that the person who had given it in mistake for a penny might correct the error in the vestry. But Noah proved obstinate; he was not accustomed to go into pulpits and Miles was. It got to the last verse of the hymn, and ultimately Miles was constrained to venture on the errand. But just as he opened the door to go into the chapel he caught sight of some one he had not seen before. His jaw dropped, he hesitated and turned round, and as the congregation went to prayer he turned hastily to the vestry, and staring in amazement at his colleague gasped out, "Whey, mon! dust know whoas here?"

"Whoa?"

"He hesna bin i' this chapil fur twenty yer an' mooar."

"Whoa?"

"Owd scratch 'ull be comin' to chapil next."

"Whoar is it, mon? Speik, wilta?"

"Reubin Tonge, an' noabry else."

Noah gave the little tailor a rough push to one side, and darted for the chapel door, but the congregation was dispersing, and so, missing his man, he came back hastily and made for the door of the vestry, where he stood watching for a sight of the visitor. Reuben was dressed in a new suit of black, with a new silk hat, a high collar and broad black stock, and looked what he really was—a substantial man of property. A more striking transformation it would be difficult to conceive, and the astonishment and curiosity of the chapel people was so great that the super and his transgressions were for the moment forgotten. And at night the minister had Reuben in his congregation again, and Miles and Noah found another half-crown in the collecting-box.

But Reuben did not come on the following Sunday, nor on the Sunday after that; and it was only on the next visit of the super that he reappeared at the chapel. What did it all mean? The only conclusion that they could reach was that it was another instance of that inveterate contrariness for which Reuben had been so long distinguished. Everything that the authorities at the chapel liked he disliked, and everything that they condemned he took up and defended. This had been his habit now for many years, and the present was only a somewhat more remarkable instance of his strange perversity.

The spring was somewhat late, the weather had indeed been genial, but it suddenly harked back and the temperature was that of mid-winter again. A Sunday or two after the strange appearance of the sandman at the chapel, Miles Grimshaw had been appointed at the most distant place on the plan and had to drive in an open conveyance. The evening turned out rough and wet and bitterly cold, and Miles was conscious as he rode behind the second minister and another "local" that he was catching cold. Next day he felt better than he expected, but towards evening he began to be unaccountably tired and listless. By bedtime he was quite feverish, and though he threatened all sorts of pains and penalties to any one who suggested the idea of a doctor, Quiet William went off to fetch one, and, returning about ten at night, suddenly ushered him into Miles's bedroom. The doctor said that Miles was in a very serious condition, and predicted that it would require every effort they could put forth to save him from rheumatic fever. Miles was indignant. The doctor was a "numyed," a "blethering quack," and several other equally objectionable things besides, and William and poor Dinah were "mopesing molly-coddles," and as for staying in bed all the doctors and all the wives in creation should not keep him in bed longer than next morning.

But next morning Miles never named getting up, he had something else to think about. He had passed a woeful night and was, if possible, crosser than ever. During the forenoon he seemed to improve a little, and for some time lay very quiet in his bed. Dinah, who had been up all night and had travelled up and down stairs numberless times, was still standing anxiously at his bedside, when a knock came at the back door.

Dinah hurried downstairs once more and opened the door very cautiously, for it was blowing a hurricane outside, and fine sleety snow was whirling about in thick clouds. It was the super. He was covered with the small snowflakes and looked cold and very thin.

"Hay, mestur! Yo'n neer come aat a mornin' loike this! Wotiver's browt yo' here o' thisunce?"

"I heard that Brother Grimshaw had taken cold on Sunday, and was very ill; how is he?"

"An' han' yo' come fro' Wallbury ta see aar Miles a day loike this?"

"Certainly! How is he? Can I see him?"

"He's up sturs. Yo con goo an see him yorsel'!" and Dinah, who was bursting into tears and scarcely knew what she either said or did, surprised the minister by hurrying off into the pantry to conceal her emotion, leaving him to find his way upstairs by himself.

The staircase was opposite the door, and Miles had heard every word that had been said. When the minister reached the little bedroom he found the tailor sitting up in his bed, and evidently trying to control his face.

"Well, Brother Grimshaw, I'm sorry to find you so unwell, but you were serving a good——"

But Miles just reached out his hand, and, taking the minister's in his, he shook it passionately, and cried through rising tears, "God bless yo," and then, suddenly releasing his grasp he turned away and buried his head in the bed clothes and could not be induced to speak a word. The super stayed some time, and Dinah was scandalised at her husband's behaviour; but it made no difference, Miles would not uncover his face; only as he was going down the stairs the minister heard a hoarse, quavering voice, broken as if by a sob, crying after him "God bless yo," and he went away with the feeling that the Scowcrofters were stranger than ever, and more difficult to understand, and that he never should get to know them.

Dinah was loud in praises of the super when he had gone, but Miles would not say a word, and even when, two days later, by which time he had thrown off the danger and was sitting up in bed, his wife began enlarging upon the good man's thoughtful and self-sacrificing visit, Miles did not join in.

In a few days the tailor was convalescent, and received permission to come down stairs, and then his wife informed him that Reuben Tonge had called twice to inquire after his condition. Miles was more surprised than ever. What could be coming over the fellow? When his cronies came in that night he mentioned the matter to them, but nobody could give even a likely guess as to what had produced this great change in their old enemy.

All day the following Sunday Miles stayed indoors, but at night there was a full attendance of his associates round the fire.

Jacky o' th' Gap ventured a disparaging remark about the super, but nobody took it up. Then Jimmy the Scutcher commenced in a similar vein, and was just turning to appeal to Miles when the door opened and in stepped, of all persons in the world, Reuben Tonge. Two or three rose from their seats in pure amazement, but nobody offered the newcomer a chair. Reuben looked coolly round, and then remarked to the master of the house, "Thar't comin' tew, Aw see."

"Aye," answered Miles, shortly, and there was an awkward pause.

Then, as the sandman seemed to be inclined to stay, Dinah came forward and asked him to sit down.

Reuben sank carelessly into a chair, drew out a short wooden pipe, and leisurely charged it, everybody present watching the operation with painful interest.

Then the visitor leaned back laxily in his chair, and contemplated the joists above his head, and, finally, without changing his position, he remarked, "Awve fun' a Christian at last as *is* a Christian."

As this was an implied reflection on all present several of the faces hardened somewhat, but nobody answered.

"Aye, an' he's a parson, tew."

The stillness deepened.

"An' a Methody parson, tew."

There was still no response, but the eyes of the company were all turned upon the speaker with quickened interest.

"He wur born amung th' quality, an' they turnt their backs on him 'cause he wur religious." Reuben paused for some response, but as none came he proceeded. "An' he gan up a thaasand a yer ta be a Methody parson."

Quiet William gave an exclamation of admiration, but nobody else showed any sign.

"An' he went a bein' a meesionaary amung the blacks. It wur a whot place, wheer white folk couldn't live, bud he kept on stoppin'."

"Bless him," muttered William, under his breath.

"An' his woife deed, bud he wouldna' leev his wark."

"That's summat loike," assented Miles, with growing interest in the story.

"An' his two little wenches deed, bud he wouldna' leeav."

The expressive eye of Jimmy began to roll about as if he were getting excited over something, as, indeed, he was.

"An' then he wur took bad hissel', and hed ta be browt whoam."

"God bless him!" shouted William, unable any longer to restrain himself.

"Bud as sewn az he get bet-ter he were fur off ageean, bud th' doctors said az if he did it ud kill him."

Every pipe in the company was sulkily smouldering because its owner had forgotten it, and was waiting breathlessly for the speaker's next word.

"Bud he went."

The interest was now painful, and even the phlegmatic Jimmy gasped, "Goa on, mon."

"He said he wanted ta translate Scriptur' into th' langu'ge o' th' country." He stopped five yer, an' they buried his owdest lad woll he were away."

"Bless him! Bless him!" broke in Dinah, "Hay, Awd loike fur't d see that felley."

Reuben glanced at the sobbing woman with a very peculiar look, and then went on. "An' when he'd finished his translating he wur welly deead. An' they browt him whoam ageean."

"An' he wur tew yer afoor he were fit fur owt."

"He met weel; he ought ta niver a dun nowt no moor—he owt t'hed a pension fro' Parliament," shouted the glowing, full-hearted Miles.

"They sent him tew a hard circuit."

"The lump-yeds, it's a shawm! It's nowt else!" shouted Abram Briggs.

And now it seemed as if Reuben had finished, for he made no attempt to proceed.

"Well! Goa on wi' thi," cried Jimmy, eagerly.

"Nay, Aw've no mooar ta say."

Then, forgetting that they were scarcely on friendly terms with the man who had told them this wonderful story, they began to quiz him with all sorts of questions about the hero they had been hearing about. Was he alive? Could they by any means ever get to see and hear him? Miles announced his purpose of going to Manchester, or even further if he could only see such a man.

"Grandest felley Aw iver yerd abaat," cried Jimmy.

## THE SUPERINTENDENT. 289

"We ne'er getten sich felloys as that at aar meesionary meetings," said Jacky, who generally was the most voluble of the critics, but who in the presence of Reuben had special reasons for silence.

"Dust think we cud get him fur aar sarmons?" inquired Miles, looking eagerly at Reuben, who was rising to depart.

"Aw darr say yo met if yo tried, but Aw yer yo dunna think mitch abaat him in Scowcrof."

"Uz? Dun we know him? Whoar is he?"

Reuben put his chair away carefully against the wall, and then standing carelessly on the mat, he replied: "Aye, Aw think some on yo knows him, his name's Lingard," and whilst shouts of amazement came from the company, Reuben, with a smirk of delight at the consternation he had caused, stepped to the door and was gone. Lingard was the name of the unpopular super.

\*　\*　\*　\*　\*

But the now all interesting minister never came to Scowcroft again, for the unseasonable and unexpected winter weather which had given Miles his bad cold proved fatal to the minister's son, who died in a few days, leaving a broken-hearted and lonely parent, who thus lost his last and only earthly tie. The good man was so broken down by his great calamity that he was compelled to go away, and when a subscription was started to pay the expenses of the holiday, the circuit stewards were surprised at the astonishing contributions that came from Scowcroft, Miles Grimshaw's donation being higher than that of the richest man in the circuit, and only exceeded by that of the eccentric sandman, Reuben Tonge.

# A SUSPICIOUS CASE.

# A SUSPICIOUS CASE.

## I.

It was Saturday afternoon—*the* Saturday afternoon of the year, in fact—at Scowcroft, the one preceding the "sarmons" day. The croft, always lively on Saturdays, now wore an unusually animated appearance, the ordinary travelling hawkers' carts having been reinforced by several strange ones of gay and rakish look. Opposite "Tay Wayter Martha's" was a gorgeous red-and-white-striped nut and brandy-snap stall, and at the other end of the row was a small stall doing apparently a large business in baloons, monkeys-up-the-stick, pea-shooters and rag dolls. In the middle of the croft, nearly opposite the chapel, a man, with thick, raucous voice, was inviting the juvenile population to invest in "A stick an' tew glawses fer a ha'penny,' whilst old Eb. Cribby and his lame daughter Lavinia were selling posies and "sarmon button-holes" out of a very shaky wheel-barrow. The smaller juveniles were gathered in little groups around these alluring "emporiums," and gazing with wide-open eyes and toffee-smeared mouths at the wonderful treasures so seductively offered for sale, whilst the older ones were crouched in doorways, in various stages of *dishabille*, cleaning Sunday boots or polishing the rarely-used best cutlery for the approaching anniversary festivities.

At the chapel Quiet William and several of the teachers were busy putting up the stage or platform, and Tom Crompton, the chapel-keeper, in a frightful condition of nervous excitement and profuse perspiration, was fetching and carrying for the stage builders one minute, and the next minute making excursions and alarums after the children who, having spent their pocket-money, were standing round the chapel gate, long sticks of wall-paper-covered treacle-toffy in their hand, and small and very green-looking apples bulging out of their pockets, every now and then venturing to peep into the porch, and thus coming into collision with some of the not too amiable stage builders.

The only door that was shut in the row was that of Miles Grimshaw's house, inside which the irascible tailor was stitching and shearing at various belated garments which were required for the coming morrow. Every now and again the future wearers of these garments came to the door to see how their coats and trousers were progressing; but as they held the door in their hands, and glanced at the flurried and anxious face of the gentle Dinah, they either retreated without asking the question that was upon their lips, or else they stopped in the middle of their first sentences and beat hasty retreats, followed by rasping sarcasms and most terrible threats from the irate tailor.

At Jimmy the Scutcher's, on the other side of the chapel, preparations for the coming Sabbath were already in an advanced state. Sarah Ann, the eldest daughter, still in her factory clothes, was cleaning the window, pausing every now and again to converse with Letty Hollows, who was standing in the next doorway, and who had her own reasons for being interested in the doings of the Scutcher's household. Inside the house Mrs. Jimmy, a tall, thin, somewhat, worn-looking person, was going about with an absent, preoccupied air, glancing every now and again at the little, drunken-looking clock on the inside wall, and then turning to gaze earnestly across the croft as if expecting some one to come over the canal bridge, as indeed she was; whilst Jimmy himself, washed and dressed, was sitting in his shirt sleeves with a long clay pipe in his mouth and a little dog-eared book in his hand, from which he was hearing Harriet Jane repeat her Sunday's "piece."

Harriet Jane was not getting on very well, her fear of her terrible father seeming to confuse and clog her memory, and Jimmy consequently wore puckers of irritation and impatience on his rugged face.

The "piece" was Longfellow's "Village Blacksmith," and Harriet Jane had reached the fourth verse, though not without hesitation and stumbling. She stood heavily on one leg, the corner of her best pinafore crumpled up in her hand ready to be used upon her frightened eyes.

She had just finished the third verse:

> When the evening sun is low.

Then she drew a long breath, and was about to commence the next verse when her eyes suddenly darkened, she gave a short gasp, and then raised her head and began to gaze helplessly at the joists above her head.

"When the evening sun is lo-o-ow."

"Oh, it's low ageean, is it? Twicest i' wun neet; it's a funny soort ov a sun."

Harriet Jane gave a little hysterical giggle, but hastened to suppress it as her father turned his terrible eye upon her.

"When the evening sun is low," she repeated, helplessly, and gave undoubted signs of approaching tears.

"Harriet Jane," drawled the Scutcher, in slow and biting tones, "Aw'm sorry for th' sun reet enuff, bud Aw conna skrike abaat it. If Aw wur thee Aw'd leeav it wheer it is, a' goa on to th' next——"

But the tortured reciter had a sudden flash

of memory, and plunged off at racehorse speed:

> He goes on Sunday to the church,
> And sits among his b'iys.

But an ominous creak from the critic's chair suddenly stopped her, and as she held her breath apprehensively her father turned to look at the clock, and then, as if addressing that article of domestic furniture as a colleague in judgment, he proceeded: "Naa, this sun's summat loike a felley, a dacent, *religious* soort of a chap; he goes to th' church an' sits amung th' b'iys"— and then suddenly whisking round and glaring fiercely at poor Harriet Jane, he shouted, "Dust know as tha's skipped a voss, thaa lumpyed?"

But just then a stentorian "Whoy!" was heard outside, and Jacky o' th' Gap, addressing a string of objurgations to his twenty-year-old grey mare, came clambering down out of his shaky old gig into the house.

"Gettin' thi piece off, wench?" he cried, as he entered. "Give it maath, lass, plenty o' maath. That's getten ta keep th' family name up, tha knows."

"Aye! hoos getten summat ta keep up, sure*li*," grunted Jimmy, as he emptied a parcel of tobacco into a big jar, and then handed the vessel to Jacky.

"Keep up!" cried Jacky, in his energetic way. "Hoo hez that! Scowcroft 'as allis been th' best place i' th' circuit fur pieces, and the best piece-sayers i' Scowcrof' haz allis cum aat o' this haase, anna they? Hast fergetten yore Caleb? There's nowt i' th' countryside cud touch him!"

And then the thin face of Mrs. Jimmy came out from behind the kitchen-door with something of an uplifted look upon it, and she said, as she offered Jacky a drink of small beer: "Dost remember th' last toime he set up, Jacky? His piece hed thorty-seven vosses in it, an' six loines in a voss?"

"Hi, sure!" cried Jacky, "an' he went through it loike steeam an' niver slipped a wod. There's now't loike him i' Lancashire, that's sartin'."

A soft light came into the worn eyes of the delighted mother, and, putting a hand gently on Jacky's shoulder, she asked, "An' wot wur it as that bump-feeling felley i' Wallbury market said abaat him?" But Jimmy, who had more than his share of the Lancashire man's dislike of open praise, either of himself or his belongings, scowled threateningly at his wife and replied sternly, "Aar Caleb's noa better nur he should be, Aw con tell thi'."

The indignant mother tossed her head a little, and was apparently about to retort somewhat hotly upon her provoking husband, when there was a short cry at the door, and Sarah Ann was seen coming in from her window-cleaning with some mysterious-looking something crouched behind her. A moment later a tall, good-looking young fellow of about twenty-two rose up from behind Sarah Ann's skirts, and with a joyous "Hew dew, all on yer?" sprang into the middle of the room.

But although he had been six months absent in his situation in Manchester, and was the only son and pride of the family, there was no embracing, no kissing. The sisters came very near to him, and looked as though but for country shame they would have liked to take him round the neck. Letty Hollows, following him in at a little distance of time stood shyly in the door-way with a light in her eyes she was trying in vain to conceal. The mother stepped back towards the kitchen-door, having suddenly become as shy as a school-girl, and heaved a great sigh, whilst pride and delight made her sad face quite beautiful for a moment. Jimmy, after a startled glance at the newcomer, turned hastily away, and fixed an apparently absorbed look upon a little oak-framed funeral-card hanging over the fire-place, and everybody looked away from everybody else with shame-faced and almost guilty looks.

There was a moment of embarrassing silence, and then Caleb suddenly remembered the presence of Jacky o' th' Gap, and relieved his own and everybody else's feelings by taking him enthusiastically by the hand, and asking him over and over again how he was. Jacky responded in a characteristically boisterous manner, and the ice having thus been broken, the younger people began to talk and ask questions with a nervous rapidity which was meant to conceal their nearly uncontrollable emotion.

In the midst of it all Letty suddenly remembered herself, and said she must be "gooin'," upon which Caleb, to the delight of all the women folk, uttered a hasty but emphatic protest, rushed at the retreating maiden, caught her cleverly in the doorway and—it could only be attributed to the unwonted excitement of the occasion—actually kissed her as she tried to escape him. Upon this Mrs. Jimmy retired into the kitchen again, to dry her eyes, and murmur a fervent "Thank God!" and the embarrassed but happy Letty accepted for the first time an oft-repeated invitation to stay to her "tay." Meanwhile, Jimmy was still engrossed in his distant study of the funeral card, and but for one spasmodic roll of his nether eye, just when the smack of the kiss was heard, nobody would have thought that he was at all conscious of what was going on around him.

When tea was ready Mrs. Jimmy frustrated a carefully-arranged plan of her daughter's for placing Caleb next to Letty, by dropping into the seat herself, and whilst the rest were busy eating and talking she was nibbling gingerly at a piece of bread and carefully studying her idolised son. And somehow the examination was not quite satisfactory, for her husband, watching her narrowly, caught her sighing once or twice, and even he was disturbed to find a tendency in himself to the same pensive exercise.

Late that night, when the rest had all retired, Jimmy sat moodily smoking by the expired fire, whilst his wife went about doing little odds and ends of work, or rather pretending to do them, but in reality waiting for her husband to commence a conversation on their beloved son.

But the Scutcher seemed a long time in beginning. At last, however, as she was piling some wood on the hob by the fire for use next morning, he leaned back in his chair and sighed sarcastically.

"Aye! feshionable breeches an' lastic-side boots."

Mary winced, drew herself up to her full height, and cried querulously, "Well, he mun dew as uther young felleys does, Aw reacon."

Jimmy blinked his eyes rapidly, poured out a great volume of smoke, blinked again, and then said, " An' a watch in his waistcut pocket, an' a cheean loike a booat rooap."

Mary had reached the kitchen door, but, stung by this second sneer at her favourite, she turned round and retorted, hotly, "He's as good as his faythur, an' a foine seet bet-ter, sa theer," and then she broke down and vanished into the kitchen, trying in vain to choke back her angry tears.

But the remorseless Jimmy was not yet content. He knew that in her heart his wife was as concerned at what they had seen in Caleb as he was himself, and in fact very much more so, and this cruel banter was his only way of discussing the matter with her.

Ten minutes passed before Mary came near him again, and when she did so it was only to demand, in her surliest tones, if he was going to bed that night; but Jimmy had to relieve his mind fully, and so he sat for a minute or two without speaking, and then drawled out, "An' a Shakespeare collar an' a goold-plated ring."

And then Mary, with a candle already in her hand, stepped into the middle of the floor, and, standing defiantly before her husband, cried through a fresh flood of indignant tears, "Aye, an' he'st hev a solid goold cheean, if he wants wun, bless him," and with this final though consciously feeble shot the distracted mother turned to the staircase and was gone.

Jimmy sat for some moments in the darkness, evidently in deep thought, and at last he heaved a long sigh, and groaned out, "It's *aar* fawt, Lord, nor 'is. Dunna punish th' lad fur his payrunt's proide. Dunna! Lord, dunna!"

## II.

Jimmy did not get to sleep until the small hours of the morning, and consequently awoke too late to go to the usual Sunday morning prayer-meeting. The sun was shining in at the bedroom window, and it was evidently going to be an ideal anniversary day. And now Jimmy began to feel that his fears of the preceding night had been a little excessive. Caleb was "nobbut a bit gallous, loike th' rest o' young chaps," and he had been rather foolish to trouble himself so much about the lad's little vanities. He would think no more about the matter. Just then he heard a burst of very un-Sabbathlike laughter, and realising that household discipline demanded his restraining presence downstairs, he made haste to dress himself, and descended the creaking stairs in his stocking feet—for slippers were unmanly luxuries in his eyes. The scene that met him when he arrived on the lower floor not only aroused his fatherly ire, but brought back all his previous night's fears. There on the hearthstone stood young Caleb, dressed in a new suit of clothes of disgracefully fashionable cut. His coat was hung over a chair back, he wore also a fine white cotton shirt, a pair of shining patent leather slippers, whilst cocked on the top of his head, at an irresistibly comical angle, was Sarah Ann's new Anniversary bonnet. Caleb, with the broad ultra-fashionable cuffs of his shirt turned up over his elbows, and a long fork in his hand, was pretending to superintend the cooking of a pound of those wonderful and famous Smithy door sausages, which the better end of the Scowcrofters always brought home as rare dainties on their occasional visits to Manchester. The girls, who were without their frocks, and had their hair in curl papers, were watching their frolicsome brother with eyes that danced with delicious fun, and even the mother was peeping out from behind the kitchen door, her face wreathed with smiles that looked all the sweeter because there was a shadow of pain behind them.

It required all Jimmy's boasted self-control to save him from a most compromising grin, but when with a supreme effort he had escaped that disgrace he assumed a look of awful sternness, glared round severely on the confused merrymakers, and then, after a terrible pause, remarked in biting tones: "Oh, Aw'm a whoam, Aw see! Aw thowt Aw wur sleepin' o'er a bar-parlour."

"Mornin', fayther!" cried Caleb, flourishing the fork, whilst Sarah Ann shyly snatched her precious new bonnet from his head. "Cum on wi' yo! Theas sausage is dun tew a toucher. Muther, dun yo know wot ther made on?"

"Naa, Caleb!" cried both the girls at once,

in deprecatory anticipation of one of their brother's old jokes.

"They makken 'em aat o' owd shoon an' hymn bewk backs daan Shudehill way, bud theas is made aat o' ceaw-heel-pie an' hair-ile. They're stunners."

The girls uttered cries of nausea, and Caleb, with a delighted chuckle, whisked the hissing sausages upon the table and called upon all the rest to "reich tew."

Jimmy drew up to the table with a face of gathering gloom, and interrupted his son in the telling of a funny story to ask a blessing.

Caleb commenced his duties as carver by selecting the brownest and most tempting sausage for his mother, who took her plate with a hand that suddenly began to shake and eyes that had a quick light in them. And then the light all at once became tears, and unable longer to control feelings that had been gathering ever since her beloved son came home, she burst out, "Bless thi, lad, Aw'm fain ta see thee," and dropped her head over her plate and blushed like a maiden; for the stern eye of her husband was upon her, and she realised that she had broken every canon of Lancashire reticence and unpardonably committed herself.

But the awkward pause that followed was not to Caleb's mind at all; he was intent upon enjoying himself and on making everybody else enjoy themselves as far as possible; and so he felt resentful at his father's sternness, and inwardly resolved to give him something to be sulky about as soon as possible.

"Caleb, when is it *yore* sarmons?" asked Sarah Ann, as she handed her brother a piece of new oven-bottom cake.

"Aar sarmons? Wot dust meean? Theas is aar sarmons."

"Ger aat wi' thi! Aw meean yore sermons i' Manchester. Thaa goos to th' schoo, dustna?"

And Caleb, glancing hastily at his mother out of one·eye, noticed that she was waiting his reply with an interest that was painful, and so, feeling still a little resentful, he glanced out of his other eye at his father, and as that worthy was looking very ostentatiously out of the window to conceal the fact that he was awaiting as eagerly as his wife for the answer, Caleb gave way to inward anger, and with a toss of his head answered, "Schoos! Aye, there's plenty o' schoos i' Manchester."

"Bud which does *thau* goo tew?" asked Sarah Ann, after a somewhat painful pause.

"Me! Me goo to th' schoo? Not me," and Caleb laughed a boisterous but not very successful laugh.

Then there was another long and embarassing pause, broken only by a heavy sigh from the mother.

"Then wheer dust put thi toime in ov a

neet?" asked Sarah Ann, and everybody looked away from everybody else as if afraid to hear what was coming. Caleb stole a long, uneasy glance at his mother, but again his resentment at their unjustifiable suspicions overcame all other feelings, and he answered defiantly, "Oh, th' Albert Gardins an' the Strawberry Gardins an' th' the*a*yter, and sich loike."

There was a sudden choking sob; mother fell back in her chair, and throwing her apron over her face, uttered a piteous wail, and Sarah Ann, rising from her chair hastily, cried almost in tears, "Dunna believe him, muther, he's lyin'. Haa could ta for shawm, Caleb."

Caleb rose from his chair and walked sulkily to the door, where he stood looking across the croft with resentment and penitence struggling together upon his face. Poor mother hastened into the scullery, where she could be heard trying to smother her sobs, and the girls sat looking down on the now despised dainty on their plates, and biting their lips to keep their tears back. As for Jimmy, he had never moved; he still sat looking through the window, but he had become sternly pale, his great left eye seeming to protrude and dominate his whole face, whilst the morsel of sausage he had in his mouth might have been poison, judging by the difficulty he had of getting rid of it. Then he turned away from the table, leaving a newly-filled cup of coffee untouched, and groping in the corner of the fire-place for his pipe, he stuck it unfilled into his mouth, and with an effort to appear unconcerned sat staring moodily at the fire.

For seven or eight minutes Caleb stood in the doorway looking fixedly before him, and only the rapid motion of his left leg gave any indication of the state of his feelings. Once or twice he turned slowly round and glanced into the house, his gaze resting each time upon the kitchen door. Then he commenced to whistle a hymn tune in low, wavering tones, turning round as he did so, and gliding towards a large picture-frame containing funeral-cards, which he began to study intently. Then he moved across the floor to the other side of the wall, where was a similar picture, and became absorbed in that. Then he transferred his attention to a small rosewood frame hanging on the inner wall near the pantry door, and containing a print of Mr. Wesley and Dr. Coke. This occupied his thoughts, at least in appearance, for quite a long time, but suddenly he glanced hastily round the room again, made a rush at the pantry door, and Jimmy, sitting still and morose by the fire, heard a scuffle and a series of short cries in the pantry, followed by a rousing kiss, and then there was a moment's silence again, and Caleb emerged from the pantry with his hair very much ruffled, and trying to hide a look of sheepish bashfulness behind an appearance of sudden and delighted recollection.

"By gum, wenches, Awd welly furgetten! Well, that *is* a mank, ony way. It must a bin mi fayther as put it aat o' mi yed wi' talkin' sa mitch."

And whilst the girls laughed rather constrainedly at this sally on their father's taciturnity, Caleb scrambled noisily upstairs and presently returned with a small parcel.

"Naa, then! Come on wi' yo! Who speiks fost?" he cried in nervous excitement, and commenced to fussily unwrap the parcel.

"Me!" cried Harriet Jane, eagerly, and Caleb thrust into her hand a packet which, when she had opened, proved to contain a quantity of tobacco.

"Naa, then, lumpyed!" he cried, delightedly, "tha'rt no wantin' thi fayther's 'bacca, sure*li*," and as his sister pettishly jerked the packet across the table towards her father's elbow, Caleb, rejoicing to think that he had so easily got over the ordeal of presentation to his sphinx-like parent, chuckled gleefully and dived his hand once more into the parcel. A pair of gloves for Sarah Ann was the next thing produced, with a serious exhortation not to let Sammy Dick "sile 'em bi squeezin' 'em whol th' collection wur bein' made."

Then came a small box containing a brooch

for Harriet Jane, who, whilst she received it, could not help noticing that a similar one was being surreptitiously slipped into her brother's pocket, and she was not therefore surprised later in the day to see Letty Hollows with a resplendent ornament pinned upon her white dress.

While this had been going on mother had stolen quietly out of the pantry and crept to Caleb's elbow, and was looking shyly down upon his parcel.

"Hey, muther!" he cried, catching sight of her, and hastily covering up something in the parcel with his hands. "Aw'd clean furgetten yo! Well! wot mun wi dew? This is a bonny mank." And then, after looking at her for a moment in well-dissembled astonishment, he went on: "Ne'er moind; Aw'll bring yo wun o' them new fancy Chignons as is comin' up. Aw will, fur shure."

But the mother, with a quiet, confident smile, gently pushed away her son's hands from what they were covering, and drew out of the parcel a beautiful new hymn-book. She stood for a moment looking down at her present, then raised her eyes for a moment to her son's face; then lifting the book, tapped Caleb lightly on the head with it and turned away hastily into the pantry again, where, hugging the gift to her breast, she reminded herself that it was only a very carelessly-dropped word that she had uttered about wanting a new hymn-book, and it was months since she had done so, and yet here it was. And putting her precious present into the window-bottom and plunging her hands into the wash-basin again, she murmured, "A lad as thinks ov his muther loike that's no goin' t' be a wastril, bless him."

---

## III.

AND whilst the proceedings narrated in the last chapter were going on around him Jimmy was sitting still and stony before the fire. He had charged his pipe and lighted it at least twice, but it had now been out for some time, and he appeared entirely unconscious of the fact, and every now and again took a long, pensive pull at it. He was greatly disturbed. Up to some two years ago Caleb had worked in the mill as a weaver. But the lad, greatly to his father's delight, had again and again declared that he wasn't going to "ston behint a loom aw his days," and though as in duty bound Jimmy had sternly reproved the lad's "proide," he had been greatly pleased at the declaration, and raised no objection beyond indulging in a characteristic jibe when Caleb announced his determination of going to the Wallbury night-school twice a week. It was a long way to go for learning, and Jimmy shrewdly reasoned with himself that if this was merely a passing whim his son would soon weary of it, and if he did stick to it that would be the clearest possible evidence that he ought to be encouraged. Caleb had stuck to it, thus falsifying all the prophesies which his father had perversely made to the proud mother, when she tried to ascertain the state of her husband's mind on the subject. At last Caleb won the first prize at the night-school for book-keeping, and was strongly recommended by his teacher to apply for a situation in Manchester as a clerk.

Jimmy, when his son made this announcement to him, treated the matter with great scorn, told him he was "gettin' tew big fur his shoon," and bade him "stick of his weyvin'." But as his father did not formally forbid the attempt, Caleb answered advertisement after advertisement until at last a favourable offer was made him.

Then, to everybody's surprise and perplexity, Caleb's mother suddenly opposed the whole thing. She would lose her son for ever, he would become a "foine gentleman"; he would forget his "owd muther," and "happen lewse his sowl."

Then the Scutcher came out in fine style. His wife's opposition had arisen far more than she was aware of herself from Jimmy's own remarks at odd moments when he was in a scoffing vein, for she had secretly great faith in his judgment. But now Jimmy rose to the occasion; with glorious inconsistency he poured lofty scorn on his wife's fears, and indignantly denied having ever expressed such views as she now reminded him of. She was a "meythering owd maddlin," and wanted to make her son a "slavvering molly-coddle." "He had ne'er expected nowt else"; the lad "hed a bit a spunk in him loike his fayther." If only he (Jimmy) had had half Caleb's chances he would have been a manager before now.

And so, of course, Caleb had his way, and went to the great city and became a clerk. And this was his third visit home in about eighteen months. On the two previous occasions his mother had been so surprised and delighted with her son's handsome, gentlemanly appearance, and so uplifted by the remarks of her female friends, that she had forgotten all her fears, and was only too willing to believe that in this case, at any rate, she had justified her husband's oft-repeated declaration that "Aw thy meyse (mice) is tigers."

And just in proportion as "mother" got over her fears and indulged her maternal pride, Jimmy, with natural contrariness, lapsed again into his old scoffing and unbelieving manner. Whenever Caleb's excellences were described in his presence he curled his expressive upper lip, and hummed and haa'd and sniffed in a most provoking manner, and listened to extracts from his son's letters with ironical, unbelieving sneers.

Now, however, this elaborate pretence of scepticism suddenly became painfully real. He had all an old-fashioned villager's mistrust of town folk and town ways. He had more than his share of Lancashire prejudice against show and bounce, and his son's manner and appearance seemed to him to justify his worst fears.

Just at this moment Harriet Jane slided towards him the little packet of fancy tobacco, and Jimmy, though he neither moved nor spoke, felt strongly tempted to snatch it up and toss it into the fire. Then lest there should be any mistake as to his appreciation of his son's gift, Jimmy got up to refill his pipe out of his own tobacco-box, only to discover that his pipe was still full. Having risen, he somehow felt it awkward to sit down again, and so still standing, he relighted his pipe and sauntered aimlessly towards the door.

Pausing a moment in the doorway, he presently wandered across the croft to the canal bridge, and stood leaning over the wall, moodily and absently contemplating the water beneath him.

"Grand day fur th' sarmons, Jimmy," cried a thin, squeaky voice behind him. Jimmy recognised the speaker by his tones, and so without moving or even turning his head he answered in his surliest manner, "It's reet enuff."

The new-comer was a tall, thin man of about thirty-five, who was the only Scowcrofter besides Caleb who was employed in Manchester, and who for several years now had carried on a leisurely and intermittent courtship with Jimmy's eldest daughter, Sarah Ann. He was employed in the same warehouse as Caleb, but though he had been there as many years as Caleb had been months, the younger man was already several places before him in rank.

Jimmy seemed more taciturn even than usual, but as his companion had come to talk, and was not inclined to let the opportunity slip, he proceeded, "Aw see yore Caleb's a whoam tew. Hay he's a wik un yore Caleb is."

Jimmy felt a sudden sinking within him, and so turning round and leaning against the bridge wall he demanded, sharply, "Whey! wot does *thaa* know abaat aar Caleb?"

"Oh, nowt! nowt! We dunna tell tales aat o' th' schoo' tha' knows, Jimmy."

Jimmy eyed the speaker steadily for several seconds, and then turning his back upon him with a look of freezing disdain, he coolly resumed his contemplation of the canal.

"Naa, Jimmy, dunna be vexed; ther's plenty wur nur yore Caleb, Aw con tell thi."

But Jimmy maintained an icy silence.

The informer fidgeted for a moment or two, then moved a little further away from his companion, and turning to look over the bridge, murmured as if to himself, "*Aw've* ne'er seen him drunk, nur goin' wi' fly women noather, an' they con say wot theyn a moind."

All at once the Scutcher wheeled round, and with white set face and blazing eyes he lifted his hand and struck out at the traducer of his son. But the coward was too wary, and stepped aside, and Jimmy went sprawling against the other side of the bridge wall.

When the fallen man picked himself up his companion was nowhere to be seen. Jimmy stood looking about him for a minute or so, then fell to contemplating the broken pipe in his hand, and finally, with a groan and something very like a curse, he strode slowly back towards home.

Then he changed his mind, not caring to face his own in that condition, and turned off up Twiggy Lane, and when at length he returned to his own house the young people had gone to join the school procession, and Jimmy found himself alone with a sorrowful-faced wife.

A single shy glance at her husband's face told Mrs. Jimmy all she needed to know. She had no idea, of course, of what had taken place on the bridge, but to her anxious mind what they had seen and heard since Caleb came home was more than sufficient to explain her husband's stern and gloomy looks. Then her heart went out to her son. They couldn't expect him to be the same as if he had stayed at home.—Oh! how she wished he had done.—But he was her only son, and it cut her to the heart to see his father so troubled about him.

"He's noa woss nor uther folks's lads if we knew aw," she murmured at last, with a heavy sigh, but Jimmy did not answer her. "It wur niver my will fur him to goa," she continued, after another long silence. Jimmy jerked himself round in his chair and seemed about to make a hot reply, but he suddenly checked himself and only looked at her with stern protesting look.

Then she went to the window, where she could see the scholars beginning to form in procession, and then turning away with a smothered cry, she came and put her hand gently on her husband's arm and said in low, coaxing, but tremulous tones, "Less tak him away, lad, afoor it's ta late."

Jimmy sprang to his feet as if he had been stung. "Woman," he cried, in fierce anguish, "thaa talks loike a meythering foo; it's ta late naa, Aw tell thi."

The Scutcher and his wife never saw the Sunday-school procession that day, although it passed their door, and when the children came home they found the atmosphere of the house so heavy with a mysterious gloom that their own tongues seemed tied, and dinner was eaten almost in silence. Caleb in particular seemed uncomfortable, and fearing that his parents had been having words about him, he tried to be gentle and conciliatory, and made every possible overture short of actual request for pardon to his silent and surly father.

Jimmy had some doubts as to whether he could go to the service in the state of mind he was in, but eventually he made an effort and insisted on his wife going with him. Both the services passed off satisfactorily; the sermons, although Jimmy found that he could only listen to them by fits and starts, satisfied him, the sum in the hands of Harriet Jane went down in its best manner, and the collection was up. Altogether the services did Jimmy good. He found himself watching with painful interest the conduct of his son, and concluded that either Caleb was a consummate hypocrite or that he was agitating himself about his boy without any just cause. During the interval between the services Jimmy heard Harriet Jane whisper to her mother that "Aar Caleb put a wholl haaf sovrin into th' box," and Jimmy was divided between a fear that so unusual a sum could not have been honestly gained, and joy at the generosity of his son.

When the evening service was over, Jimmy found himself able to join his old friends at

Miles's, and presently got so animated in a discussion on the afternoon's sermon that for the moment he quite forgot his fears. Recollecting himself, however, in good time, he left the tailor's house earlier than usual, and was just settling himself down to a go-to-bed pipe when the door was suddenly burst open, and with a wailing scream Letty Hollows came staggering into the house crying, "They'n tan him! Oh, they'n tan him."

Letty's cry was immediately drowned in another, and Caleb's mother, with a piercing shriek, flung herself upon the weeping girl.

"Wot?" cried Sarah Ann, coming rushing downstairs. "Whoa? Whoa's tan him? Whoa an they tan?"

"Caleb!" cried the unhappy Letty. "They'n tan him. Th' bobies fro' Manchester as tan him, an' ther comin' here."

As she spoke two policemen entered the house from behind her and immediately began to explain. Something had gone wrong at the office, and Caleb was suspected. They had come in a gig, and had met Caleb in the lane courting Letty. They had arrested him at once, and two of them had driven off to Manchester with the prisoner, whilst they (the speakers) had stayed behind to search the house.

## IV.

For some minutes nothing was heard in the house but the sobs and wails of the distracted mother and sweetheart, mingled with incoherent protestations from Caleb's sisters.

"He browt summat wi' him when he coom whoam, didn't he?" said one of the officers at length. "We mun see it."

"Nay yo' winna! He browt nowt, and yoll see nowt," and with streaming eyes and suddenly-defiant looks the wretched mother rose to her feet and stood at the staircase door to prevent the search.

"Bud he towd uz sa hissel," remonstrated the officer gently; "he said he hed a carpet bag."

"He hadna! Aw tell yo' he hadna! Fur shame o' yursels, yo' hard-herted wastrils."

"Well! We mun see at ony rate."

"Nay, yo winna! Yoll no goo up thoose sturs ta-neet. O-o-h, ha' marcy, will you! Lord, do *Thaa* ha' marcy!" and the distracted mother leaned against the staircase door as if her son were behind it, and they were seeking his life, and she was resolved to lose her own to save him.

"Dunna muther! dunna!" said Sarah Ann, soothingly, though her face wore a look of surprise and shame that her mother should thus plunge recklessly into falsehood.

But "mother" still clung to the staircase door, and leaning her tear-stained face against it she sobbed, "Theyn tempted him tew it! Theyn tempted him! he'd ne'er a dun it of hissel'," and then, after a moment or two of passionate sobbing, she went on, "Haa could ta, Caleb! Haa could ta! tha's brokken thi muther's hert."

But at this moment there was the noise of a chair being pushed violently over the sanded floor, and the next instant Jimmy, white to the lips and in a perfect passion of indignation, strode over to his weeping wife, and seizing her violently by the shoulders and pressing her against the door, so that she was compelled to show her anguished face, he shouted, hoarsely, "Woman, art *thaa* aar Caleb's mother?"

"Aw am! Aw am! God help me!" was the wailing reply.

"An' does thaa believe az aar Caleb, *aar* Caleb's a thief an' a liar an' a wastril?" and with face all a-work and expressive eye rolling fearfully about Jimmy stood glaring at the sobbing woman before him. "If Aw thowt tha did," he went on, "if Aw thowt tha did, sithi, Aw'd—A'wd fell thi ta my feet!" and then releasing the now-terrified woman from his grasp he pushed her away from the door, and, flinging it wide open, he turned to the officers, and cried, "Goa up wi' yo'! Seearch wheer yo'n a moind. An' goo tew his lodgin's i' Manchester, an' seearch theer, an' if yo' foind owt, if yo' foind owt ageean him, see yo', yo' con tak' him to th' New Bailey an' hang him—aye, an' his owd fayther wi' him."

And thus did Jimmy and his wife illustrate in their own persons the different effect upon different temperaments of the same great love. In the mother it took the form of anxious solicitude and a Thomas-like apprehensiveness which made belief in misfortune to her beloved fatally easy, and in the father it brushed away all petty prejudices, and laid bare the broad foundations of an attachment and trust which misfortune could only increase.

By this time the neighbours had got to know what was going on, and came hurrying in to offer sympathy and get fuller information. Jimmy treated the women with a merciful indifference, for which they were very grateful; but the men who entered were met by the Scutcher with such stares of challenging inquiry that they lapsed one after the other into discreetest silence, and were fain to wait to discover Jimmy's attitude on the question before they ventured to express any opinion.

This divided the company into two parties—one standing round Jimmy in moody, wondering silence, and the other trying to soothe Mrs. Jimmy's sorrows with loud lamentations of their own.

Then Quiet William came in, and at once set the tongues of the men loose, expressing himself in tones as empathetic as those just used by the Scutcher as to his confidence in Caleb's innocence.

Taking their cue from William, the rest became equally certain and much more demonstrative as to the final issue of the matter. Then they began to cross-question the weeping Letty as to the exact occurrences connected with Caleb's arrest, and as this gave food for further discussion everybody had an opinion and everybody else a reminiscence that bore more or less directly on the case. The debate had been proceeding for some minutes, and Miles Grimshaw was just finishing an emphatic little homily to Mrs. Jimmy, the chief point of which was that it was a trial and would "Aw cum reet, tha'll see," when somebody suddenly missed Jimmy. Search was made for him in vain, and it soon became evident that the distracted father had started off for Manchester. Then William announced that he must be going, but he was so mysteriously hurried in his manner that everybody guessed in a moment that he had gone after Jimmy. It was some twenty odd miles to the great city, but both the men knew every inch of the road, having in earlier days tramped it many a time carrying "cuts" on their heads. William overtook his old friend very soon, but little was said between them, and they jogged along together with heavy hearts through the still summer night.

Never to be forgotten were the hours of that weary night to Jimmy's household. The distracted mother sat rocking herself to and fro and moaning out her unavailing lamentations, and the girls, scarcely less affected, clung to each other and hung on the necks of sympathising neighbours. One by one their friends left them until only Dinah Grimshaw and Quiet William's kindly little wife remained. The morning dawned very early, but brought no relief, and as hour followed hour the sufferers began to expect news, though they could not understand how it was to reach them. Breakfast time came, and Dinah did her best to make the sorrowing women take some refreshment, but with little success. Jacky o' th' Gap had brought his trap down, and offered to drive them all to the city, and though the poor mother was all for going, Miles and Noah, the grocer, advised that nothing should be done until some tidings had been received. Ten o'clock came, and eleven, but still no news. Noon arrived, and Mrs. Jimmy was almost getting beyond control.

Just, however, as the hands were coming home from the mill to dinner a boy on a pony drove up to the croft and asked for the Scutcher's house. A moment later he had

# A SUSPICIOUS CASE.

handed a telegram—the first they had ever received—to Sarah Ann at the door. Before the trembling girl could open it, however, it was snatched out of her hand, and her mother, hugging the flimsy packet to her heart, began to moan and weep afresh.

"Oppen it, muther! oppen it!"

"Aw darna! Aw darna!" moaned the wretched woman.

"Then let me oppen it. Dew, muther!"

"Aw darna! Aw darna!"

"Cum, cum, wench," said Dinah Grimshaw, coaxingly, and, stealing an arm round her friend, she drew the telegram from the trembling fingers and handed it to Sarah Ann.

But the daughter, only a little less excited than her mother, fumbled so with the envelope that Miles, who had heard the news and came running in, snatched it from her, and, tearing it open, glanced hastily at the contents, and then, casting the fateful document into the air, he cried out wildly, "Aw said sa! Aw said sa! an' Awm reet!"

This shout brought in the little crowd that had gathered about the door, and when Miles had thus got a larger congregation he sought for the telegram, carefully smoothed it out, and then, after an impressive pause, read:

All right—a mistake. Coming home.—CALEB.

The present chronicler has no power to

describe the scene that followed, and must leave it to the imagination of his readers. Everybody had been right. Nobody had ever had any doubts as to the innocence of him who was now the hero of the hour. They all knew Caleb and his folks too well to think that he could have done anything wrong.

Mother, however, was only half convinced. It " was only sent to th' 'sizes," and Caleb was "bailed aat." At the least he had lost his shop (situation), and would have to go to " weyving" again, though she confessed afterwards that on the whole she would rather have liked that. But the more dubious " mother " was the more confident the rest became, and she listened with a hungry eagerness to all their reasons for being sure that her fears were groundless.

About tea-time the three absentees returned, and then the mystery was explained. Pilfering from the petty cash had been going on in the Manchester office for some time, and the cashier had been driven almost to his wits' end to discover the culprit. Latterly suspicion had seemed to point to Caleb, and after he had left for home on the previous Saturday discoveries had been made which seemed to confirm the suspicions. The police had been called in, with consequences of which we are aware, and Caleb had been arrested in the manner already described. Then a message had been sent to the junior partner, who was away on his holidays. That gentleman, who was a fiery, impetuous little man, had returned at once, and when, upon arriving at the office on Monday morning, he had been told that Caleb was the culprit and was now in prison, he had flown into a great rage, called the cashier a grinning idiot, and then darting across the room he had seized a sallow-faced clerk by the neck and shaken him until the wretched man had been fain to confess and beg for mercy. Then the irate little man had called for a cab and driven at top speed to the police station, where he had called the chief inspector a lunatic, and then after a few words of explanation had dragged Caleb out of the place, and with a kick behind had ordered him off home for a week and sent him staggering into the arms of Quiet William, who, with the now triumphant Jimmy, was waiting in the passage outside.

When the joy of the reception had somewhat subsided and a bountiful tea had been partaken of, Jimmy lounged out of the house to his place at Miles's fireside, and Caleb got Letty Hollows into a corner and made her blush again and again as he reminded her of the compromising things she had said when "th' bobbies were takkin' me," and Letty really looked so very pretty as she blushed that her lover might have committed himself before company, but that she drew away from him and pretended to want to speak to Sarah Ann very particularly. Meanwhile, Quiet William was sitting and staring at the empty fire-place, with a musing but delighted expression on his big face. Presently he glanced round slyly into the corner occupied by the courters, and then, beckoning Mrs. Jimmy to him, he jerked his thumb over his left shoulder and said in a soft undertone, "Aw thowt az tha said az he didna goo to th' schoo'."

And a shadow came back for a moment into the mother's face as she answered, with a little sigh, "He towd uz sa his-sel'."

And William put out his great hand, and, pulling her nearer to him until he could whisper into her ear, answered huskily, "Whey, woman! he's th' Secretnary."

And as soft, grateful tears rose into the red eyes of the mother, William began to feel very moist under the eyelashes himself, and so, pausing a moment to recover possession of himself, but gazing earnestly all the while down into the swimming eyes before him, he presently cleared his throat, and, bending forward, said, " An' tha towd me az he went to th' thea*y*ter an' th' Strawberry Gardins."

"Well, he does, doesn't he?" And there was a painful eagerness in the eyes that looked so wistfully into William's.

"Whey, wench! he's nee'r bin theer in his loife. He spends his neets teichin' in a neet schoo'."

And then the overwrought mother, lifting her thin arms, cried out, "Bless the Lord! bless the Lord!" And William ducked down his head and buried his face in his hands; and as the young people flocked round their mother, demanding what was the matter, William softly stole away, and a few minutes later was sitting with his cronies at the tailor's house.

Here the first excitement of the conversation on the topic of the hour had subsided somewhat, and there was a little lull as William arrived. When the big man had charged his pipe, however, Jacky o' th' Gap, looking steadily at the smoke that was issuing in thick volumes from William's mouth, heaved a long sigh, and said slowly: "Aye ther's sum foine lads bin turnt aat ov aar schoo'."

And Jimmy gave most welcome and satisfactory signs of having returned to his normal condition by replying, with all his customary contradictoriness, "Aye, an sum wastrils tew."

A long meditative silence followed, but presently Jacky returned to the attack. Taking his pipe out of his mouth, and leaning forward and scowling at Jimmy as he tapped his knee with the stem of his churchwarden, he cried in a tone that challenged and defied contradiction,

"Yore Caleb ull be a pardner yond ofoor he dees."

And Jimmy made the reply which everybody expected from him when, after a somewhat scornful and unbelieving pause, he answered, "Aye, when pigs flies."

# REUBEN CLEANS HIS SLATE.

# REUBEN CLEANS HIS SLATE.

## I.

"WEYSHIN'-UP mugs! Stew mugs! Whaite sand an' *rub*-bin' sto———" and the familiar cry ended in a long fit of coughing as the sandman drew up before a little row of stone cottages just at the corner where Cinder Hill Lane ran into the Wallbury High Road. "Pablo, lad," gasped the hawker, laying his hand on the pony's back and struggling to get his breath, "we're gettin' owd, thee an' me; weest sewn be done fur if things goos on o' thisunce," and as his face again became purple he bent down and went off into another long cough.

"Hay, Reubin, yo dew saand bad! Wot-iver's ta dew wi yo?" The speaker was a short, trim little woman of about thirty-seven. She had a broad, serious brow and black wavy hair, whilst her cheeks still wore some of the bloom of youth, and her soft, dark eyes looked at the coughing sandman with sympathetic distress. She wore a pink print dress, with white spots in it, which, though somewhat faded and neatly patched on the bodice in two or three places, still became her well and set off her very natty figure.

"It's losening, wench, it's losening," gasped the sandman, and in confirmation of his statement he went off immediately into another fit of coughing.

"Hay, mon! bud yo arr badly. Yo shuld'na be aat wi' a cowf loike that. Cum into th' haase, an' Aw'll gi' yo summat warm."

At another time the surly old hawker would have declined this invitation, but this was one of the few women he had learned to respect, and his cough had really exhausted him, and so, with a crusty grunt, he followed her into the cottage. In a few minutes the sympathetic little woman had set him in an armchair by the fire, and was busy mixing him a glass of black currant tea, into which she dropped a few drops of brandy, and as he held the smoking glass in his hand and sipped at it, he heaved a sigh and began to look round the room. It was scrupulously clean; the window-blind and the table-top were almost equally white, the three little fuchsia-pots in the window had been "ruddled" until they looked as red almost as paint, the fire-irons shone in a high state of polish, and the mahogany chest of drawers reflected the fire almost as in a glass. It was a long time since Reuben had seen so sweet a little nest, and his heart warmed towards the owner of it as he looked again and again at the brightness around him. And then the active little woman began to advise him about keeping his feet dry and wearing goose grease on brown paper on his chest, and a bacon collop round his neck at nights, and finished by handing him two little packets of herbs, "cumfrey and horehound," with minute and oft-repeated instructions as to how they were to be brewed and how often the decoction was to be taken. And Reuben, wondering at his own mildness, took the little packet, and with a muttered and strangely bashful "Thank thi, wench," rejoined Pablo in the road.

As they went along Reuben seemed to be lost in meditation; then he stopped, and, turning round, stood looking back at the little cottage he had just left. Then he hurried forward to overtake his cart, and in a moment or two he had brought his steed to a standstill in the road, and once more turned to gaze down the road. Then, as if struck with a sudden thought, he darted forward, and seizing Pablo by the rein he brought him to a standstill, and then pulling the animal's head half round and pointing with his whip down the road he cried, "Hoos poor, an' hoos hafe-clemmed, and hoos worked ta death, and hoos a Methody, but sithi, Pablo! hoos *ten* times happier tin yore Reuben," and there was sorrow and regret and keen disappointment in his face, and he shook his head mournfully.

After giving his master as much time as he thought the subject demanded, Pablo started again on his journey, leaving Reuben still standing and staring down the road. Presently the sandman made a sudden dart after his pony, and seizing the bridle once more with an impatient jerk, he cried, half angrily, "Sithi, thaa owd haythen thaa! If thaa doesna be sharp and ger on wi' thi deein thall live ta see yore Reubin a Methody! Aye, an' a gradely Methody tew!"

And then another mood came over the disturbed man, and taking the pony gently by the reins he began to lead him along the road. He was looking straight before him now, and sadness and vain regret were in his face. Then he heaved a heavy sigh, and jerking his thumb over his shoulder in the direction of the cottage he had left he muttered, "Hoo wudna *lewk* at me! Aw tell thi, Pablo," and he turned to the pony once more as if it had raised some objection, "hoo wudna lewk at me. Awm rich, an' cud mak' her into a lady, an' her childer into swells, and hoos next dur to th' bastile, an hoo wudna lewk at me," and Pablo plodded doggedly on as if this was an extraordinary and unaccountable lapse on the part of his master, of which it was not worth his while as a self-respecting and experienced animal to take too serious notice.

When they turned the corner of Lark Lane

they of course came in sight of the sandman's cottage, and as they did so Reuben's countenance changed, and an amused, half mischievous look came into his eyes.

"Bi Gum, Pablo!" he cried "we're coppt! We're fairly coppt this time! Naa fur it."

There was a perambulator standing at the cottage door, and somebody evidently well acquainted with the mysterious and complicated system of door fastenings in vogue there was already in possession of the house. The sandman did his best to look penitent and apologetic as he entered, but a smile lurked about the corners of his big mouth. On the hearthstone stood a bright-looking, well-dressed young woman, who might be a little under or a little over thirty. It was Mrs. Grace Westall, *née* Tonge, and she was dandling a baby up and down as she talked.

"Father! How could you! Was there ever such an aggravating man!"

The sandman walked meekly to his seat.

"Didn't I tell you not to go out for a week? Oh, I could shake you, you old a—a—maddlin'," and Grace, who as the mill-owner's wife now usually talked decent English, or at any rate Lancashire English, slipped unconsciously in her pretty indignation into the dialect.

The sandman grinned, but never spoke. Grace since her marriage and consequent elevation in station had become quite an imperious little domestic tyrant, especially toward her father, and Reuben liked her better in this character than he had ever done as his meek and dutiful daughter, and when she went into one of her pretty tantrums Reuben delighted to sit and watch her.

"You're worse! I can see you are worse! And you might well!" and the irate lady tossed back her long yellow curls and shook her head threateningly at her parent.

Then she took a little walk across the rug with the baby, and then glancing scornfully at the table she cried, more indignantly than ever, "And look at that table! A week's pots unwashed! What are they doing there? Where are those lazy charwomen I sent?"

But the sandman only grinned the more.

"Where are they, I say?"

"Aw sent 'em whoam."

"Sent 'em home! And what for, pray?"

"They aw wanted ta merry me."

And in spite of herself Grace had to laugh, which was what her father most of all desired.

"Marry you! I wish one of 'em would, I do for sure!"

After a moment's pause, during which Grace was tossing her baby up and down, Reuben drawled out, "Aw wur thinkin' o' puttin' up ta Long Sally—bud hoo happen wodn't ha' me." And Grace rippled out a long, merry laugh, for Long Sally was about the ugliest and most intemperate old woman in the parish, and a character to boot.

And then Grace tucked up her dress-sleeves and carried away the dirty pots, and announced that she was going to send her servant down to "fettle up." Then she made some tea, during which last operation Reuben went out and put up Pablo.

Grace was just rolling down her sleeves again and preparing to take up the baby, who was becoming fretful, when her father returned from the stable.

"Father," she said, turning to him quite seriously, "I really wish you would find some decent body and wed her. You won't come and live at the house, and you can't go on like this. You are gettin' older." But the twinkle in Reuben's eye set her off laughing again, and she hastened away to her own residence.

The sandman, who had followed his daughter to the door, sauntered slowly and absently back into his house; then he put his hands into his trousers pockets and stood looking through the window with a far-away and somewhat pensive expression on his square, strong face. Then he took off his coat and hung it behind the door, and once more resumed his gaze through the window. A little sigh escaped him, and turning round he took the little bundles of herbs out of his coat pocket and stood looking at them. Then he laid them on the table, glanced again through the window, and with another little sigh walked to the door. From the door he wandered into the stable and began to inspect his four-footed friend once more. He groped in the manger to feel for the corn, then he picked up a bucket and offered the ragged looking animal a drink. Once more he sighed, and this time more heavily, and then, standing away a little and appearing to take a long careful look at his old companion, he murmured, "Neaw, neaw, Pablo! It winna dew, lad! Thee an' me's ta owd fur that sooart o' wark!" and then as he withdrew towards the door with another and longer sigh he continued, "Bud sumbri 'ull ger a bargin' some day, they will fur sewer, lad."

As Reuben stepped into the lane, and stood fumbling absently with the fastening of the stable door, he caught the patter of little clogs coming along, and the murmur of children's voices, and turning round he beheld two youngsters, the children of the widow of whom he was at that moment thinking.

"Hello! Lizer," he cried, with a clumsy affectation of eagerness and surprise, "wheer arr yo goin'?"

The eldest of the two children stopped, and began to look frightened as the sandman sauntered towards them. "We're goin' whoam tew arr baggin'," she answered timidly, and stepped back a little.

"Aye!" exclaimed Reuben in pretended surprise, "an' what dew yo hev fur yur baggin'?"

"Traycle butty-cake an' tay."

The sandman seemed overwhelmed with astonishment for a moment, and then he asked, "An' wot dun yo hev fur yur dinners?"

The little girl hesitated as if she were not quite sure whether these were proper questions to answer, and then she replied "Bacon collops, a—a—a—when we han ony."

The sandman seemed more surprised than ever, and presently went on, "An' wot dun yo hev when yo hanna ony collops?"

Lizer hesitated again, glanced timidly back down the lane, looked up again into the face of her interrogator, and then answered almost in a whisper, "Nowt."

The hawker lifted his heavy brows higher than ever, and demanded hastily, "An' wot dun yo dew then?"

The little one was embarrassed; surely her questioner was asking very unjustifiable questions. She would evidently have very much preferred to run away, but she had quite her share of the Scowcroft children's fear of the sandman, and so presently she stammered, "Then my muther prays."

Reuben's hard eyes suddenly became most unwontedly dim; he choked back a novel rising in his throat, and asked, in a voice that annoyed him by its huskiness, "An' wot then?"

Lizer seemed surprised at the question, and with a little look of remonstrance and astonishment she answered, "Oh! ther's allis summat comes then."

The sandman wheeled suddenly round, and hastened indoors as if little Lizer had struck him—as indeed she had.

---

## II.

Now Reuben had not in the least exaggerated when he had described the condition and circumstances of Kitty Wallwork, the widow, to his faithful steed. Since the death of her husband some four years before she had found the struggle of life very hard indeed, and had many a time been reduced to the direst straits. She lived by baking and selling bread and tea-cakes, and by doing a little washing. She had her full share of that proper pride which hates to acknowledge poverty, and her feelings on this point were intensified by the recollection that her present condition was an ample justification of the evil prophecies of her neighbours when she had defied public opinion by marrying into an unpopular family. Moreover, though modest and quiet in her general demeanour, Kitty was a very ambitious woman, and strove to forget her present difficulties in highly-coloured day-dreams of the future of her children. If only she could get over three or four more years; but that was the difficulty, and every now and again she felt as if she had got to the last extreme and would have to give in. And things had reached an acute stage at the time when she had her little interview with the sandman, and she could not help wishing, as she watched his creaking old cart go down the road, that she had a little of the money which rumour credited him with possessing and for which he had so little use.

But it was no use wishing and fretting; the winter was coming, her needs were great, and she must work whilst she had the chance, so she heaved another little sigh, threw her shawl over her head, and hurried off to do a little work for the Misses Garlick at the farm.

This employment, to her great joy, lasted all that evening and the next day, and when she arrived home on the following evening she was greatly astonished to find her little coal-shed crammed to overflowing with coals that would, with the care she had learned to exercise, last her all the winter. But who had sent them? The children knew nothing. Owd Hecky next door was blind, and pleaded that as a reason for his ignorance, though he did not say, as he might have done, that a load had also been given to him as the price of his silence. The other neighbours all went out to work, except Martha Myers at the end of the row, and she was away from home. Who could it be?

And presently it struck her that it must be the sandman, only it was so very unlike him, and his character was so bad, that if it were he, there must be some suspicious reason behind the generosity. She mentioned her idea to little Liza over a frugal supper, and the child then remembered her interview with the sandman, and detailed it to her mother. Yes, it was the sandman without a doubt, and almost immediately poor Reuben was forgotten in the widow's gratitude to her Maker. He had answered her prayers, and *did* work in mysterious ways indeed, when He had answered her prayers by sending her help through such a channel. Then she began to fear whether it was right that she should accept help from a hard-hearted, money-grubbing old wretch like Reuben. But she got over that by reminding herself of stories she had read in tracts in which God had sent help to His children in distress from people quite as unlikely as Reuben, and that night the little ones looked up into their mother's half-transfigured face with solemn wonder as she poured out her thanksgiving to her Maker for fulfilling His promises and helping the widow in distress.

She was out when next the sandman came on his rounds, and it was several days before she got an opportunity of thanking him.

One morning, however, as she was busy baking, with the door open, a shadow fell across the entrance, and a rough voice demanded, "Dust want owt, Kitty?" It was Reuben, of course. He was seated on the little stone table outside the door, and looked as unconcerned as usual.

"Aye, Aw want *thee*. Aw want ta thank——"

"Me! Thaa wants me! Bi Gum, Kitty, Awm fain——"

"Neaw! Neaw!" cried the widow, hastily, whilst a faint blush rose to her face. "Aw dunna meean that; Aw want ta thank thi——"

But again, and with obvious intention, Reuben interrupted her.

"Aar Grace wur saying t'other day as Aw owt get marrit."

And Kitty ducked her head down and drew a short breath, and then she went on, "Aw want ta than——"

"Thaa wants! Neer moind what *thaa* wants, *Aw* wants a woife."

Kitty felt that the situation was getting ridiculous; she could feel her face beginning to burn, and yet she was sure that the sandman was only joking. And he had been very good to her; there was evidently some good in him somewhere.

Could she say anything that would do him good and set him thinking in serious directions? She paused a moment, stole a rapid glance at her visitor as he sat on the stone table. Poor man! perhaps nobody ever had spoken to him for his good. She would try.

"There's summat else as thaa waants mooar tin a woife, Reuben."

And then she caught her breath, fearing that she had ventured too far, for the sandman was credited with a dreadful temper.

"Wot's that?" demanded Reuben, eagerly.

And Kitty bent her head over her dough, and answered, timidly, "A cleean slate, lad."

But there was no explosion as she had expected; there was no reply at all, in fact; and a moment later she heard the wheels of the sandcart begin to creak slowly, and when she raised her head her strange wooer had disappeared.

And then Kitty began to accuse herself of all kinds of transgressions; she had repaid Reuben's kindness by offending him; she had flown in the face of Providence just when God had sent her most unexpected help. She had given way to pride, and had robbed her children by slighting the help they all so much needed. Once more she had let her tongue get her into trouble. Oh, what a foolish and wicked woman she was!

For two days poor Kitty continued to torture

herself about her mistake, and had resolved a score of times that when next the sandman came on his rounds she would make ample amends for her ingratitude.

On the Saturday morning whilst she was blackleading the firegrate, and was therefore very hot and dirty, she was surprised to hear the old familiar cry of the sandman about two hours earlier than the usual time. Why was he coming just then? She would finish hastily and wash herself before he reached her door; she could not possibly talk to him in that condition. But before she had finished her shining grate she heard a rough "Whoy wi thi" outside, and almost instantly the door opened, and the strong face of the hawker looked in upon her.

"An' soa when thaa gets wed it'll be tew a felley wi a clean slate, will it?" cried Reuben, holding the door in his hand.

And Kitty, annoyed to be caught in that condition, especially when she wanted to be nice to the sandman, replied, without ever turning round, "It will that."

"Oh."

And before she could rise to her feet or stop him the sandman had banged the door and was leading his pony down the road.

What a provoking man he was, and what an unlucky and foolish woman was she! The very coals on the fire which she now poked so angrily were his gift, and she could not even be civil to him. Besides, she had no rubbing-stone and could not finish her work without. What was she to do? Next day was Sunday, and the sandman occasionally came to chapel now, she would look out for him then and give him her thanks. Yes; that would be a very good opportunity, for Reuben was not likely to be able to evade the issue as he had done last time if she spoke to him at the chapel door.

But that Sabbath Reuben did not appear, and she had, perforce, to wait until his next round. On the day but one after, she finished her baking earlier than usual, and left her door open so that she could hear him as soon as he was in the neighbourhood. She had also put on her second-best dress which, alas! was just then her first-best too; and having given her hair just a little touch, she sat waiting for him to approach.

Creak! creak! creak! he was coming; as soon as he stopped at old Hecky's she would go out to him.

Creak! creak! went the cart. He must be opposite the door now, but she dare not look.

Creak! creak! Why, he must be going past!

Kitty felt suddenly faint; turned to look round the house as if to ask the various pieces of furniture to behold this astonishing thing and explain what it meant; and before she could either move or speak, the pony and cart and owner too were past.

Kitty sank back into her seat and felt very much inclined to cry. She could have stopped him by calling after him, of course; but why had he gone past? He had certainly never done that before. He was offended, and well he might be! And Kitty did not know, of course, that whilst she was sitting staring at the fuchsias Reuben was standing some distance down the road and gazing back at her cottage with much the same expression on his face as stood at that moment on her own.

Later in the same day she heard news. Old Martha Myers, who had returned home again, came in evidently full of some very toothsome gossip. The Black Lion, more commonly known as "Th' Hole i' thi' Wall," a low beerhouse on the outskirts of Scowcroft, was to be closed. More wonderful still, for the house, though of evil repute, was known to pay well; it had just come out that Reuben the sandman had been the owner of the place for some time, and that it was his action that was causing it to be closed. Kitty was more perplexed than ever. She scarcely dared to hope that her few words to the old hawker had had anything to do with the matter, and still, if he had made up his mind to act on her suggestion, this was about the first and best thing he could have done.

Kitty began to feel worried about the matter. When the little ones had been got off to bed she sat down to have a good long meditation about the subject, but had scarcely composed herself when a cart stopped at the door, and a man bearing a sack of flour and a heavy parcel strode into the house. To all her protestations that the goods were not for her the man opposed an obstinate heedlessness, and presently left her more bewildered than ever. When he had gone she opened the parcel, which proved to contain two dresses, one a good stuff of fashionable pattern, and the other—oh, marvel of marvels—a real black silk!

But the wonders of this most wonderful day were not over yet. Kitty had just reduced herself by strenuous efforts to something like calmness, and was deciding that of course these were gifts from the strange sandman, which she could on no account accept, when a step was heard on the flags outside, the door opened, and in walked, of all persons, the sandman himself.

"Oh, thart theer aar ta," he remarked, and then with the utmost coolness walked over to the chair on the other side of the fireplace and sat down.

An exclamation of surprise rose to the widow's lips as she saw him enter, but his perfect self-possession and his changed appearance stopped her, and she rose slowly from her seat and stood there staring helplessly at him. She had never seen him look like this. He did not wear his ordinary dirty every-day clothes, neither had he on those gorgeous best blacks which he affected when he came to chapel on Sundays. It was a neat and evidently new suit of dark mixture, which fitted him uncommonly well. Besides that he was shaved, and his short, stumpy beard had been carefully trimmed, and Kitty saw to her surprise that he was after all a good-looking man.

As the widow stood looking at her visitor she suddenly began to feel very awkward. She realised that she must look like a shy schoolgirl. All the same she felt powerless to move. Why was she so helpless? She always did feel helpless in the presence of this man. She understood now why people were so much afraid of him. She was afraid of him herself. Presently, with a painful effort, she managed to say, "Hay, Reuben, Aw'm glad tha's cum, Aw —Aw—Aw—them coils——"

"Naa, then, theer thaa art agean! Dunna bother me abaat th' coils." And the sandman sounded angry, as he made an impatient gesture with the arm that was leaning on the other side of the table.

Kitty could feel her heart beating, and had to lean against the table for support. Oh, why was she so "sawft" just when she needed to be cool and firm? There were several things she had to say to her visitor, and now for the life of her she could not decide which to mention first.

Presently she ventured very penitently, "Aw wur—Aw've bin ill off this last wik fur wot Aw said tew thi."

And Reuben wheeled half round in his chair, and cried eagerly, "Oh, tha's changed thi moind, then hast?"

"Neaw! neaw! Aw dunna meean that! Aw meean abaat wot Aw said abaat clean——"

But the sandman perversely misunderstood her, and broke in impatiently, "Wot's a toathre coils! Ha' sum sense, woman, an' think o' thi childer."

"Bud, Rewbin"—and Kitty tried to be calm and speak firmly—"Aw conna! Aw darna! It's no' reet, tha knows."

"Reet!" shouted Reuben, jumping to his feet in anger. "Is it reet ta clem thiself, an' clem thi childer, an' chuck ther chonces away wi' proide! Is that reet?"

Kitty was bewildered; this masterful man frightened her and paralysed her; she could not even think clearly. At last she said, timidly, "Aw trusten i' Providence——"

"Providence!" broke in the sandman; and striding across the floor towards the kitchen door he suddenly wheeled round, and cried, excitedly, "That's it! that's it! That's th' way wi' aw yo' cantin' Methodys; Yo' talken abaat Providence, an' yo' pray ta Providence, an' then when He sends ya wot yo' wanten yo' conna tak' it fur proide!"

But Reuben had gone a little too far, and Kitty felt her spirit rising. "Rewbin," she commenced very firmly, but once more the irate sandman broke in—"Sithi, Kitty, wilt ha' me an' cumfort an' plenty o' brass, an' cloathes fur thi childer, an' summat ta leeav 'em when tha dees—wilta or wilta not?"

But the woman in Kitty was aroused now. What kind of love-making was this? The idea of being proposed to by a man in a passion! It was monstrous! She drew herself up proudly, took a long breath, and then answered, "Ha' thi? *Thee!* Neaw, nor if tha'd ten toimes as mitch, sa theer."

Reuben stood looking at her from head to foot. He seemed all at once to have become quite calm. And still he looked her over until all the courage went out of her, and she began to tremble. Then he drew his breath, walked quietly to the door, and was just departing when he turned round again, and said slowly, "Kitty, Aw want thi an' Awst *have* thi. An' if tha sends that flaar an' stuff back Awst send *twict* as mich," and closing the door very deliberately he was gone.

## III.

Left to herself Kitty sank into the nearest chair and burst into tears. But just then she heard the pattering of little feet on the floor above her head, and a moment later her whole family was clinging around her and demanding what was "ta dew." Poor children! They had become of late only too accustomed to strange men coming to the house and "saucing" their mother. They had seen her cry more than once after the "rentman" or the "c'llector" had called, but this was a new voice they had heard shouting downstairs. Who could this be? And this tender, clinging child-sympathy—the most touching of all consolations—softened the mother more than ever, and for some moments she could only soothe them and hug them to her breast. Then she told them that it was only the sandman, and showed them the big sack of flour, and told them that he had given it to them.

"Then aar yo' skriking 'cause yore happy, muther?" asked little Lizer, wistfully.

"Aye, chilt, aye," sobbed the mother, and coaxed them back to rest.

Then the harassed woman went downstairs again and sat before the fire and wept. And somehow the crying relieved her, and she presently found herself sitting and gazing absently into the fading fire.

After a little while she began to smile, and presently she laughed outright. Really, her wooer's extraordinary mode of proposing was too ridiculous. But it was certainly in harmony with everything she had ever heard of him; he never did anything like anybody else. Then she became serious again as the grave question of accepting or otherwise of Reuben's gifts presented itself to her mind. He had a reputation for being generous in his own peculiar way, and was reputed to be very well off. Why shouldn't she swallow her pride and accept his help for her children's sake? And there might after all be something in what the man had said about Providence providing for her, and she rejecting. Perhaps God had seen she was proud, and had taken this way of helping in order to cure her of her sin. Poor soul! It was easy enough for her to think badly of herself.

But this proposal! That seemed to complicate everything. If Reuben was simply trying to buy her there was an end of it, she could not bear the thought. And every now and again the idea of the possibility of accepting the sandman passed through her mind. But somehow she always shirked the thing, and preferred to argue the matter with herself without reference to this element of the case. Again and again her thoughts went out to her children and their needs, and at last she stole off to rest, but only to toss about and brood until the small hours of the morning.

The children had their promised cakes when they came down to breakfast next day, but not from Reuben's sack. Kitty had not quite settled that question yet. Then she took another look at the tempting dresses, the silk absorbing her thoughts for quite a long time, until at last she thrust it nervously from her, hastily threw the wrapper over it and carried it upstairs. Not to keep, of course, but only to be safe from harm until she should be able to make up her mind.

As she was finishing her own breakfast, who should come hurrying in but Peter, the grocer's assistant, to know if she could bake bread for a funeral on the morrow. The bread would have to be made at once if she did, for it must be neither too new nor too old. "Yes," she said, in answer to Peter's inquiry and without giving herself time to think, and then as the messenger departed, she turned to Reuben's sack and began to look at it very earnestly. She had used all her own stock of flour to make the children's cakes, there was no time to go for more, or at least she tried to think there was not—was it another Providence that this order should come in like this, to compel her to decide?

Perhaps it was. She got up and went to the

sack and took hold of the tied neck. Then she let it go somewhat hastily and drew her hands away. Then she sighed and looked the bag over again very slowly. She might open it and just see what kind of flour it was. It might be common, and that would save her the trouble of deciding for herself. The flour was the very kind she always used. It must be Providence! She put her hands in to feel it, and then Ah! and then, in a moment or two she had taken a portion out and was busy kneading it in her mug, with a clouded and anxious face.

And that day Kitty was trying to pacify her conscience by reminding herself how easily Reuben could spare the things she had taken from him. Then she told herself she would be very kind to him when next she saw him. As for the dresses, she was firmly resolved that nothing in the world should persuade her to accept them, she would make him take them back the very next time he called, and when he did come she would thank him for all he had done, whatever he might say. Once or twice the question of marriage passed through her mind, but each time she dismissed it as something not to be considered.

On the third day Reuben turned up as usual, and, to her great surprise, was as bland as she had ever known him in her life—which was not saying much. He made no allusion to the last interview, and actually came into the house without being asked. Everything was in her favour, and she at once plunged into her thanks. Reuben frowned slightly when she commenced, but patiently heard her out. "Well, hast done thi nomminny?" he asked when she paused for breath. "Aye," she replied, surprised at the mildness of his tone.

"Then let that dew fer allis. Aw conner abide sich foo-scutter" (silly talk); and then without another word he strode out of the house towards his pony.

"Rewbin! Here, Rewbin, cum back wi' thi."

But the sandman held on his way.

Kitty was so eager that she rushed out of the house. "Rewbin, tha mun tak yond dress-pieces back. Aw conna' keep em."

And Reuben turned round, and flourishing his whip at her, answered, "Aw'll gi' thi dress-pieces if tha doesnna' goo back," and then wheeling round again, unconcernedly resumed his journey.

During the next few days Kitty and the sandman gradually became more and more friendly. The hawker now called on one pretence or another nearly every day, and on those days on which he did not appear Kitty was alarmed to discover that she strangely missed him. Meanwhile the children grew plump and rosy once more, and she dared not think of what would become of them if she broke with her benefactor. To her great relief Reuben never broached the subject of marriage, and only showed his old temper when she attempted to revive discussion on the question of the dresses. All the same, she resolved and resolved again that she would never wear them. In fact, she told herself every time she thought of them that she dare not. She noticed also that Reuben was now most exemplary in his attendance at the chapel, and she was delighted to hear her old leader declare as they came from the class one night that the sandman was turning over a new leaf, and would be a "dacent Methody afoor lung."

By this time also she had saved a little towards her back rent, but was surprised and rather uneasy that for two weeks the landlord's agent had not called. The third week-end came, and still the "rentman" did not appear, and so on Monday morning after a very uncomfortable Sunday Kitty hastened down to the agent's house to avert the coming danger. For she could see in this man's absence nothing but expulsion from her home.

The agent took her back rent quite eagerly, and then, when she asked timidly why he had not called, he looked up at her from his desk with a glance of surprise, and demanded, "Whey dustna know as th' haases is sowd?"

"Sowd! Neaw! Whoa tew?"

"Rewbin."

And Kitty went home with a very uncomfortable feeling in her mind. She must stop this. Reuben was almost keeping her, and he was doing these things as a means of winning her for himself. It was not right that she should deceive him. Neither was it right that she should be living on a man who was nothing to her. It was not decent; it looked very ugly indeed when she fairly faced it. But the children! Oh, what would become of them if Reuben ceased to help her. And they were looking so bonny just now; even little Milly, the delicate one, was getting quite strong and rosy.

On the other hand, the flour was getting done, and now she could not conceive how she had ever done without it, and the prospect of having to buy again in small quantities seemed very dreadful to her. Oh, what should she do? What *could* she do?

And that very night Reuben came again and almost immediately introduced the dreaded topic. Kitty was terrified. What a man this was: she never felt less able to contend than she did just then. Could he read her heart? Why had he waited until this day of her weakness?

"Neaw! neaw! neaw! Dunna, Rewbin, dunna!" And she put her hands upon her ears and refused to listen.

And the sandman, instead of "flyin' up" as

she expected, waited until she was a little calmer, and then gently and gradually brought her back to the subject. He talked about having watched her ever since her husband's death, and being much impressed by her quiet devotion to her children. He praised the children, and said what a pity it would be not to give them a "chonce." Then he spoke of his own position, and how easy it would be to make her comfortable for life, and so on, and so on.

He was thinking of giving up the sand-cart and retiring and "livin' different," which gave Kitty the sweet feeling that perhaps the few words about cleaning his slate had not been in vain. And so this strange man talked and reasoned and coaxed until at last poor Kitty, with visions of a future for her children, blended with a feeling of helplessness in the presence of this overpowering lover, consented, and Reuben went away a satisfied man.

And next day another sack of flour arrived, and a side of home-cured bacon, and a piece of cloth to make dresses for the children, and Kitty tried to crowd back her feelings into some remote corner of her mind, and be happy for the sake of the little ones.

But it was no use. It seemed as if a legion of tormenting spirits had got into her soul, and were stirring up her whole nature to rebellion. She could not be quiet. She could not rest anywhere, and when she went to bed she could not, and did not, sleep. Next morning she got up very early and started off to the sandman's to beg him to release her from from her promise, but Reuben had already left home, and though she looked out for him all day he never appeared. At night, however, he came to see her, but as soon as she put eyes upon him all Kitty's resolution melted away, and do what she would, she could not muster courage to tell him what she felt.

A week passed, a week of sleeplessness and anguish for the poor widow, and at last she began to realise that, however he might take it, Reuben must be told, or she would lose her reason. By this time she had begun to feel sorry for the sandman. She had led him on, she had selfishly accepted gifts which would give him a false impression. And she had found him out. Under that rough exterior there was a real kind heart, and it was wicked of her to take his love when she could give him none in return. Oh, what a base woman she had been! But she would put it right now. And then she prayed, and as she prayed grew calmer. Yes! she could do it now, and would do. Reuben was too good to be treated like that.

The sandman seemed brighter and happier when he came that night, and Kitty's heart sank again as she looked at him. She had resolved to speak as soon as she saw him, lest she should be too much afraid afterwards. But now that he was here, her tongue seemed tied, and she welcomed him in silence. As he took his seat in his favourite chair and accepted the lighted spill she offered him, he looked up very earnestly and searchingly into her face, but said nothing.

Kitty felt as if she were choking, but for the life of her she could not speak.

Presently the sandman turned slightly round in his chair, and said in a tone of gentle anxiety, "Thaa doesna' lewk weel, wench! wot's up wi' thi?" and there was a chord of sadness and regret in his tones that went to Kitty's heart. It was the one touch needed to set her free, and with a heartbreaking sob she dropped on her knees at Reuben's side and burst into a passion of tears.

The sandman sat strangely still as she wept, looking down upon her with a mournful moisture in his small, sharp eyes, and at last he leaned forward, put his hand on her hair, and gently stroking it, murmured, "Poor wench!" And Kitty, whilst a new spasm of sorrow went through her frame, sobbed on and did not move.

After a little while Reuben leaned forward again, and with the gentlest of touches upon her hair, asked, slowly, "Kitty, tha'rt nor happy abaat this wedding?"

Kitty was still weeping, though she listened with painful interest to every word he spoke.

Presently, as she did not reply, he proceeded, "A yung woman loike thee conna take tew an owd chap loike me—an' him a wastril tew! conta?"

And still Kitty did not reply, only she was holding her breath and listening with tearful wonder for what he was going to say next, for it was evident he had not done.

"An' tha did it for th' sake o' thi childer, did t'na, wench?"

And Reuben's tones were more mournfully sympathetic than ever. Kitty had a feeling that she was listening to a totally new Reuben, such a one as she had never either heard of or imagined.

And then there was a pause. She felt it was time for her to speak, but what she was hearing was so delightful, and withal so wonderful that she felt she wanted to hear more. But Reuben was in no haste to proceed, and she was just about to lift her red and tearful face, when the sandman bent over her, and, laying his hand solemnly on her head, said, "God bless thi, Kitty! God bless thi!"

Kitty's frame was shaken with a new paroxysm of feeling; she sobbed and sobbed again, and then she rose to her feet and blessed the sandman with an intensity and passion that amazed him. Then she declared that he was far too good for her. He was an angel; let the world say what it liked, she knew. He was an angel; he was "nowt else."

Then she stopped and stepped back, and stood looking at him with wonder and admiration shining through her tears; but before she could speak he said, "Aw'll let thi off merrying me, Kitty, up a wun condition."

"Nay, tha winna! Awst no be let off. Awd merry thi naa, if tha hedna a bodle."

Reuben smiled a sad sort of smile, and then repeated slowly. "Up a wun condition."

"An' wot's that?"

"Az tha lets me help ta keep theeas childer."

And in spite of a fresh burst of tears and many emphatic protests on Kitty's part the sandman had his way. She was to pay no rent and receive whatever he might send; and as Kitty poured out her overflowing gratitude for the twentieth time the sandman sauntered to the door, and as he opened it and was departing he turned round and said, in his old, hard, rasping voice, "Awst start o' cleeanin' my slate afoor lung."

## IV.

THERE was a large company at Miles's; all the regular frequenters were there and one or two additional ones. The fire burnt brightly, the lamp shed a cheerful light over the company, and the region of the fireplace was thick with tobacco smoke.

Quiet William was descanting with glowing face on the recent and most delightful change that had come over Reuben the sandman.

"Aw've seen it cumin' fur months," he cried; "an' it's cumin' gradely, naa; he'll be a member i' less than twelve months, see if he isna."

Just at this point the door opened and Juddy Hicks, the clogger, a man of about five-and-thirty, came sauntering in, and soon settled into a seat.

"Well, it's the coppest thing as iver Aw knowed," said Noah.

The scutcher, who was seated on the further side of the fireplace, looked earnestly for a moment at the last speaker, and then said, in his slow, oracular way, "If yond mon turns o'er gradely there's a chonce fur th' divil, that's Aw."

"Oh, yore takin' abaat *him*, arr yo'," broke in the new comer, though no name had been named, and there was contempt and irony in his pronunciation of the "*him*."

"Three or four pairs of eyes were turned inquiringly upon the speaker, and quiet William began to frown, but nobody spoke.

"Aye," laughed Juddy, sarcastically, "a bonny mon to turn *he* is."

> "And whilst the lamp holds out to burn,
> The vilest sinner may return,"

quoted William, in loud rebuking terms.

Juddy laughed another hard unbelieving laugh, and then he said, "Does yo' chaps meean ta say as yo' dunna know wot he comes to th' chapil fur?"

Quiet William rose from his seat, and standing over the traducer of the absent Reuben, he cried, in stern tones, "He cums ta worship God, wot else?"

Juddy leaned further back in his chair, and looking with a grin at William, he cried, "William, he cums a cooartin'."

There was a dead pause, and those present turned and looked at each other with surprise and curiosity in their faces.

"Whoar is he cooartin'?" demanded William, without moving from before Juddy's chair.

"Whey, Kitty Wallwork, fur sewer; an' funny cooartin' it is, tew."

And in a few moments Juddy had told his tale. Everybody knew. The sandman was going to the house every night, and sometimes in the daytime, too. He had bought Kitty's house, and Kitty herself had altogether changed her appearance, &c., &c. "They're cooartin' reet enough, bud it's a sooart a cooartin' az Aw dunna loike th' lewk on, that's aw"; and Juddy finished by a mysterious little cough.

Astonishment, disappointment, and rising disgust sat on every countenance, and at last, after looking helplessly at Jimmy for some moments, Miles gasped out, "Whey, mon! hoos nowt na bet-ter tin a kept woman."

And Jimmy, after taking time to think, replied, "Hoo met as weel be livin' tally wi' him at wunce."

And then William, who had all this time been standing over Juddy, turned round, and in tones strangely intense and bitter, he cried, "Yo' letheryeds! Yo' numskulls! Aw conna bide ta lewk at yo'," and with a gesture of disgust he strode to the door and was gone.

Now Juddy had very particular reasons of his own for being interested in the doings of Kitty and Reuben. The fact was he was casting sheep's-eyes on the widow himself. He had fancied her before she married his old companion, Kitty's first husband, but had been prevented from proposing because of his poverty, for he was only an indifferent hand at his business, having picked it up after he attained manhood. Since Kitty had been free again he had been constantly making up his mind to approach her, but was deterred by the fact that he was no better off than he had been previously, and Kitty's three children made the task of maintenance more difficult. He therefore had been about the first person to discover the relationship between the widow and Reuben, and had watched them with a very jealous eye. But he was in the sandman's debt, almost hopelessly so, in fact, and therefore dare not cross him. During the last few days, however, he had heard so often about the scandal that he thought he might safely speak; the matter seemed to be common property, and even if it got to Reuben's ears it was very unlikely that the sandman would suspect him. Juddy was a very decent fellow as a rule, but when a man is jealous he sometimes gets beyond his own control.

William, when he left the tailor's, made straight away to Kitty's house. She was one of his members, and he had a special responsibility for her. He resolved as he went to be very faithful and have the matter ended once for all, but when he arrived the widow was so very glad to see him, and evidently so very unsuspicious, that he found it difficult to commence what he intended to say. Abandoning, however, his first plan, he tried to bring round the conversation towards Reuben, and Kitty seemed so very glad to speak about the sandman, and expressed herself so delightedly, and yet so innocently, about the signs of reform which had appeared in his recent conduct, that William grew ashamed and angry again at the innuendoes to which he had listened, and eventually left without giving any hint of his original purpose in coming. When he got outside he stood wavering in the twilight for a few moments, and then started off to interview Reuben. This was, of course, a much more formidable task than talking to Kitty; but William reflected that he might perhaps make the sandman see what he meant without actually telling what he had heard, and unless Reuben were a very much worse person than he supposed that would be sufficient. But Reuben was not at home, and so William returned homewards, and as the evening was not yet far gone he passed his own cottage and went on to Miles's again.

The company had thinned during his absence, but those who remained were still discussing the unsavoury subject with which he had left them.

As he sank with a little sigh into his seat, Miles, who was standing before the fire and looking very grim and emphatic, having evidently just delivered himself of some very conclusive and all-silencing verdict, turned to him and cried with fierce, defiant emphasis, "Naa, then! ther mun be noan o' thi shilly-shally wark abaat this. Yond woman's name cums off th' bewk at wunct! Mind that, naa."

And William, the quiet, gentle William, rose to his feet, and shaking his great fist in his brother-in-law's face whilst his own flamed with anger, he cried, "If yond wench's name cums off th' bewks *moine* cums off, tew." And then after drawing his breath he went on, "If tha'd hawf as cleean a slate as hoo hez tha'd be a foine seet bet-ter mon tin tha art."

But though William had not found courage to tell Kitty of the rumours that were going about, there were others who had no such scruples, and she heard of it the very next day, and heard of it in its most brutally suggestive form. It went to her heart like a stab—all the light seemed to have suddenly gone out of her life, and she blamed herself with cruel perseverance for her lack of thoughtfulness in the matter. However, now that she did realise all that it meant, she must take immediate and decisive action. As soon as it grew near to the time at which Reuben would come, if he did come, though, as a matter of fact, he scarcely ever called now except on his rounds, she locked the door and put out the light, that she might appear to be out, and next morning she took her children and walked all the way to a small farm a mile on the other side of Wallbury, where she spent the next fortnight with some distant relations. She might probably have stayed longer, for it appeared impossible for her to go back to Scowcroft, and yet she could not decide what else to do; but at the end of this time she realised that the evil tidings had reached the farm, and there was a sudden cooling of her welcome. The next day she returned to her home.

In the meantime Reuben had discovered what was the matter also. He had been amazed and nonplussed when he discovered that Kitty had disappeared without leaving any trace behind, and in his concern he began to make all sorts of inquiries. And these questions of his, of course, only confirmed the suspicions of those to whom they were made that there had been something between Kitty and him, and that Kitty had gone out of the way to escape him. Little by little, by a hint here and a look there, Reuben discovered that something was wrong, and that somehow he was considered to be responsible for it. But he got at no facts, and so, worried and anxious, he began to get angry and desperate. The night following the day upon which Kitty came home he slouched into the "Red Cat," and called for a glass of spirits. Avoiding the parlour, he dropped into a little apartment which had been formed by partitioning off a little space behind the "tap." In this position he could hear what was going on in the bar-parlour without being seen, though at the time he never thought of it. He was very miserable. He had been trying to do some little towards "cleaning his slate," and all that had come of it was a nasty scandal and deep trouble to a woman he loved. A few months ago he would not have cared about the scandal; he had rather gloried in outraging public sentiment, in fact; but now, after some months of long and painful struggling to be better, he felt the thing very keenly indeed.

Just then he heard Kitty's name mentioned, and pricked up his ears. And then it all came out. The speaker was not detailing the story, but was evidently speaking of something that was common property, and so Reuben had to pick up the facts bit by bit. The laughs and jeers of the men who were talking fell on his ears without in the least distressing him; he was listening only for the facts. Little by little the true position of affairs was made clear to him, and as the conversation branched off into speculations as to where Kitty had gone, Reuben rose to his feet and stole slowly home.

As he was giving a last look at his steed before retiring to rest that night, he said, mournfully, "Pablo, lad; slate cleaning's hard wark! it's harder tin Aw thowt it 'ud be!" And then as he was leaving the stable he turned suddenly and impatiently round again, and just as if the animal had been saying something with which he did not agree, he cried, fiercely, "Aw tell thi ther is! Ther's monny a wun! Isn't aar Grace a Christian? an' Quiet William! an—an—an—Kitty, God bless her! Aye, an Awst be a Christian tew if Aw con, an' tha con say wot tha's a moind! Awve tan nooatice o' thee lung enuff, thaa owd haythen thaa!"

Next day Reuben had an interview with Quiet William, and by roundabout methods got from him a shrewd suspicion as to who had first told him the rumours. Then he took a walk round by Kitty's, and discovered to his delight that she had returned, but he carefully avoided being seen by either the widow or her children.

Two days later, as Juddy the clogger sat at his work in the little building which he used for the purpose, and which had once been a butcher's shop, the door opened, and Reuben, looking, Juddy thought, very stern, walked in.

"Awm cumin' a Setterda! Aw'll pay thi awf a sovrin a Setterda, Aw, Aw will fer sewer!" cried Juddy, in great agitation.

But the sandman stood looking sadly and a little scornfully on the clogger, and never spoke.

"Aw've hed ta pay Cheetham's fur owler wood, but Aw'll pay thi summat o' Setterda, Aw will."

But Reuben's mysterious silence began to affect the clogger, and so he ventured to steal a look at his visitor, and as he did so he went suddenly cold as he remembered that Reuben might have called about what he had said about Kitty.

The sandman drew two pieces of paper from his pocket and held them up. "Dust see theeas, Juddy?" One of the papers was an I O U for £20, the other contained memoranda of certain repayments.

"Well, Aw'll pay, Aw tell thi. Aw'll pay summat o' Setterda."

Reuben walked to the fire and put the papers in, and stood watching them burn.

Juddy dropped the clog that lay upon his knee and stood up in sheer amazement.

"Wot the ferrups hast dun that fur?" he demanded, sulkily; but the mysterious sandman made no reply.

Juddy watched the papers burn for some time, and was just raising his head to speak when his visitor said, slowly, "Juddy, Aw believe thaa loikes Kitty Wallbrook, dustna?"

"Well, what bi that? Wot hast brunt them papers fur?"

Ignoring the latter part of Juddy's question, Reuben went on, "Whey dustna merry her, then?"

"Haa con Aw merry when Awm i' debt? Wot hast brunt them papers fur?"

The sandman paused, looked down for a moment at his feet, and then said, "Then tha'd merry her if thaa could affoard—if thaa could keep her?"

"Merry her! Aye, would Aw if hoo'd ha me. But wot hast brunt——"

But the sandman stopped him by a hasty wave of the hand, "Niver name them papers ta me ageean—hoos woth hevin' lad."

"Hoo *is* that," cried Juddy, very earnestly.

"Juddy," said Reuben, with strange eagerness, "hoos pure goold, Kitty is. Th' mon az gets her 'ull be weel off if he's no' woth a fardin'."

There was a chord in Reuben's voice that somehow touched the clogger, and so he blurted out all at once, "Aw yerd az *yo* wer efther her."

Reuben was now gazing pensively out through the dirty little window, and presently, with a long soft sigh, he said, "Aw think ta weel on her ta tee her tew an owd felley loike me—an' besoide, hoo wouldna ha' me, lad."

They talked for some time after that, and in the end Juddy was made to understand that his debt was forgiven him, and that if he could get Kitty's consent to marry him the sandman would make some sort of provision for Kitty's future and give them a good start in life.

Juddy was overwhelmed; again and again he tried to thank his eccentric friend, but he soon found that that was the one thing that angered the sandman.

When Reuben had gone Juddy gave himself up to all kinds of delicious speculations and wonderings. He tried several times to finish repairing the clogs upon which he was engaged when the sandman called, but found it impossible to stick to any kind of work. One moment he was melted down with gratitude at the sandman's generosity, and the next he was trying to arrange how he must propose to Kitty. Once he kicked over his clogging stool in sheer frolicsomeness, and the next moment he burst out singing,

"Cum, Mary, link thi' arm i' moine."

Presently, however, a thoughtful mood came upon him, and standing where Reuben had stood some little time before he stared hard and abstractedly through the window, and muttered "If owd Reuben's a wastril Aw wouldna gi mitch fur sum o' th' chapil folk's chonces."

Now Reuben's intention had been, after seeing Juddy, to go over and arrange matters as far as need be with Kitty, but he had been so satisfied with Juddy's eagerness that he thought that he might safely leave matters to take their own course. And on the whole he rather preferred not to go near Kitty at this juncture.

A week later Juddy, with overflowing gratitude and thanks he dared not speak, reported to the sandman that he had "getten her."

Reuben replied with a surly grunt that reminded the younger man of the Reuben of other days, and then commanded him to go and tell Liger, the village carpenter, to put a shop-front into the large cottage that stood at the far corner of Twiggy Lane, "and," he added, thrusting a bundle of title deeds into his hands, " see az tha taks cur o' them an' keeps thi maath shut."

The deeds made Kitty the owner of the property indicated, and accompanying them was an envelope containing a banknote, presumably to pay for the alterations.

About two months later Juddy and Kitty were married; and though Reuben was known to be at the church whilst the ceremony was being performed, he refused very peremptorily Juddy's oft-repeated invitation to the breakfast. In the meantime, however, Juddy had taken good care that the truth about Kitty's relations with the sandman should be known to the village, even though it involved certain severe reflections on himself. Quiet William was triumphant, and sat listening to Juddy's explanations with beaming face. The others pretended to receive the story with doubt, and Miles and Jimmy ventured on the profound and original prophecy that "Them az lives lungest 'ull see th' mooast."

"See! they will that!" cried William, excitedly. "They'll see Rewbin Tonge i' th' Society afoor he dees, that's wot the'll see."

And William proved to be right, for Reuben attended William's own class the very next time it met.

One evening, about a month after Kitty's marriage, Reuben went home after a visit to the new clog-shop, and after partaking of supper he sauntered into the stable to take a final look at his faithful steed before he retired.

Pablo was lying down; but as this was no unusual thing, he bent down and gave him an affectionate slap on the back. And then he drew back and touched the beast with his foot.

# REUBEN CLEANS HIS SLATE.

Yes; there was no doubt of it, Pablo was dead. Reuben stood looking at his old comrade mournfully for a few moments, and then with a quaver in his voice he said, "An' tha's gen o'er at last!" And then after another heavy sigh he added, "Well, if *tha's* gen o'er *Awst* give o'er tew."

The sandman kept his vow; the old sand-cart appeared no more in Scowcroft; but when he had quietly buried his old friend in the paddock at the country end of his house, he heaved another heavy sigh and said, "An' naa Aw *will* start o' cleeanin' my slate."

And next Sabbath he was found teaching the infants in the Scowcroft Sunday-school.

THE END.

LONDON:
W. SPEAIGHT AND SONS, PRINTERS,
FETTER LANE, E.C.

# Novels and Stories

PUBLISHED BY

## JAMES CLARKE AND CO.,

13 & 14, Fleet Street, London.

---

**THE VICAR OF LANGTHWAITE.** A Novel.
    By **Lily Watson.** New Edition, in One Vol., with Introductory Note by the **Right Hon. W. E. Gladstone.** With frontispiece. Crown 8vo, cloth, 5s.

    MR. GLADSTONE expresses his "*satisfaction at the publication of a work, written with ability and in an attractive manner, which exhibits from a favouring point of view the social, moral, and spiritual facts of English Non-conforming life.*"

**UNKNOWN TO HERSELF:** A Novel.
    By **Laurie Lansfeldt.** Crown 8vo, cloth, 6s.

    "*A clever novel.*"—SCOTSMAN.
    "*The various dramatic incidents are splendidly wrought up.*"
    —DUNDEE ADVERTISER.

**ON LONDON STONES:** A Novel.
    By **Catherine March (Carl Swerdna).** Crown 8vo, cloth, 6s.

    "*Each character is minutely drawn and not overdrawn, and the catastrophe, though sensational, is exactly what we feel must have happened. . . . Well worked up. . . . We can thoroughly recommend the book.*"—THE GUARDIAN.

    "*No recent novel has given us more pleasure of the quiet kind than 'On London Stones.'*"—LITERATURE.

**THE DUTCH IN THE MEDWAY:** A Story of the time of Charles II.
    By **Charles Macfarlane.** With a Foreword by **S. R. Crockett.** New edition, cloth, 3s. 6d.

**HOW THE CHILDREN RAISED THE WIND.**
By **Edna Lyall.** Illustrated Edition. Fcap. 8vo, cloth, gilt top, 1s. 6d.

**THE MIST ON THE MOORS:** A Romance of North Cornwall.
By **Joseph Hocking,** Author of "The Story of Andrew Fairfax," "All Men are Liars," &c. Paper, 1s.; cloth, 1s. 6d.

**THE BLINDNESS OF MADGE TYNDALL:** A Novelette.
By **Silas K. Hocking.** Paper, 1s.; cloth, 1s. 6d.

**A MORNING MIST:** A Novel.
By **Sarah Tytler.** Crown 8vo, cloth, 5s.

**MISS DEVEREUX, SPINSTER:** A Novel.
By **Agnes Giberne.** New Edition. Crown 8vo, cloth, 5s.

**A MAN'S MISTAKE:** A Novel.
By **Minnie Worboise.** Crown 8vo, cloth, 5s.

---

## Marianne Farningham's Novels and Stories.

**A WINDOW IN PARIS:** A Story of the Franco-German War.
By **Marianne Farningham.**

**1900?** A Forecast and a Story.
By **Marianne Farningham.** Second Edition. Crown 8vo, cloth, 3s. 6d.

**THE CLARENCE FAMILY;** or, Brothers and Sisters.
By **Marianne Farningham.** Fcap. 8vo, cloth, 1s. 6d.

**THE CATHEDRAL SHADOW.**
By **Marianne Farningham.** Fifth Thousand. Crown 8vo, cloth, 3s. 6d.

**WHAT OF THE NIGHT?** A Temperance Tale of the Times.
By **Marianne Farningham.** Fourth Thousand. Crown 8vo, illuminated cover, 1s.

## NOVELS BY AMELIA E. BARR.

JOHN GREENLEAF WHITTIER (Quaker poet), writing to Mrs. Barr in 1890 from his home in Massachusetts, said:

"*But for failing health and sight, which make even a brief note a painful effort, I should long ago have told thee how much I admire thy* 'Friend Olivia.' . . . I HAVE READ EVERY BOOK OF THINE WITH GREAT INTEREST."

**A Rose of a Hundred Leaves.** With Numerous Illustrations. Crown 8vo, cloth extra, 6s.

**Friend Olivia.** A Quaker Story of the Time of the Commonwealth. Crown 8vo, cloth, 6s.

*Three Shillings and Sixpence each.*

**The Beads of Tasmer.**
**A Sister to Esau.**
**She Loved a Sailor.**
**The Last of the MacAllisters.**
**Woven of Love and Glory.**
**Feet of Clay.** (With Portrait of Author.)
**The Household of MacNeil.**
**In Spite of Himself.**
**A Border Shepherdess.**
**Paul and Christina.**
**The Squire of Sandal Side.**
**The Bow of Orange Ribbon.**
**Between Two Loves.**
**A Daughter of Fife.**
**Jan Vedder's Wife.** (*Also cheap edition, paper,* 1s. 6d.)
**The Harvest of the Wind, and Other Stories.** Crown 8vo, paper, 1s.

## NOVELS BY EMMA JANE WORBOISE.

*Crown 8vo, uniformly bound in cloth, Three Shillings and Sixpence each.*

Thornycroft Hall
Millicent Kendrick
St. Beetha's
Violet Vaughan
Margaret Torrington
The Fortunes of Cyril Denham
Singlehurst Manor
Overdale
Grey and Gold
Mr. Montmorency's Money
Nobly Born
Chrystabel
Canonbury Holt
Husbands and Wives
The House of Bondage
Emilia's Inheritance
Father Fabian
Oliver Westwood
Lady Clarissa
Grey House at Endlestone
Robert Wreford's Daughter
The Brudenells of Brude
The Heirs of Errington
Joan Carisbroke
A Woman's Patience
The Story of Penelope
Sissie
The Abbey Mill
Warleigh's Trust
Esther Wynne
Fortune's Favourite
His Next of Kin
Campion Court
Evelyn's Story
Lottie Lonsdale
Sir Julian's Wife
The Lillingstones
The Wife's Trials

*Three Shillings each.*

Married Life; OR, THE STORY OF PHILIP AND EDITH.
Our New House; OR, KEEPING UP APPEARANCES.
Heartsease in the Family.
Maude Bolingbroke.
Amy Wilton.
Helen Bury.

*One Shilling and Sixpence.*

Charles Eversley's Choice.

13 & 14, FLEET STREET, LONDON.

# New and Forthcoming Books

Published by

James Clarke & Co.,

13 & 14, Fleet Street,

London.

*October, 1899.*

13 & 14, FLEET STREET,
LONDON.

*October, 1898.*

# James Clarke & Co.'s New and Forthcoming Books.

## Fiction.

**J. Bloun-delle Burton.**

THE SCOURGE OF GOD: A Romance of Religious Persecution.

By **John Bloundelle-Burton**, Author of "Across the Salt Seas," "The Clash of Arms," "In the Day of Adversity," &c. Crown 8vo, cloth, 6s.

*Pictures of Lancashire Life.*

**John Ack-worth.**

THE SCOWCROFT CRITICS.

By **John Ackworth**, Author of "Clog-shop Chronicles" and "Beckside Lights." Crown 8vo, art linen, gilt top, 3s. 6d.

"Clog-shop Chronicles" is now in its Ninth Thousand.

## FORTHCOMING BOOKS.

**Marianne Farningham.**

*New Work by Marianne Farningham.*

**A PARIS WINDOW: A Romance of the days of the Franco-German War.** Based upon fact.

By **Marianne Farningham.** Crown 8vo, cloth, 5s.

The Story falls in the days of the Siege of Paris and the Commune, and is based on materials gathered from those who lived through that awful time.

---

**Emma Jane Worboise.**

*New Uniform Edition of Emma Jane Worboise's Novels.*

**OVERDALE: the Story of a Pervert.**

By **Emma Jane Worboise.** Crown 8vo, gilt top, art linen, 3s. 6d.

**ST. BEETHA'S; or, the Heiress of Arne.**

By **Emma Jane Worboise.** Crown 8vo, gilt top, art linen, 3s. 6d.

**JOAN CARISBROKE.**

By **Emma Jane Worboise.** Crown 8vo, gilt top, art linen, 3s. 6d.

**GREY AND GOLD.**

By **Emma Jane Worboise.** Crown 8vo, gilt top, art linen, 3s. 6d.

These are the first volumes of a New Uniform Edition of the Novels of Emma Jane Worboise. They are entirely reset in new type, printed on a specially-made paper, and bound uniformly in a crimson art-linen, with gilt tops.

# FORTHCOMING BOOKS.

**Mary Hartier.**

*A Devonshire Story.*
CHAPEL FOLK.
> By Mary Hartier. Crown 8vo, cloth, 3s. 6d.

## Small Books on Great Subjects.

*New Volumes.*

**Stopford A. Brooke.**

THE SHIP OF THE SOUL, And Other Papers.
> By Stopford A. Brooke, M.A. Pott 8vo, buckram, 1s. 6d. [*November.*

**R. J. Campbell.**

THE MAKING OF AN APOSTLE.
> By R. J. Campbell, of Brighton. Pott 8vo, buckram, 1s. 6d. [*October.*

**R. F. Horton.**

THE CONQUERED WORLD, And Other Papers. [*Ready.*
> By Robert F. Horton, M.A., D.D. Pott 8vo, buckram, 1s. 6d.

*For Christmas and the New Year.*

**Geo. Matheson.**

THE BIBLE DEFINITION OF RELIGION.
> By George Matheson, M.A., D.D., Senior Minister of the Parish of St. Bernard's, Edinburgh. On deckle-edge paper, with red border-lines and decorated wrapper, in envelope, suitable for use as a Christmas and New Year greeting. Price 1s.

## FORTHCOMING BOOKS.

**C. Silvester Horne.**

*A Gift-book for the Sorrowing.*

**THE ORDEAL OF FAITH.**

By C. Silvester Horne, M.A. Meditations on the Book of Job, designed as a "ministry of consolation to some who are pierced with many sorrows." Fcap. 8vo, handsomely bound in cloth, gilt top, 2s. 6d.

---

**J. E. Ritchie.**

*New Book by Christopher Crayon.*

**CHRISTOPHER CRAYON'S RECOLLECTIONS:** The Life and Times of the late James Ewing Ritchie as Told by Himself. With Portrait. Cr. 8vo, cloth, 3s. 6d.

---

**T. Witton Davies.**

**MAGIC, DIVINATION AND DEMONOLOGY AMONG THE HEBREWS AND THEIR NEIGHBOURS,** Including an Examination of Biblical References and of the Biblical Terms.

By T. Witton Davies, B.A., Ph.D., Lecturer in Semitic Languages, University College, Bangor, and Professor of Old Testament Literature at the Bangor Baptist College. Crown 8vo, cloth, 3s. 6d.

---

**N. Fox.**

**CHRIST IN THE DAILY MEAL,** or the Ordinance of the Breaking of Bread.

By Norman Fox, D.D. Cr. 8vo, 3s.

## FORTHCOMING BOOKS.

**L. W. Bacon.**
**J. Bryce.**

*Introduced by the* RIGHT HON. JAMES BRYCE, M.P.

A HISTORY OF AMERICAN CHRISTIANITY.

By L. W. Bacon, with Introduction by the Right. Hon. James Bryce, M.P. Crown 8vo, cloth.

---

**J. Brierley.**

STUDIES OF THE SOUL.

By J. Brierley ('J.B.' of *The Christian World*). Crown 8vo, cloth, gilt top, 6s.

Dr. HORTON says that he "*prefers this book to the best-written books he has lighted on for a year past.*"

---

**A. H. Moncur Sime.**

THE LITERARY LIFE OF EDINBURGH.
By A. H. Moncur Sime. Pott 8vo, cloth, 1s.

Dr. GEORGE MATHESON says:—"I am simply charmed with your historical sketch. It presents in terse and vigorous language, and with graphic power of delineation, a picture which in the space of half-an-hour will make the citizen of the modern Athens master of the literary history of Edinburgh, and which every Edinburgh citizen ought to buy. A brochure like this makes the mouth water; it awakens my thirst for a literary Home Rule in Scotland such as we had in the days of THE EDINBURGH REVIEW."

Sir LEWIS MORRIS says:—"It is a very intellectual sketch of the life of the Northern capital, and contains much that will be fresh to most readers. The style is bright throughout and very pleasing."

## The Polychrome Bible.

**Paul Haupt, H. Howard Furness.**

A New English Translation of the Books of the Bible. Printed in Colours exhibiting the Composite Structure of the Books. With Explanatory Notes and Pictorial Illustrations from Nature and from Ancient Monuments of Egypt, Assyria, Palestine, &c. Prepared by Eminent Biblical Scholars of Europe and America, and edited with the assistance of **Horace Howard Furness,** by **Paul Haupt,** Johns Hopkins University, Baltimore.

Volumes Ready or Nearly Ready :—

**C. J. Ball**

THE BOOK OF GENESIS. Translated, with Notes, by **C. J. Ball, M.A.,** Chaplain of Lincoln's Inn, Editor of the "Variorum Apocrypha." [*May, 1899.*

**H. E. Ryle.**

THE BOOK OF EXODUS. Translated, with Notes, by **Herbert E. Ryle, D.D.,** President of Queen's College, Cambridge, and Hulsean Professor of Divinity.

**S. R. Driver, H. A. White.**

THE BOOK OF LEVITICUS. Translated, with Notes, by **S. R. Driver, D.D.,** Regius Professor of Hebrew and Canon of Christ Church, Oxford, one of the Revisers of the Authorised Version, and **H. A. White, M.A.,** Fellow of New College, Oxford. 114 pp., printed in two colours (65 pp. translation, 50 pp. notes). Four full-page illustrations (one in colours), and

**S. R. Driver, H. A. White.**

four illustrations in the Notes. Cloth, gilt top, price 6s. net.    [*Ready.*

"Leviticus has fared badly. It has been regarded either as a mass of uninteresting and obsolete ritual or as a quarry for incredible allegorising. Driver and White have rescued it from the double reproach. It is a book of genuine historical and religious worth, and every chapter overflows with interest. They simply restored it as it is. And it is most precious and stimulating. There is little variety of colouring of course, but the translation is beyond anything yet done into English, and the notes are full and pertinent. There are four full-page plates and four smaller illustrations."
—EXPOSITORY TIMES.

"A version that will make the sense of the original more clearly intelligible to the English reader than any existing version. . . . The notes as a whole are admirable; it would be difficult, and even impossible, for the English reader to find elsewhere in any convenient form such help in the interpretation of Leviticus."
—G. BUCHANAN GRAY IN "THE CHRISTIAN WORLD."

"The names of the translators, Canon Driver and Mr. H. A. White, are ample guarantees for the high scholarship and critical soundness of the work. The translation is, it is hardly necessary to say, exact. It may be more to the purpose to add that it is also in clear idiomatic English."
—MANCHESTER GUARDIAN.

"The notes will be found most useful, both in explaining the structure of the book and in elucidating its meaning; and, in short, the volume cannot fail to prove most serviceable to such as may desire to study minutely, in the light of the latest scientific criticism, this ancient law-book."—SCOTSMAN.

"The translation and notes are scholarly and suggestive. The translation is specially interesting and valuable."—GLASGOW HERALD.

"Dr. Driver's name will serve in Britain as a guarantee of the thoroughness of the scholarship and fineness of judgment displayed in this volume. . . . The fruits of immense labour are most reverently and instructively presented in this fine volume."
—ARBROATH HERALD.

"That the work will be a valuable, indeed an invaluable, contribution to the progress of Biblical study, no one can doubt."—GOOD WORDS.

# FORTHCOMING BOOKS.

> "*Any one reading it can see at once how, according to this 'Higher Criticism,' the book has been constructed.... The high reputation of the chief editor of this volume for Hebrew scholarship is well known, and naturally claims the most careful study for any work that is issued by him.*"
> —NORTH BRITISH DAILY MAIL.

> "*A work which cannot be ignored.*"
> —CAMBRIDGE INDEPENDENT PRESS.

**J. A. Paterson.**

THE BOOK OF NUMBERS. Translated, with Notes, by J. A. Paterson, D.D., Professor at the Theological Seminary, Edinburgh. [*May, 1899.*

**G. A. Smith.**

THE BOOK OF DEUTERONOMY. Translated, with Notes, by George Adam Smith, D.D., LL.D., Professor of Hebrew and Old Testament Exegesis at the Free Church College, Glasgow. [*May, 1899.*

**W. H. Bennett.**

THE BOOK OF JOSHUA. Translated, with Notes, by W. H. Bennett, M.A., Professor of Hebrew and Old Testament Exegesis at Hackney and New Colleges, London. [*December.*

**G. F. Moore.**

THE BOOK OF JUDGES. Translated, with Notes, by G. F. Moore, D.D., Professor of Hebrew in Andover Theological Seminary. 98 pp., printed in seven colours (42 pp. translation, 56 pp. notes). Seven full-page illustrations (including a map in colours), twenty illustrations in the Notes. Cloth, gilt top, price 6s. net. [*Ready.*

> "*I admire the skill with which the most necessary information on the origin of the book is here com-*

municated to the English reader, and the fulness and yet conciseness of the notes. As to the colours which indicate the sources of the existing composite work, I can by no means sympathise with the laughers who have begun to show themselves. If the public are to be enabled to see what analytic criticism comes to, such a plan as Dr. Haupt has devised, and Professor Moore and others have endeavoured to carry out, was indispensable. As a specimen of fine prose I would gladly quote the story of Jephthah's daughter, but it may be enough to invite the reader to get the book, and turn to the passage at once."
—Dr. Cheyne in "The Expositor."

"The translation is in clear, strong, dignified modern English. The explanatory notes are concise, to the point and adequate. The map and illustrations are just what is required to throw light on the book."
—Manchester Guardian.

"Professor G. F. Moore, of Andover, stands in the front rank of Old Testament students. His English rendering is readable, though it looks to faithfulness first and to style only in the second place. His notes are pointed and helpful; his criticism is free and thoroughgoing, without becoming either precipitate or showy."
—Critical Review.

---

**J. Wellhausen, H. Howard Furness.**

**THE BOOK OF PSALMS.** Translated by J. Wellhausen, D.D., Professor of Semitic Languages at Göttingen, and H. Howard Furness, Ph.D., LL.D., Editor of "The Variorum Shakespeare." 224 pp. (161 pp. translation, 63 pp. notes, including an Appendix on the Music of the Ancient Hebrews). Eight full-page illustrations (one in colours), and fifty-three illustrations in the Notes and Appendix. Cloth, gilt top, price 10s. 6d. net.  [Ready.

"The most beautiful version of the Hebrew Psalms which exists in our language."
—Dr. Cheyne in "The Expositor."

"The 'Psalms' are translated and edited by Professor Wellhausen. The German translations are rendered into English by Mr. Furness. And the effect is, we can only say, magnificent. Here for the first time the

## FORTHCOMING BOOKS.

*English reader is enabled to understand obscure places in the Psalms, and at the same time to catch the roll of the rhythm and to feel that the Psalms are poems."*—DAILY CHRONICLE.

*"The Psalms, which have been translated by the greatest Biblical critic in Europe or the world, Professor Wellhausen, are distinguished externally from the other books by being absolutely colourless. This, of course, does not mean that they are not of very different epochs of Jewish history, and Professor Wellhausen's treatment of these and analogous questions is worthy of the scholar who has done more to throw light upon the composition of the books of the Old Testament than all of his predecessors."*
—DAILY TELEGRAPH.

**T. K. Cheyne.**

### THE BOOK OF THE PROPHET ISAIAH.
Translated, with Notes, by T. K. Cheyne, D.D., Oriel Professor of the Interpretation of Holy Scripture at Oxford, and Canon of Rochester. 216 pp., printed in seven colours (128 pp. translation, 88 pp. notes). Nine full-page illustrations and twenty-eight illustrations in Notes. Cloth, gilt top, price 10s. 6d. net.
[*Ready.*

*"If the reader of the Polychrome Isaiah feels that he has before him a totally different book from the familiar Isaiah of the English Bible, he will not feel that he has lost, but gained; for while his new Isaiah is far easier to understand, it possesses no less of the inspired passion and power and truth which have always made the Book of Isaiah the favourite book of the Old Testament."*—DAILY CHRONICLE.

*"By far the most important of the three first volumes which have just seen the light is the Book of Isaiah, by Professor Cheyne, whose previous writings on the Old Testament are widely known and highly appreciated. He is at once the most lucid, dispassionate, and cautious of English scholars, and the uninitiated reader, to whatever school of theology he may belong, can fully commit himself to his guidance."*
—DAILY TELEGRAPH.

FORTHCOMING BOOKS. 13

G. H. Toy.

**THE BOOK OF THE PROPHET EZEKIEL.** Translated, with Notes, by **C. H. Toy, D.D.**, Professor of Hebrew and Lecturer on Biblical Literature in Harvard University. [*December.*

E. T. Bartlett,
J. P. Peters,
F. W. Farrar.

**THE BIBLE; FOR HOME AND SCHOOL.** Arranged by **Ed. T. Bartlett, M.A.**, Dean of the Protestant Episcopal Divinity School in Philadelphia, and **John P. Peters, Ph.D.**, Professor of the Old Testament Languages and Literature in the Protestant Episcopal Divinity School in Philadelphia. With Introduction by **Rev. F. W. Farrar, D.D.**, Dean of Canterbury. In ten monthly parts, 1s. each. In One Vol., cloth, 8vo, 10s. 6d.

DEAN FARRAR says:—"*An important contribution to the training of the young in truths which God has revealed to us by His Holy Book, as it is read in the light of that advancing knowledge which is itself a part of the Divine enlightenment which He vouchsafes to all mankind, as always, fragmentarily and multifariously, yet progressively 'in many parts and in many manners.'*"

W. H. Bennett,
W. F. Adeney.

**THE BIBLE STORY.** Re-told for Young People.

The OLD TESTAMENT STORY, by **W. H. Bennett, M.A.** (sometime Fellow of St. John's College, Cambridge), Professor of Hebrew and Old Testament Exegesis at Hackney and New Colleges, London. The NEW TESTAMENT STORY by **W. F. Adeney, M.A.**, Professor of New Testa-

**W. H. Bennett, W. F. Adeney.**

ment Greek Exegesis, at New College, London. With illustrations and 4 maps.

This book is designed to supply the want of such a presentation of the narratives contained in the Bible as shall be suitable for the reading of young people. The results of recent Historical Research and Biblical Criticism are brought to bear on the story, to throw light on it and also to prevent misapprehensions. The book is reduced to reasonable dimensions, by the omission of those portions of the narrative which are less suitable for young people, and also of incidents not essential to the story. In this way the salient features are emphasized and some sense of proportion observed, while there is scope for those dramatic elements which have always fascinated young readers of the Bible.

---

*Fourth Edition (completing 12,000 copies).*

**W. F. Adeney.**

HOW TO READ THE BIBLE. Hints for Sunday-School Teachers and other Bible Students.

By **Walter F. Adeney, M.A.**, Professor of New Testament Exegesis, &c., New College, London, and Author of "The Theology of the New Testament" (Theological Educator), "The Canticles and Lamentations," "Ezra, Nehemiah, and Esther" (Expositor's Bible), &c. Pott 8vo, in paper, 1s.; in cloth, 1s. 6d.

*"This little book aims at being a most elementary introduction to the study of the Bible. To many readers much of it will appear to be a perfectly superfluous reiteration of the most obvious truths. But it*

*is a singular fact that warnings that never need to be uttered, and directions that never need to be laid down, in regard to the study of any other work in the world's literature, are imperatively called for to prevent the student of Scripture from being ensnared by the most outrageous devices of misinterpretation."*

---

*Dr. Horton on Romanism.*

**R. F. Horton.**

**ENGLAND'S DANGER.** Romanism and National Decay—St. Peter and the Rock — Truth — Protestantism — Holy Scripture—Purgatory.

By **Robert F. Horton, M.A., D.D.** Fourth Edition. Fcap. 8vo, 6d.

---

**Minnie Elligott.**

**A HELPING HAND TO MOTHERS.**

By **Minnie Elligott.** Fcap. 8vo, paper, 6d.

The AUTHOR says: *"In submitting this little book to Mothers I hope I am rendering a slight service to those who, while earnestly desirous of bringing up their children on healthy principles, are frequently at a loss how to act, simply from lack of experience. The first baby is often the victim of divers experiments which would never be tried were its wants and requirements properly understood. I have endeavoured to show what these are, and to point out how the children of parents whose means are limited may be as well trained and cared for as those of mothers and fathers in affluent circumstances."*

---

**R. A. Armstrong.**

**FAITH AND DOUBT IN THE CENTURY'S POETS.**

By **Richard A. Armstrong, B.A.** Fcap. 8vo, 2s. 6d.

Prose and Verse by Mary E. Manners, H. E. Inman, Kate Lee, A. Dixon, S. D. Constance, and many others.

Illustrated by Louis Wain, E. A. Mason, Felix Leigh, Harry Dixon, A. T. Elwes, T. Cromwell Lawrence, G. Stoddart, &c.

**THE ROSEBUD ANNUAL, 1899.** With about 200 Original Illustrations. In handsome cloth binding, 4s.

*As a Reward Book, Birthday or Christmas Present for a child, "The Rosebud Annual" still stands unrivalled. The short stories in prose and verse are full of healthy humour, and while free from goody-goodiness, convey many a lesson in a quiet way. Every picture in the book was specially drawn for it, and nearly all the birds of the air, the beasts of the field and the fish in the sea are represented in various comical attitudes. There are also songs with music.*

What the Papers say about THE ROSEBUD :

THE TIMES : "*Few more lively.*"
DAILY GRAPHIC : "*Vast resources in the way of amusement.*"
DAILY NEWS : "*Looks particularly attractive.*"
WESTMINSTER GAZETTE : "*One of the best.*"
DAILY TELEGRAPH : "*Splendidly printed.*"
STAR : "*Storehouse of innocent humour and gaiety.*"
PALL MALL GAZETTE : "*No more charming picture-book.*"
SCOTSMAN : "*That pleasant and well-known nursery monthly.*"
LIVERPOOL POST : "*A treasure of delight.*"
LEEDS MERCURY : "*Fascinating.*"
BRADFORD OBSERVER : "*Full of fun and laughter.*"
ABERDEEN FREE PRESS : "*Ideal.*"
BRISTOL MERCURY : *Delightful. . . admirable little magazine.*"
GLASGOW HERALD : "*Sure of a rapturous welcome.*"
DUNDEE ADVERTISER : "*Crammed full of good things.*"
BIRMINGHAM POST : "*Well adapted for very little folks.*"
NEWCASTLE CHRONICLE : "*None more entertaining.*"
NEWCASTLE LEADER : "*Well worth the money.*"
DERBY GAZETTE : "*Charmingly got up.*"
HUDDERSFIELD EXAMINER : "*We know of nothing better.*"
OXFORD CHRONICLE : "*Bound to be treasured.*"
MIDLAND FREE PRESS : "*An old and ever-welcome friend.*"
PRESTON GUARDIAN : "*The Nursery 'Punch.'*"
LLOYD'S NEWS : "*A veritable mine of wealth for the juveniles.*"
PUNCH : "*Gorgeously gay.*"
ST. JAMES'S BUDGET : "*Sure to be a favourite.*"
BOOK AND NEWS TRADE GAZETTE : "*Will always find a big sale.*"

www.ingramcontent.com/pod-product-compliance
Lightning Source LLC
Chambersburg PA
CBHW051246300426
44114CB00011B/917